The Fox Terrier:
Smooth and Wire

Anna Katherine Nicholas
Marcia A. Foy

Title page photo: The great Ch. Sunnybrook Spot On who scored so brilliant a Best in Show and Group winning career for Mrs. Robert V. Clark, Jr., Springfield Kennels, Middleburg, Virginia, then retired to become the friend and family member of Dan Kiedrowski, La Honda, California. Peter Green handled this excellent and spectacular Fox Terrier throughout his American career. Spot On as a sire founded a dynasty of Best in Show wires.

In Appreciation

The authors acknowledge, with sincere thanks, the help and co-operation of the many breeders who have added to the interest of this book with kennel stories and photos. Our deep gratitude to Ric, Peter, George, Woody, and Chris for the wonderful photos they've shared with us.

Distributed in the UNITED STATES by T.F.H. Publications, Inc., One T.F.H. Plaza, Neptune City, NJ 07753; in CANADA to the Pet Trade by H & L Pet Supplies Inc., 27 Kingston Crescent, Kitchener, Ontario N2B 2T6; Rolf C. Hagen Ltd., 3225 Sartelon Street, Montreal 382 Quebec; in CANADA to the Book Trade by Macmillan of Canada (A Division of Canada Publishing Corporation), 164 Commander Boulevard, Agincourt, Ontario M1S 3C7; in ENGLAND by T.F.H. Publications Limited, Cliveden House/Priors Way/Bray, Maidenhead, Berkshire SL6 2HP, England; in AUSTRALIA AND THE SOUTH PACIFIC by T.F.H. (Australia) Pty. Ltd., Box 149, Brookvale 2100 N.S.W., Australia; in NEW ZEALAND by Ross Haines & Son, Ltd., 18 Monmouth Street, Grey Lynn, Auckland 2, New Zealand; in the PHILIPPINES by Bio-Research, 5 Lippay Street, San Lorenzo Village, Makati Rizal; in SOUTH AFRICA by Multipet Pty. Ltd., 30 Turners Avenue, Durban 4001. Published by T.F.H. Publications, Inc. Manufactured in the United States of America by T.F.H. Publications, Inc.

Contents

About the Authors

Anna Katherine Nicholas

Since early childhood, Anna Katherine Nicholas has been involved with dogs. Her first pets were a Boston Terrier, an Airedale, and a German Shepherd Dog. Then, in 1925, came the first of the Pekingese, a gift from a friend who raised them. Now her home is shared with two Miniature Poodles and numerous Beagles.

Miss Nicholas is best known throughout the Dog Fancy as a writer and as a judge. Her first magazine article, published in *Dog News* magazine around 1930, was about Pekingese, and this was followed by a widely acclaimed breed column, "Peeking at the Pekingese," which appeared for at least two decades, originally in *Dogdom*, then, following the demise of that publication, in *Popular Dogs*. During the 1940s she was a Boxer columnist for *Pure-Bred Dogs/American Kennel Gazette* and for *Boxer Briefs*. More recently many of her articles, geared to interest fanciers of every breed, have appeared in *Popular Dogs, Pure-Bred Dogs/American Kennel Gazette, Show Dogs, Dog Fancy, The World of the Working Dog,* and for both the Canadian publications, *The Dog Fancier* and *Dogs in Canada.* Her *Dog World* column, "Here, There and Everywhere," was the Dog Writers' Association of America winner of the Best Series in a Dog Magazine Award for 1979. Another feature article of hers, "Faster Is Not Better," published in *Canine Chronicle,* received Honorable Mention on another occasion.

In 1970 Miss Nicholas won the Dog Writers' Association Award for the Best Technical Book of the Year with her *Nicholas Guide to Dog Judging.* In 1979 the revision of this book again won this award, the first time ever that a revision has been so honored by this organization. Other important dog writer awards which Miss Nicholas has gained over the years have been the Gaines "Fido" and the *Kennel Review* "Winkies," these both on two occasions and each in the Dog Writer of the Year category.

It was during the 1930s that Miss Nicholas's first book, *The Pekingese,* appeared in print, published by the Judy Publishing Company. This book, and its second edition, sold out quickly and is now a collector's item, as is *The Skye Terrier Book* which was published during the 1960s by the Skye Terrier Club of America.

During recent years, Miss Nicholas has been writing books consistently for T.F.H. These include *Successful Dog Show Exhibiting, The Book of the Rottweiler, The Book of the Poodle, The Book of the Labrador Retriever, The Book of the English Springer Spaniel, The Book of the Golden Retriever, The Book of the German Shepherd Dog, The Book of the Shetland Sheepdog, The Book of the Miniature Schnauzer, The World of Doberman Pinschers,* and *The World of Rottweilers.* Plus, in another T.F.H. series, *The Maltese, The Keeshond, The Chow Chow, The Poodle, The Boxer, The Beagle, The Basset Hound, The Dachshund* (the latter three co-authored with Marcia A. Foy), *The German Pointer, The Collie, The Weimaraner, The Great Dane, The Dalmatian,* and numerous other titles. In the KW series she has done *Rottweilers, Weimaraners,* and *Norwegian Elkhounds.* And she has written American chapters for two popular English books purchased and published in the United States by T.F.H., *The Staffordshire Bull Terrier* and *The Jack Russell Terrier.*

Miss Nicholas's association with T.F.H. began in the early 1970s when she co-authored for them five books with Joan Brearley. These are *The Wonderful World of Beagles and Beagling* (also honored by the Dog Writers Association), *This is the Bichon Frise, The Book of the Pekingese, The Book of the Boxer,* and *This is the Skye Terrier.*

Since 1934 Miss Nicholas has been a popular dog show judge, officiating at prestigious events throughout the United States and Canada. She is presently approved for all Hounds, all Terriers, all Toys and all Non-Sporting; plus all Pointers, English and Gordon Setters, Vizslas, Weimaraners, and Wirehaired Pointing Griffons in the Sporting Group and Boxers and Dobermans in Working. In 1970 she became only the third woman ever to have judged Best in Show at the famous Westminster Kennel Club event at Madison Square Garden in New York City, where she has officiated as well on some sixteen other occasions over the years. She has also officiated at such events as Santa Barbara, Chicago International, Morris and Essex, Trenton, Westchester, etc., in the United States; the Sportsman's and the Metropolitan among numerous others in Canada; and Specialty shows in several dozen breeds in both countries. She has judged in almost every one of the United States and in four of the Canadian Provinces. Her dislike of air travel has caused her to refrain from acceptance of the constant invitations to officiate in other parts of the world.

6

Marcia A. Foy

Marcia A. Foy was born in Chicago and raised in the suburbs of the North Shore. From early childhood she loved dogs and had many breeds at one time or another as pets, including Pekes, a Basset, a Gordon Setter, and Miniature Poodles.

Her first show dog was a Kerry Blue Terrier, That's Dundel of Delwin, who came from the noted Delwin Kennels of Ed Sayres, Sr. She showed this dog for the first time in 1945, when she was eleven years old.

Marcia moved East in 1960, at which time she acquired her first Beagles. Among those she has owned and shown are the unforgettable Champion Kings Creek Triple Threat; his son Champion Rockaplenty's Wild Oats (who now belongs to A.K.N.); the magnificent bitch, Trippe's daughter, Champion Foyscroft Triple Lena Wor Lo; the multi-Group winners Champion Junior's Foyscroft Wild Kid and the 13" Champion Jo Mar's Repeat Performance; and many others. Although she has raised only a limited number of litters, she has bred a goodly number of champions, among them dogs who have provided foundation stock for other successful kennels.

Interest in Beagles is shared by a very special love of Poodles, a breed which has long been one of her favorites.

It was in 1976 that Marcia officiated for the first time as a judge, an experience which she has grown to thoroughly enjoy. Her first breeds were Beagles and Dachshunds. Currently she is approved for all Hounds and the Hound Group, all of the Terriers, Poodles and Best in Show. Her judging assignments take her on a wide course of travel each year, and she has officiated at leading shows throughout the United States and in most of Canada. One of her earliest assignments was that of the National Beagle Club Sweepstakes at Aldie, and she has also judged the Blossom Valley Beagle Club Specialty in California, along with dozens of all-breed shows.

Marcia has been largely instrumental in having persuaded the Southern New York Beagle Club, of which she is an Honorary Member, to hold an annual conformation Specialty, which it now does in conjunction with the Westchester Kennel Club each September—most successfully, we might add!

At Crufts in May 1957. Two great British handlers and Mr. William W. Brainard the judge: Ernie Sharp (*left*) handling Ch. Caradoc House Spruce to Reserve Best in Show. Purchased by Mrs. Joseph Urmston. Best of Opposite Sex, Ch. Bluebird Radwyre Ruby. Tommy Brampton (*right*) handling.

Ch. Donna Fortuna shows by her quality why the kennels of Mr. Francis Redmond were so highly esteemed throughout the early days of the breed. Mr. Redmond was noted for the quality of his dogs and for his tremendous knowledge of Fox Terriers. Truly he was the dean of Fox Terrier fanciers in Great Britain.

Chapter 1

Origin of the Fox Terrier

The Fox Terriers, both Wire and Smooth, have been popular breeds over a great many years, the Smooth being the earlier known and more popular of the two. As with most terrier breeds, the roots of their origin are in the British Isles, although their development through the early years was on somewhat different lines from one another.

The Smooth Fox Terrier is believed to have developed through crosses which included Beagles, Bull Terriers, Greyhounds, and the Smooth Coated Black and Tan Terriers. The Wires, on the other hand, the newer of the two breeds by about 15-20 years, is felt to be directly descended from the *rough coated* black and tan working terriers of Derbyshire, Durham and Wales.

The principal demand upon a Fox Terrier of the 19th century and earlier was its ability to rout a fox from underground. The important physical characteristics of the dogs then were strength and power to travel well; and white was the favored color, permitting the dog to be easily seen and identified so as not to be confused with the fox by an over-eager huntsman.

In earliest times, the Smooths and Wires were bred together; thus there is some of both in each of the breeds. Interestingly, we have read that a Smooth dog, Jock, mated to a bitch of unknown heritage named Trap and wearing a rough (or Wire) coat, were behind many of the great early Wires.

The Kennel Club in England was established in 1873. The Smooths and Wires received separate stud book registers in 1876,

9

at which time the Standard of the Breed (applicable to both) was drawn up and approved. So well done was this standard that it has served practically in its original form (except for a two-pound weight reduction) since that time.

During the early days of breed and type establishment, considerable breeding was done back and forth between the Smooths and the Wires, largely to refine type in the Wire to conform with the elegant silhouette, length and refinement of head and predominantly white coloring of the Smooth. So far as we know, it has been many years since this crossbreeding was undertaken, correct type in both having long since been well established.

The Fox Terrier Club of England was founded in 1872 under the auspices of Mr. Harding-Cox, Mr. Burbridge, Mr. Dixon, and other gentlemen involved with the breed during that period. Soon after them came Her Grace, the Duchess of Newcastle, Captain Tudor Crosthwaite, Roscoe Bradley, Sidney Castle, and Reverend Rosslyn Bruce. Others of note were Baron Van der Hoop and the notable experts George Raper, Walter Glynn, and Theo. Marples among others. And on all sides we have read tributes to Francis Redmond for his invaluable furthering of the best interests of the Smooth.

The first Specialty Show of the Fox Terrier Club of England was held in 1877, for which turned out what we are sure must have been a very exciting entry of 220, judged by Mr. Bassett. Quite a compliment, with a newly organized club and a first Specialty for the breed!

We have read that the Fox Terrier Club of England was the third earliest Specialty Club organized in Great Britain, having been just one year behind the Bulldog Club and the Dandie Dinmont Club.

In 1913 a second club for Fox Terriers was founded—the Wire Foxterrier Association. Both of these clubs are to this day still operating, healthy, active and wealthy, involved in every function for the improvement and advancement of their breeds. A.E.G. Way was the first President of the Wire Foxterrier Association; others involved in the founding of this group included C.G. Anne and Calvery Butler.

Additionally, numerous organizations have been formed in Great Britain over the years to encourage and protect the working abilities and instincts of the breed.

Ch. Dusky Reine, born in 1899, was one of the very best of the early Wires. Owned by Mr. Enfield in England, this is one of several noted Dusky Wires on the early British show scene.

The first dog show ever held anywhere was in England, at Newcastle-on-Tyne in 1859 (which you will note was even before the founding of the English Kennel Club). Pointers and Setters were the only breeds and total entry there. Later that same year, a show was held at Birmingham (its first and Great Britain's second) at which Smooth Fox Terriers were entered in a "miscellaneous" class. Three years later, at this same show, there was classification for Smooth Fox Terriers.

It was at Birmingham's second show, under the heading "miscellaneous," that Wires appeared in competition in 1860. It took the Wires until Darlington in 1869 to earn separate classification, as "Rough Coated Terriers." But at Birmingham they were listed as "Wire-Haired Terriers," their official breed for registration until 1882 when the English Kennel Club reclassified them in the stud book as Wire Haired Fox Terriers.

A splendid British Wire from 1929. Ch. Thet Tetrarch, by Ch. Eden Aristocrat, was a homebred that belonged to Miss L.M. Dixon.

This is a Kennel Club Challenge Certificate awarded at Crufts Dog Show in England during February 1975. The winning of three C.Cs. gives a dog in England the title of "Champion." They are offered at only a limited number of selected shows (all-breed and Specialty) during the course of each year. Courtesy of Frank Jones, Jonwyre Terrier Kennels.

CRUFTS DOG SHOW - FEBRUARY 7th & 8th 1975

Breed   FOX TERRIER (SMOOTH)   Sex   DOG

Kennel Club
Challenge Certificate

I am clearly of opinion that

Champion Jonwyre's Galaxy
(Name of Exhibit)

owned by   Mr. F. Jones
(Name of Owner)

is of such outstanding merit as to be worthy of the title of Champion.

(Signed)

Barbara H. Stapley (Judge)

Chapter 2

Fox Terriers in Great Britain

The British Isles have long been known and acknowledged as the home of great Terriers. For not only did the terrier breeds originate and develop there, but it is still the place where breeders, exhibitors and professional handlers go to find and purchase the outstanding members of these breeds—almost to the extent that people will sometimes facetiously remark that it is a wonder any are left considering the number taken to other countries. Yet there always do seem to be new, good, young exciting terriers coming along, which in itself speaks eloquently of the talent the British have in raising great ones.

In the United States, when one shows dogs, one is most generally eager for a First in Group Award or for a Best in Show. Not so in England. There the special emphasis is on the earning and completion of the championship title; and a Group or Best in Show win pales by comparison to this in the eyes of the British exhibitor. Probably this is largely due to the fact that a championship in the U.K. is by no means an easy thing to attain, not nearly so easy as in the States. To begin with, Great Britain has only 40 General Championship Shows (all breed events), plus a moderate number of breed championship events at which Challenge Certificates (for championship) are available. The number of Challenge Certificates available to each breed each year is based upon the previous year's championship show entries. Thus the more numerically popular the breed in the dog show ring, the more Challenge Certificates become available to members of that breed. For example, during 1985 just 22 sets of Challenge Certificates were allotted to Fox Terriers for each coat. Another custom making a championship especially prized in the U.K. is the fact that there are no non-regular classes for dogs who already are champions; thus they compete against the non-champions in the regular classes, actually "challenging" them to win the C.C. card. Obviously competition under these circumstances is a lot tougher and of usually better quality than where the class entries can pick up their points for title without ever defeating a single dog already finished!

A Challenge Certificate winner can come from any scheduled class and frequently must defeat champions in that class to do so. Thus, in a sense, the entry of a dog is *challenging* those who are already champions to beat them if they can. Sometimes they do, in which case the C.C. merely adds to those in a dog's record without doing anything for all those eager young hopefuls gathered. A dog whose championship has been completed (this takes the winning of three Challenge Certificates from three different judges) after that can compete *only* in the Open Class.

Obviously this adds tremendously to the quality of competition and to the value of winning a C.C. There are exhibitors who continue to show their champions as such, which can cause a real problem for those who are trying to make up a title, as often a dog (champion or otherwise) on a winning streak can use up half or more of the entire year's available champions, leaving thin pickings for those trying to become *new* champions. The system is good, though, since a dog who has *gained* the title has very likely genuinely *deserved* it. There cannot be "cheap" champions under such a method for, with the champions meeting the new faces in the competition for C.C., they *must* be worthwhile for making the grade over the better known faces.

Another highly valued British award is the Junior Warrant. This one is a Kennel Club award which is accompanied by a suitable certificate. It is earned on the point system, a total of 25 points being earned for first prize wins in the following manner. First Prize in a class at a Championship Show where C.C.s are on offer nets the winner three points. In a breed class at a non-championship rated Open Show, a first prize class win earns a single

Malmsey Shadow, well-known English Smooth, handled by her breeder, Frank Jones, Jonwyre Terrier Kennels, Heywood, Lancs., England.

point toward the Junior Warrant. Placements other than first do not count in the Junior Warrant tabulation. Frank Jones, of Jonwyre Kennels and the English *Dog World* magazine, has sent us this information, and adds to it the comment, "The difficulty of attaining a Junior Warrant is the time of year and the number of shows one is able to attend. It really requires an early start in the year if one is to get into a sufficient number of shows to make up a winner for this award."

The numerical size of dog shows in Great Britain is almost mind-boggling. For instance, Crufts in 1986 drew over 11,000, and soon will be increased from a three-day to a four-day event. Each day has its own catalogue covering the breeds which will be

15

in competition that day. But Crufts is not the only show with huge turnouts. For example, Frank Jones tells us that the Ladies Kennel Association Show, in December 1985, drew an entry of 22,000 in its two-day event. And there are other championship events in that same category.

Open Shows in Great Britain are smaller, far more informal, and a win at that type of show is exactly that—a win on the day. It carries no weight toward championship honors, although Groups and Best in Show are awarded. But it is the Challenge Certificates and the title they add up to that is the chief concern and most sought-after goal of the British Dog Fancy.

We are proud of the warm response we have received in the preparation of this book, and pleased at the quality of the kennel stories the following pages include.

BOREHAM

The Boreham Smooth Fox Terriers are owned by Mr. and Mrs J.T. Winstanley at Damerham near Fordingbridge, Hampshire. The kennel has been in existence for more than sixty years. The Boreham prefix had been registered with the Kennel Club in 1922 by Mrs. Winstanley's father, Dr. R.M. Miller, S. So., who owned his first Fox Terrier, a Wire, while a student at Cambridge University, and one in France during the first World War.

After their marriage, Dr. and Mrs. Miller lived at a village named Boreham Street, from which this kennel prefix came, used to identify their own dogs in the beginning, then later those owned by their daughter, Mrs. Winstanley.

The Millers moved to Rudgwick in 1926, a village on the border of Sussex and Surrey. There the original stock was a daughter of Cromwell Ochrette from Mr. Bradley, and a bitch called Mabonnie who was a daughter of Miss Watteau. (Actually Dr. Miller had also owned Cromwell Ochrette, but he had returned her to Mr. Bradley when he was in France.) To these two Smooth bitches another one, called Morna, was added following the move to Rudgwick. It is these three bitches who stand behind all of the modern Boreham Smooth Fox Terriers.

The first of the champions was in 1931, a great granddaughter of Cromwell Ochrette named Champion Boreham Bister. A son of hers, Champion Boreham Bisdon, won the F.T.C. Gold Cup at age seven months and had gained his title by a month later. These

Ch. Gedstar Petronella, a descendant of the Boreham line, bred and campaigned by Eileen Geddes, Gedstar Kennels. A noted English winner.

Ch. Boreham Ballet Star, born in 1968, has made a good show record for Boreham Kennels, Mrs. J.T. Winstanley, Fordingbridge, Hants, England.

17

Ch. Boreham Baranova, the Top Smooth Bitch of all time, imported and owned by Mrs. E. Stewart Simmons. She is a full sister to Bonanza from an earlier litter by Eng. Ch. Newmaidley Whistling Jeremy ex the Top English Producing Bitch of all time, Eng. Ch. Boreham Ballerina.

were followed by Champion Chipstead Malaprop, Champion Boreham Belscie, Gold Cup winner in 1945 and 1946, and their last champion was made up in the ownership of Captain Ashcroft, Champion Boreham Bendigo. After Dr. Miller retired, very few dogs were shown, but the bitch line was kept.

It was not until 1962 that the present owner of Boreham Kennels, Mrs. Winstanley, had her own first Smooth as a pet for her children. This was Boreham Bequest, who became the dam of American Champion Boreham Barrister. Mrs. Winstanley shared the Boreham prefix with her mother following the death of Dr. Miller. Boreham Bacchante, who came to her in 1966, was to be the foundation of her own Smooth line, being from the old Boreham stock. Everything that Mrs. Winstanley has bred since then and many of today's most famous Smooths are descended from her Smooth line.

In 1968 Champion Boreham Ballerina produced Champion Boreham Burlesque, Champion Boreham Briar Rose, and Champion Boreham Ballet Star. This lovely bitch also produced seven champions in the United States, Canada and Germany; these include American Champion Boreham Black Domino, American Champion Boreham Baranova and American Champion Boreham

18

Bonanza; Canadian and American Champion Boreham Buoyant and Canadian and American Champion Boreham Butterfly and the latter's sister, American Champion Boreham Belle Etoile. She also produced Boreham Blossomtime, the dam of Champion Mossvalley Blossomtime, the dam of Mossvalley Maytime and granddam of Champion Mossvalley Mimosa.

Boreham Bacaret, sister to Ballerina, is the great granddam of the twin winners, Champion Glenure Theo and Champion Glenure Myrtle who were consistent and exciting British winners during 1985 and 1986.

Champion Boreham Briar Rose, owned and campaigned by Mr. Peter Winfield, is the dam of Champion Riber Ricochet and Champion Riber Rosemean.

Champion Boreham Ballet Star, who won the Fox Terrier Club Gold Cup in 1975 and 1976, produced Champion Boreham Bluepoint and Champion Boreham Bagatells plus six champions and international champions abroad. She also produced Boreham Brioletta, granddam of Champion Gedstar Petronella, bred and campaigned by Mrs. Geddes; and Boreham Belinda, dam of Champion Roxway Evita, bred and campaigned by Mr. and Miss Strong.

Champion Boreham Bagatelle produced Champion Cantervey Cavellette for Mrs. Kate Evans and is the granddam of Champion Rarity of Riber.

Champion Boreham Bluepoint is the dam of Champion Boreham Blueblack, winner of 12 Challenge Certificates and the Fox Terrier Club Gold Cup in 1981 and a Terrier Group—the sire at present of three champions, two American champions, and an International champion.

Mrs. Winstanley maintains a very small kennel at present: Bluepoint, Bluebell and Belinda; a daughter of Belinda's, Belladonna; and a litter from Belinda by Bluebeard. Only about one litter annually is bred there.

JONWYRE

The Jonwyre Terrier Kennels, belonging to Frank Jones at Heywood, Lancashire, was founded in 1957 with a Wire female, English and American Champion Emprise Sensational, one of Mrs. Urmston's imports (back in the days when this lady was Mrs. Leonard J. Smit).

After brief success with this one, other Wires were introduced to the kennel. Then, in 1962, the Smooths were added. The foundation Smooth bitch was Distillry Snowdrop, by the famous Debough, who figures in numerous pedigrees of that period. Himself a Championship winner, Debough was sired by the famed Champion Herman Parthing Loyal Lad. This was the particular bloodline Mr. Jones had been wanting, featuring well-bred dogs of sound construction. Indeed something to build upon!

During 1962, Frank Jones joined the ranks of the professional handlers, at the very bottom of the ladder. It was a hard school he found! His first Smooth client was Mr. Joe Russell from Londonderry, who at that time was the inspector for the Royal Ulster Society For the Protection of Animals—a worthy charity. One day a feeble, heartbroken old lady came into his office with two Smooth Fox Terrier puppies, one of each sex, intent on putting the pair to sleep as she could neither sell them nor give them away to caring homes. Inspector Russell refused to put the puppies to sleep, offering the old lady five pounds (about $8) for the puppies, which she gladly accepted. One of these puppies became Champion Spaceman in Mr. Jones's hands, the other a winning female.

Champion Spaceman and Distillry Snowdrop were sired by the same dog, the C.C. winning Debough. The obvious mating was planned in due course with one female retained from among the puppies to set the pattern for the future. She became Stargazer of Jonwyre, not the exact type required, but she did an amount of winning. In turn she was bred to Champion Maryholm Sureline, an ideally sized stallion with an impeccable pedigree. This joining produced Cosmonaut of Jonwyre, exported to America. Unfortunately he died soon after taking his first points in the States. Before leaving Mr. Jones, he had been bred to a newly introduced bloodline containing Champion Maryholm Sureline. Cosmonaut ex Monocle of Jonwyre (named due to her one black eye patch) produced Venus of Jonwyre. Mr. Jones was delighted to find himself now getting the results towards which he had been aiming. But still not quite satisfied, he next introduced still another bloodline into his carefully laid plans. This was a black and white female, another gift, light of bone, but most beautifully bred, from the Harkaway line noted for wonderful legs and feet, very dominant features of a truly first class Smooth. This was Etyne Leda, a problem dog in some ways who would fight her own shadow,

The noted Cosmonaut of Jonwyre owned by Frank Jones, Jonwyre Terriers, England.

The import, Ebony Eyecatcher of Foxden, handled by Frank Jones, Jonwyre Kennels, England. Owned by Mrs. James A. Farrell, Jr., Darien, Connecticut.

but wonderful with humans. She was bred to a Venus son and produced Jonwyre's Spacegirl. She proved the ideal brood and was lightly shown.

During this time Spaceman changed ownership, returning to Northern Ireland for stud work. He just would not settle down there and was constantly unhappy. Thus he was returned to Mr. Jones, we are happy to record, where he lived out a long and happy life in the surroundings he knew and loved so well.

Eventually Spacegirl was bred to Champion Spaceman. The much strived for result was two male puppies of very obvious distinction. One of them eventually became English and American Champion Jonwyre's Galaxy of Foxden.

These two puppies were of equal quality with very little about one to prefer above the other. It was not possible to keep both, and the deciding factor became the very slightly longer foreface. So at eight weeks of age, Galaxy joined a local family household, where his call name became "Deano." The litter brother was a lovely dog, but he hated the show ring for some unknown reason, which proved a deep disappointment. Deano's brother was passed on to a friend in Scotland, with the hopes that with individual attention he would eventually come together. Within a week he was killed instantly by a large truck while chasing a rabbit.

Meanwhile, Deano was growing into a most beautiful dog—wonderfully reared; lead, car and house trained. As Deano became a grown dog, his mating instincts took over, causing him to literally howl the place down when a female of any unknown parentage came in heat. This is where fate took a hand. Deano was returned to Mr. Jones for a week, while the "girl next door" returned to normal. But that did not do the trick, and Deano was gifted back to Mr. Jones. At eight months of age this gorgeous dog had all the worldly wiles. To quote Mr. Jones, it was "unbelievable that he was all mine." Deano was a big pup, well bodied for his age. Experience has taught Mr. Jones that it is often best to learn to wait. So Deano was kept out of the champion show circuit until he was 14 months old. Then he came out at Manchester in March—two first prizes! His first Challenge Certificate came the end of May from the Junior Class. At just one show he was placed third—his lowest placement and the only third that he ever received.

Deano won the treasured Junior Warrant in quick time (25 points are required; one first at a championship show gives three points). Deano attended 16 championship shows prior to joining the Foxden Kennel in the United States. His tally was the Junior Warrant, 10 Challenge Certificates with Best of Breed; two Reserve Challenge Certificates which included Crufts; two Reserve Groups (once or twice in a decade a Smooth wins a Terrier Group in England) plus several Best in Show awards at Specialty and Variety shows. Deano was the Top Smooth Fox Terrier in the British Isles, and repeated this double in the United States the following two years.

Could lightning strike twice? It did! A Jonwyre Smooth repeated these achievements again in 1976 and 1977 with another home-bred, English and American Champion Jonwyre's Galore.

1976 was the Centennial of the Fox Terrier Club in England and many of the overseas contingent who attended saw Galaxy's first champion daughter, Boreham Ballet Star, win Best of Breed. Galore was Best Junior. This was the second time Ballet Star was Best of Breed for the year. Previously she had topped all of the Smooths, and again was Best in Show.

Champion Jonwyres Galore's sire was Greenbelt Tri Star, gifted to Mr. Jones like almost all of his Smooths, but unfortunately he came to Mr. Jones too late in life for the best to be gotten out of him. Galore won a C.C. and several Reserves. At six months, to quote Mr. Jones, Gal was rather lacking in height, which she had made up as she matured. She won 12 Challenge Certificates, seven consecutively, eight of them accompanied by Best of Breed (including Crufts in 1977) and the Junior Warrant. During that period Mr. Jones handled five other Challenge Certificate winners. In 1977, after the Windsor Show, Gal joined Deano at Foxden.

Frank Jones acquired Corriebroom Leprechaun at about this same period. She was from a champion bitch by Spaceman, her sire a complete outcross on his sire's side, Champion Newmaidely Whistling Jeremy. Frank's aim was to have three champion producing broods. However, she was a disappointment to him with her three litters, each by a different stud dog. But two generations further on, up came a lovely champion who at the present time has a Championship Certificate winning daughter.

Mr. Jones has since given up handling, reduced his young stock, giving them to serve with great success as foundation stock for other kennels, having been invited to join *Dog World*, the world's largest weekly canine paper, as the Staff Show Representative. This position takes him from home a good deal, as well as demanding much of his time. And so, while he still owns a number of dogs, he now concentrates on his magazine duties and on judging. The youngsters have, as mentioned, gone to new homes but the "golden oldies" will remain at Jonwyre until they are called to that happy hunting ground. Frank Jones comments, with the feeling all who truly love dogs share, that "they have given me great pleasure over the years and many challenges." To which he adds, "the success of the Jonwyre Smooths has come from other kennels—cast-offs, I have just realized on looking back. I have purchased only one Smooth female for just a handful of dollars. In some sort of way, success need not cost a small fortune. One requires an eye—and one big lot of luck."

MARYHOLM

Maryholm Fox Terriers, at Dumfrees, Scotland, are owned by Mr. A. Clanachan, a gentleman who has owned and worked with terriers since the 1930's. Sad to say, it was necessary that some of his Fox Terriers be dispersed in 1939 when he entered the armed forces for World War II. But at the end of the war he managed to locate some of his original line in a bitch called Maryholm Sweet Bit (by Solus Congress from Maryholm Sweet Briar), and this bitch, bred to Champion Laurel Wreath, produced for him Champion Maryholm Spun Gold, born in 1948, a Smooth of tremen-

Ch. Maryholm Spun Gold, a famous Scottish-bred Smooth Fox Terrier, belonged to Mr. A. Clanachan, Maryholm Kennels, Dumfries, Scotland. A tremendously important and influential Smooth dog of the 1950s.

dous quality, with whom the modern Maryholms were established.

By the mid-1950's, Mr. Clanachan had a splendid stud force of both Smooths and Wire Haireds. The former were led by Spun Gold and Champion Maryholm Simon as well as Maryholm St. Patrick. The top dog among the Wires was Champion Maryholm Northern Monarch and Champion Maryholm Mighty Good, while youngsters on the stud force included the Smooth, Maryholm St. Patrick; and the Wire, Maryholm Warranted. At this time, I have read of Mr. Clanachan described as "one of the leading breeders and exhibitors of Fox Terriers in Great Britain," with special mention made of the fact that he has won all-breed Bests in Show at championship events with both his Smooths and his Wires.

By the 1960's, Maryholm had gained even further acclaim as "the leading kennel of Fox Terriers in Scotland," a position held due to the consistency of its winnings in both coats at the prestigious championship shows. Champion Maryholm Sureline had become top star among the Smooths, he by Laurel of Din ex Champion Maryholm Sweetmeat. His credit lines included the Challenge Certificate and Best of Breed at Crufts in 1960, by which time he had also become a popular sire of winners.

Then there was Maryholm Nornay Mainsail, by Champion Maryholm Shamrock (litter sister to Champion Maryholm Sureline). Mainsail lost no time in making his presence felt in the show ring and as a sire. Many were the offers to buy him when he made his show debut, but Mr. Clanachan was hanging on to him hoping that he might take the place of Champion Maryholm Spun Gold who had died at the age of 13 ½ years. It is interesting that Mainsail was from a noted young bitch, Maryholm Shamrock, had been purchased by Mesdames Coward and Soubry of Nornay Saddler fame and that Mainsail was from the first breeding of this bitch after their acquisition of her.

Eng. Ch. Maryholm Northern Monark was a very famous and important Wire of the 1950s. Owned by Mr. A. Clanachan, Maryholm, Dumfries, Scotland, he exemplifies the outstanding type and quality found in the Maryholm Wires as well as their Smooths.

Eng. Ch. Rarity of Riber in 1983. Winning the Terrier Group at the East of England Championship Show handled by Frances Winfield. A famous Challenge Certificate winner with many honors on the credit list.

Champion Maryholm Sailaway, Maryholm Stepaway and Maryholm Strollaway were other young studs there in the early 1960's while among the bitches, Champion Maryholm Sweetmeat at age six-and-a-half years was looking fit to hold her own against the best younger winners. Champion Maryholm Silver Lady was another bitch of true quality, along with her daughters Champion Maryholm Silver Locket and Champion Maryholm Silver Snowflake, winners of C.C. at Crufts 1960, and Reserve C.C. there respectively. All of them are a credit indeed to any top flight kennel.

Mr. Clanachan has always firmly believed that to be a truly successful breeder, one must have quality bitches. Correct temperament is another priority.

RIBER

Riber Smooth Fox Terriers are owned by Peter and Frances Winfield at Mapperley, Derby. These breeders are known for the outstandingly high quality of their Smooths, their winners having many prestigious honors to their credit.

Pride of place in the kennel would seem to be occupied by a magnificent bitch, English Champion Rarity of Riber, whom we

27

picture winning the Terrier Group at East of England Championship Show in 1983, owner-handled by Mrs. Winfield. Rarity has to her credit the winning of: 11 Challenge Certificates and Bests of Breed (eight of them while still a puppy); a Reserve C.C.; the Terrier Group at East of England under judge Mrs. Barbara Tull; and second in the Terrier Group at Leicester Championship Show. She was Best of Breed at Crufts in 1984 and Best in Show at the Smooth Specialty that same year. She was shown only on 13 occasions, retiring at 18 months' age unbeaten in her classes. She was also one of the Top 30 Dogs in the U.K., all breeds, in 1983. Her wins as a puppy created a post-war and possibly all time record in the breed, Mrs. Winfield tells us.

Rarity is a daughter of Champion Riber Ricochet, who was born in 1979 by Champion Watteau Ploughman ex Champion Boreham Briar Rose, the latter by Champion Riber Ramsey.

The famous Eng. Ch. Riber Ramsey, by Riber Rockafella ex Riber Side Saddle, an outstanding sire and show dog from the Riber Smooths, owned by Peter and Frances Winfield, Mapperley, Derby, England.

Teesford Tartan, born in 1970, was bred and owned by Mr. and Mrs. F. Brown and is the sire of many winners including Teesford Twinkle and Teesford Tartar. A Challenge Certificate winner; a Best of Breed winner and winner of Reserve C.Cs.

The late Champion Riber Ramsey, was born in October 1972 and died in January 1985. A son of Riber Rockefella ex Riber Side Saddle, he was the sire of eight U.K. Champions and dominant in most British Smooth pedigrees today. He won his first Challenge Certificate and Best of Breed at seven months, and four of his C.C.s as a puppy.

TEESFORD

Teesford Smooth Fox Terriers, owned by Mr. and Mrs. F. Brown at Darlington, Durham have not continued breeding since 1977, the last of their bitches having been Teesford Teaser, the dam of American Champion Higrola Horatio of Britlea and his litter sister English Champion Higrola Harriet of Britlea. Harriet was the dam of American Champion Britlea Bizet, the sire of Best of Breed at Crufts in 1984 and 1985.

29

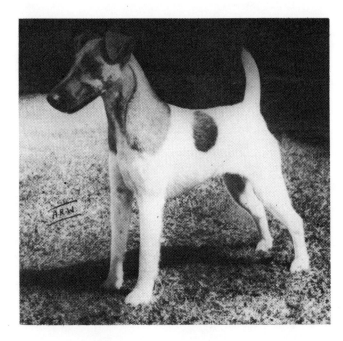

Am. Ch. Teesford Twinkle, one of the outstanding Smooths from Mr. and Mrs. F. Brown's Teesford Kennels, Darlington, England. Sold to the U.S. after winning a C.C. and two Reserves in England. Born in 1974. Photo courtesy of Mrs. Brown.

Teesford was active in the Smooth Fox Terrier world in Great Britain from 1921 until 1977. This present bitch line began in 1950, and has lasted unbroken to the present day, producing many winners on very sparing breeding of never more than one litter a year.

Among the outstanding Smooths carrying the Teesford kennel prefix are Teesford Tartan, born in 1970, a homebred by Mid Day Sun ex Teesford Tilly, winner of the Challenge Certificate, Best of Breed and Best in Show, Fox Terrier Club, 1971; the C.C. and Best of Breed at Paignton in 1972; and three Reserve C.Cs; plus being the sire of many winners, among them Teesford Twinkle and Teesford Tartar.

Teesford Twink was born in 1971, a Junior Warrant winner, sired by Watteau Pittlea Cherokee ex Teesford Tara. Herself the winner of a Challenge Certificate and two Reserves, she was the dam of Teesford Twinkle, Teesford Teaser, and Champion Teesford Trier as well as the granddam of American Champion Higrola Horatio of Britlea.

American Champion Teesford Twinkle was born in 1974, by Teesford Tartan ex Teesford Twink. A Challenge Certificate winner in 1976, she also had gained two Reserve C.C.s in England prior to her sale to the United States.

One of the most famed of all the dogs from this kennel, Champion Teesford Trier, was born in 1975 by Teesford Tartar ex Teesford Twink. Winner of nine Challenge Certificates, four Bests of Breed, five Reserve, this Smooth's notable wins also included the C.C. and Best of Breed at Crufts in 1978; the Challenge Certificate and Best in Show at the Smooth Fox Terrier Association in 1978; and the C.C. and Best of Breed at Crufts in 1979. Trier was sold to Dr. Dagradi in Italy, where we are certain this great Smooth's quality was beneficial to the breed.

WATTEAU

Watteau, probably the most famous name in Smooth history, was founded at the start of this century by Mr. Frank Calvert Butler, father of Mrs. Mary Blake and grandfather of Mrs. Antonia Thornton, present owners of the Watteau prefix. The first Smooth Fox Terrier Champion from here was Miss Watteau, who finished in 1911; and from her name came the prefix attached to all the terriers from this kennel. Although Smooth Fox Terriers are the sole residents today, there have been champions in Wire Fox Terriers, Airedales, Kerry Blues, Irish, Cairns and Scotties, all in Mr. Butler's name. Mrs. Blake bred some Miniature Smooth Dachshunds after the war, and in fact bred one champion in this breed. However, it is the Smooths who have made the biggest impact.

Watteau Kennels are at West Scrafton, North Yorkshire. During the war, most of the kennel was dispersed, and by the end of hostilities there was just one Wire bitch remaining. This was exchanged for a Smooth bitch, Brooklands Mist, and through her came the present day Watteau Smooths; not by what she produced, but by her success in the show ring which served as an encouragement to breed and show with still more success. At this point, and until the death of Mr. Herbert Johnson, Watteau and Brooklands Kennels were complementary to one another, both lines being similar, and yet both could use the other's stud dogs to good effect. Mr. Johnson had been kennel manager to Mr. Calvert Butler and on the latter's death started his own kennel with the Brooklands prefix. Mrs. Antonia Thornton notes that "To Mr. Johnson must go a large debt of gratitude as without his encouragement, good sense, and knowledge, the kennel would not have continued."

Ch. Watteau Midas, the first champion Smooth bred in Mrs. A. Blake's name. Born in 1948 by the great Ch. Laurel Wreath out of Brooklands Ebony Belle, who was a granddaughter of Watteau Kathleen. A dog of tremendous impact on the breed of the 1950s and thereafter. Owned by Mrs. Blake, Watteau Kennels, West Scrafton, England.

The first dog to be bred to win his championship in Mrs. Blake's name was Champion Watteau Midas. He was whelped in 1948 by the great Champion Laurel Wreath out of Brooklands Ebony Belle, a granddaughter of Watteau Kathleen who in turn was by Watteau Cheerio out of Watteau Wild Rose, thus connecting post-war Watteaus with pre-war. Midas did not live very long, and in fact died at only four years of age; but in that short time he had a profound effect on modern Smooths and it has been said that he was responsible for putting outstanding heads on the Smooths of the 1950's. Midas sired several champions, the most important being Champion Brooklands Black Prince who in turn sired Champion Brooklands Lucky Wishbone, he the sire of

Champion Watteau Chorister, double grandsire of Champion Watteau Snuff Box, American Champion Watteau Musical Box, etc.

Following Midas came the bitch Champion Watteau Songstress, bred by Mr. A.D. Kay. She was a granddaughter of Midas and proved to be an influential brood bitch. Her son, Champion Watteau Chorister, played a tremendous part in the success of the kennel in the 1950s and 1960s. Together with Watteau Marylyn (by Champion Hampole Tinkler), they produced at least one champion in every litter; i.e., Champion Watteau Sonata, Champion Watteau Rhapsody, Champion Watteau Madrigal, Champion Watteau Cantata, and Champion Brooklands Present; also Watteau Cantor who was exported to France, where he sired a number of good dogs; and Watteau Concerto, who became a stud force of some repute in Germany.

Ch. Watteau Chorister, a dog of enormous importance to the progress of Watteau Smooths during the 1950s and 1960s. Mrs. A. Blake, owner, Watteau Smooths, West Scrafton, England.

Ch. Watteau Ploughman, winner of 17 Challenge Certificates and was Best in Show at England's National Terrier Championship event in 1980 and at the Smooth Fox Terrier Association's Championship Shows in 1980 and 1982. His progeny include such noted British winners as Ch. Riber Ricochet, Ch. Riber Rosemead, and Ch. Vertway Bothy Boy before his exportation to Dr. Dagradi in Italy. Watteau Kennels, Mrs. A. Blake, West Scrafton, England.

Chorister was also the sire of Beechbank Olive, who in turn produced Champion Watteau Snuff Box, the winner of 23 Challenge Certificates, the Fox Terrier Club's Gold Cup in two successive years, and was the sire of some influential stud dogs. Beechbank Olive only had one litter for the Watteau Kennels, but it was a truly memorable one. As well as Snuff Box, there were American Champion Watteau Musical Box and Continental Champion Watteau Phone Call, the latter exported to Mr. Gerhardt in Holland.

Snuff Box himself was the sire of Miss Linda Beak's Champions Newmaidley Vodka and Joshua; Miss Barbara Stapley's Champion Harkaway Lancashire Lad (the sire of Champion Burmar Ted, grandsire of Champion Riber Ramsey); Mr. and Mrs. Farrell's

American Champion Foremark Ebony Box of Foxden, and Champion Hermon Mirage. He also sired a total of 20 American champions, including the littermates Watteau Snifter, Snufsed, and Sneeze. A marvelous record indeed for a dog who never left the U.K.!

Snufsed made an important contribution to Watteau prior to his departure to live at Crag Crest Kennels in the United States. He was mated to an Irish-bred bitch, Lincrove Linnet (a granddaughter of Chorister), whose litter produced two English champions and an American and Canadian champion: Watteau Happy Talk, Watteau Small Talk, and Watteau Last Word of Foxden. Happy Talk proved to be an excellent show bitch, winning six Challenge Certificates and a Terrier Group, then produced Champion Watteau Lyrical (by Champion Watteau Madrigal) and Champion Watteau Chief Barker (by Champion Karnilo Chieftain before his exportation to Foxden Kennels). Chief Barker went to Norway where he made a splendid impression both in the ring and as a stud dog. His litter brother, Watteau Cross Talk, did equally well in Germany. But it was from Lyrical that the continued saga of the Watteaus came!

Lyrical was mated to Champion Ellastone Firecrest, producing Champion Watteau Ballad and Champion Watteau Sonnet, both of whom were to become American champions prior to Ballad being repatriated. Perhaps Lyrical's most prominent litter was by Champion Maryholm Stockmark, which included Champion Watteau Ploughman and his sister Watteau Landgirl. Ploughman met with enormous success in the show ring, earning 17 Challenge Certificates, and was Best in Show at the National Terrier Championship Show in 1980 and at the Smooth Fox Terrier Association's Championship Shows in 1980 and 1982. In turn, he sired Champion Riber Ricochet, Champion Riber Rosemead, and Champion Vertway Bothy Boy before his exportation to Dr. Dagradi in Italy.

This pretty much brings us up to the present day of the Watteau story. Many other dogs have been bred here and it is hoped many will be bred in the future, although on a much reduced scale. In the kennel are Watteau Witchcraft, a daughter of Watteau Landgirl by Champion Sirandra of Maryholm; and her two sons by Champion Vertway Bothy Boy. This is the present! You have just read the past. And we look forward to the future.

Ch. Deko Dragoon, a marvelously headed dog who produced well, was influential in the world of Wires. He was brought here by John Coghlin of Wales, who was responsible for the Deko prefix, well-known through Deko Druid, and Deko Dryad as well as Dragoon. You'll see them in your Wire pedigrees! This photo of Dragoon is with the compliments of Mrs. Betsey Dossett to whom it was given by Mr. Coghlin prior to his return to Wales. Mr. Coghlin is handling him to a good win under Mrs. John Marvin.

36

Chapter 3

Fox Terriers in the United States

Development of Fox Terriers in the United States started somewhere during the middle 1860s, so far as has been officially recorded. Unofficially, however, it is known that these dogs, particularly the Smooths, were widely seen and known here from several decades earlier. The pity is that no official records were kept that long ago and so detailed particulars are lost to following generations.

It was during the summer of 1862 that a Smooth appeared at a dog show here, the first of the breed seen in competition. The early names associated with Fox Terriers in America were those of Smooths, which were dominant at that time. The "greats" then included Belvoir Joe, from Belvoir Kennels, who sired Belgrave Joe, so highly esteemed that thousands have seen his glass-enclosed skeleton on display in the offices of the American Kennel Club in New York City. But Belvoir was not alone in the possession of memorable Smooths. The Grove had its "stars" in Old Jock and Old Tartar. The Oakley was noted as the home of Old Trap. And Quorn also had its share of quality.

Following these earliest Smooths were New Forest, Splinter, and Vesuvian. Splinter became especially memorable as the sire of Venio who was progenitor of the line which descended to Visto, Vibro, Eton Blue, Dark Blue, Oxonian, Orkney, and eventually to Orkadian, whose three sons merged the early days with later generations. They were Cromwell Ochre, Orluke, and Southboro Sandman.

Arthur Wardle's famous painting, "The Totterbridge Eleven." These are Smooth Fox Terriers from 1897. A print of this painting is in the collection of the authors.

Cromwell Ochre sired Beggerman, Blybro Top Note, and Ochre's Legacy. Orluke's progeny included Flornell Lucky Pebble and Adonis. Southbury Sandman accounted for Brockford Dandy. All of these dogs had tremendous beneficial impact on the development of the American Smooth Fox Terrier. Students of pedigree research will find that Orkadian descendants encompass many of America's most notable winning Smooths from America's most prestigious kennels.

The American Fox Terrier Club was founded in 1885 at a meeting held during the Westminster Kennel Club Dog Show in New York City, the heart at that time of important United States show dog activities. Organizing members included Mr. Lewis Rutherford who, with his brother Winthrop, did tremendous service to the breed here, and left a legacy of Fox Terrier quality behind them in the form of their Warren Smooths and their Rutherford descendants. Lewis Rutherford was the club's first president, with John E. Thayer and Edward Kelly also serving in official capacities.

Despite the fact that many students of the breed feel strongly that the Wire Fox Terrier was by far the earlier of the two breeds, the Smooths are the ones who dominated the scene here until around 1915.

The American Fox Terrier Club, upon its organization, adopted for its own use the standard which had been drawn up by the Fox Terrier Club of England in 1876. It is interesting to note that while the Fox Terrier Club of England is the third oldest specialty club in existence, the American Fox Terrier Club was the first to become an American Kennel Club Member Specialty Club, although slightly pre-dated in longevity by the American Spaniel Club, the Fox Terrier people having applied for and received membership approval ahead of the Spaniel folk.

The official seal of the American Fox Terrier Club is now one hundred years old having appeared originally in 1886 and been used for the first time in the Specialty Catalogue of 1887.

For its initial Specialty Show in 1886, the American Fox Terrier Club brought to America the gentleman to whom I have frequently seen reference made as "the most notable Smooth breeder of his day": Francis Redmond of England. Whether it was a reflection of that fact or of the smaller interest in Wires than in Smooths then, or a combination of both, the total entry consisted of 75 Smooths, but merely four Wires.

The relative popularity of the Smooth Fox Terrier vs. the Wire Fox Terrier in the United States has moved back and forth over the decades. At some periods the Smooths have been in the lead numerically; at others it has been the Wires. Looking at the overall picture from the beginning of the 20th century to the present day, the authors feel that the Wires have dominated a greater portion of the time although there have been periods (the advent of Saddler, The Brat, etc., among them) when the Smooths have been neatly ahead numerically, at least so far as show recognition and entries are concerned.

Since it was the Smooths who were in the dominant position at that time, we shall speak first of the outstanding early dogs and breeders and of some of their accomplishments; then do likewise with the Wires.

Winthrop Rutherford served the American Fox Terrier Club as its President from 1896-1920, then again from 1931 until he passed on in 1944. This remarkable gentleman accomplished much of

Brokenhurst Sting, born in 1877, was bred by Mr. H. Gibson. Of very famous parentage, he was a son of two noted Fox Terriers, Joe and Bettle. A splendid example of a quality Smooth from the 1870s.

benefit to the breed, especially the Smooths, and dogs from Warren Kennels can be found consolidated into many breeding programs of the 1930s-1940s period. The kennel was carried on by Hugo Rutherford well beyond the time of Winthrop's death, always maintaining the value he placed on quality.

From the Rutherfords' kennel came the first and only dog to date to win the supreme honor of Best in Show there *on three consecutive occasions,* plus being the first Fox Terrier to gain the club's top award, as it was at the very first three Westminsters that Warren Remedy was victorious, in 1907, 1908 and 1909. It is doubtful that Remedy's three Bests in Show at this prestigious and highly competitive event will ever be duplicated. Thus Warren Remedy holds a unique position in the world of American show dogs. In honor of Remedy's Westminster record, he is the dog portrayed in the gorgeous crystal figurine, created by Ric Chashoudian, which is presented by the Quaker Oats Dog Food Division to the winners of their Annual Top Show Dog Awards; needless to say, a treasure of untold value to each fortunate winner!

The Smooth tradition at Westminster continued for a fourth year when another representative of the breed, Champion Sabine Rarebit from the outstanding Sabine Kennels belonging to F.H. Farwell in Texas, trotted right into Warren Remedy's pawprints by making it four Westminster "bests" in a row for Smooths in 1910. Thus the first four Westminster Bests in Show became a series of Smooth Fox Terrier triumphs.

As a comment on the wide swing of the Fox Terrier pendulum, we must remark that in the 76-year period between Sabine Rarebit's victory there and the present time, *no Smooth has again taken a Westminster Best in Show!* Numerous Wires have done so, as we shall relate shortly; but for the Smooths it has been a long dry period, not even broken by the presence of such "greats" as Champion Sabine Fernlike, who came close to making it with Best American-bred in Show in 1920; Champion Nornay Saddler, in whose stunning show career this was the one great disappointment to his owner Jim Austin; Saddler's son, Champion Desert Deputy, who also was a "near miss" in 1942 when he took Best American-bred in Show for his owners, Mr. and Mrs. W. Holden White; and Champion Ttarb The Brat, who has broken all previous Smooth records in the show ring, and who won the 1982 Terrier Group there.

This is the authors' favorite painting of early Fox Terriers. It depicts, *left to right*, the "Rough Coat" or Wire, Bristles; *center*, the Smooth, Hyde's Buffet, these two owned by S.E. Shirley; and on the *right*, the Smooth Fox Terrier, Bloom, owned by Mr. F. Burbidge.

It was Champion Nornay Saddler who, upon his arrival in American show rings late in the 1930's, turned what at the time had become very definite Wire dominance back to the Smooths. Saddler was a "wonder dog" who appealed immediately and strongly to the American fancy. He was brought over to Mr. Austin from England by his breeders, Mr. and Mrs. Frank Coward, and Saddler became Mr. Austin's constant companion, and quite probably his greatest pride. He was the hero of a book Jim Austin had written especially to tell his story! (I know of only one other show dog of whom this is true, the Irish Setter Champion Milson O'Boy owned by Mrs. Cheever Porter); he was the record-holding Smooth of his day with a tremendously imposing list of victories, especially so when one considers that there were far fewer dog shows at that time than now. He seemed to be almost invincible. And as a sire, he left a strong and valuable heritage. So wide was the admiration felt for Saddler that almost everyone who had Smooths was eager to use his services as a sire. Consequently, his influence was widely felt and has lived on through many generations. Between his arrival in the United States and 1946, Saddler sired more American Smooth champions than did any other dog. His son, Champion Desert Deputy, was third in line as a producer at that time (second place to Danesgate Debtor).

Nornay Saddler was entered in the Open Dog Class at Westminster in 1937 when he was little more than a puppy. His career did not get off to a propitious start as the writer recalls; but once he had started "rolling" there seemed to be no stopping him. His greatest win was undoubtedly was that of Best in Show at the Morris and Essex Kennel Club, which classic was the largest U.S.A. dog show at that time.

Wissaboo Kennels were owned by Jim Austin and Mrs. Austin's daughter Madeleine West who was called "Wissie." Saddler was only one of many outstanding terriers there. One of their early dogs, Champion Foxden Chorister, had been purchased from Mr. and Mrs. James A. Farrell, Jr., by Mrs. Austin.

A very large and high quality kennel of the same period was Andely, owned by Mrs. Barbara Lowe Fallass at Cross River, New York. They were the importers of such dogs as Buckland of Andely and Oneway Storm, among others. Andely Kennels produced a formidable number of champions, with dogs from here to be found in the breeding programs of many other kennels.

Ch. Nornay Saddler, for many years record holder in the breed, was born in 1936 and came to America at an early age. His show record stood at 55 Bests in Show, including Morris and Essex, at that time America's largest dog show; 59 Terrier Groups; and 88 Bests Smooth. He was the sire of many champions and behind numerous successful breeding programs. Owned by Wissaboo Kennels, Old Westbury, New York.

Ch. Desert Deputy, son of Ch. Nornay Saddler ex Braw Lass, born January 8, 1939. A multiple Best in Show and Group winner; an outstanding sire. Owned by Mr. and Mrs. W. Holden White, Foxspan Kennels, Chagrin Falls, Ohio. Deputy won the Terrier Group at Westminster and was Best American-bred in Show there in 1942.

Foxden Kennels were also very much in the picture at this time (you will find their kennel story later along in the book), with Mr. and Mrs. James A. Farrell, Jr., already high on the winners lists.

E. Coe Kerr, at Syosset, New York, was another fancier whose dogs were to be reckoned with, his being under the care and guidance of that outstanding terrier expert, Percy Roberts. Champion Lad Fra Syke was an important Smooth from this kennel, as were Champion Flornell Standard, Champion Flornell Special, and Champion Millhill Lingster Don.

Jere R. Collins, at one point in the 1930s-40s period, was second only to Mrs. Fallass in number of Smooth homebred champions. An early dog of his, Fox Trail As Usual, sired by Champion Danesgate Debtor, had progeny proving much in demand. He also had a bitch named Upper Crust by this same sire. The Collins family (Jere and his parents, Dr. and Mrs. Collins), at that time, could always be found at Fox Terrier ringsides at shows in the Eastern area. Later on they moved to England, where Keeshonden grew to dominate their dog interest.

Long time Fox Terrier fans will love this nostalgia builder! It appeared originally in the November 1, 1940 issue of *Vogue* magazine. Judge Mrs. Duncan Y. Henderson. Exhibitors, from the *left,* Mac Silver, Luther Lewis, Percy Roberts, and Tom Gately.

M.J. Nicholas, author A.K.N.'s Dad, with his noted Smooth Fox Terrier Ch. Pocono Prince under his arm in this informal snapshot of the 1930s–1940s period. Mr. Nicholas was for many years Secretary to the American Fox Terrier Club and its Delegate to the A.K.C.

A truly top notch breeder and exhibitor was John P.S. Harrison, owner of Etona Kennels. A brother of the U.S. Ambassador to Switzerland, Jack in the 1930s and 1940s was among our most astute and loyal fanciers. Despite being very much hampered by crippling arthritis he often was in the ring with his own dogs. Jack had a lively sense of humor and was always on the button where the dogs were concerned. The stunning Champion Alwen Foxcatcher and his son Champion Upper Boy of Etona were two of Jack's most successful. Foxcatcher was a sire who well reproduced his quality, thus had an imposing list of winning champions to his credit. Two others of Jack Harrison's Smooths who are well remembered include the Best in Show winning Champion Oppidan of Etona and the lovely bitch Champion Tilwall Tryst, a Foxcatcher daughter, who was widely admired during her successful career.

Battle Cry Kennels, owned by Mrs. Stewart Simmons, and Stoney Meadows, owned by Mr. and Mrs. W. Potter Wear (Mrs. Simmons and Mrs. Wear are sisters), have long raised outstanding Smooth Fox Terriers, and are still doing so today, in the Philadelphia and Maryland areas.

A dog named Pocono Prince was owned by my Dad, M.J. Nicholas, during the thirties-into-forties period. Under Leonard

Intl. Ch. Gallant Fox of Wildoaks owned by Mrs. R.C. Bondy of Goldens Bridge, New York. This great Terrier, one of the best of his day, was born in December of 1929, a son of Ch. Crackley Supreme out of a noted matron, Ch. Gains Great Surprise.

Brumby's expert handling, he defeated practically every Smooth in competition with the exception of Saddler, after which he went to live in Colorado, where eventually he joined the dogs at Even So Kennels belonging to Agnes Miner. Teddy was a truly lovely "Smooth" and a great favorite with our entire family due to his just plain good sense. Unfortunately we lived at that time in a New York City apartment with some half dozen Pekes, and since the Pekes were a feisty crew, we felt uneasy at mixing the two breeds together as housepets or we would never have parted with "Teddy." Both of his Colorado owners loved him dearly and were proud of owning him; and he sired some nice youngsters for his owners there.

One of the "old-timers" in Smooths was Robert Sedgewick, who bred and showed some very handsome dogs. Then that wonderful gentleman George Hartman at Lampeter, Pennsylvania, owner of Wirehart Kennels, became as famous for his Smooths as for his Wires with a splendid representation of quality in both these breeds. The Robert Neffs were interested in both coats, too. Their kennel name was Fenbor. Mrs. T. Huntley Christman, in Connecticut, bred good Smooths under the Twinbark prefix, as well as some splendid Poodles.

Some of the Smooths I personally have most admired over the years have been those from Downsbragh Kennels belonging to Mr. and Mrs. William Brainard. I was especially impressed by Champion Downsbragh Two O'Clock Fox; but there were a number of notables among the other Smooths there, too, who made outstanding show records.

In summation, Champion Nornay Saddler held the record as America's top winning Smooth and, I believe, among all Terriers over a goodly period of time. However, records in Saddler's day were made on many fewer opportunities to show dogs than later became the case; thus the possibilities of gaining vast numbers of points and wins were nothing compared to what they had been. The 55 times Best in Show won by Saddler (including the Morris and Essex Kennel Club event), backed up by 59 Terrier Groups and 88 times Best Smooth Fox Terrier, was an astronomical figure at the time they occurred. And the Group-Best in Show ratio is remarkable at any time!

Longshore K.C. in 1946. Author A.K.N. awards Best in Show to Ch. Crackley Startrite of Wildoaks, one of the famous winners, this an importation, from Mrs. Richard C. Bondy's noted kennel of Wire Fox Terriers which has been among the most successful ever in this breed, located at Goldens Bridge, New York.

By the time Brat joined the dog show scene, the dog show calendar had grown beyond the wildest expectations of any of us "old timers." Of course a mind-boggling assortment of opportunities to win also resulted, provided one had a great dog and the energy to really travel about a bit. Ed Dalton and Dr. John Van Zandt gave the Brat every opportunity, and he was more than equal to it. We salute these two "greats," at the same time wondering who will be the *next* Smooth to reach new and perhaps even greater heights than ever previously attained.

So much for the historic Smooths, and on to Wires who set the pattern here.

It was in 1882 at the Westminster Kennel Club Dog Show in New York that the earliest Wire Fox Terrier seen in the American Dog show ring appeared. This was Tyke, owned by John E.I. Grainger, New York City (a founder-member of the American Fox Terrier Club). Tyke had been imported from Great Britain, purchased from the breeder, Mr. Carrick. This entry was in the Miscellaneous Class, where Tyke won first prize. In total, Tyke made four annual appearances at Westminster, coming away with a blue ribbon on each of these occasions, the last at 11 years of age.

The turnout of 11 Wires at Westminster in 1883 was truly an

Left: Ch. Hallwyre Hard Cash owned by the Great All Rounder Forrest Hall, Dallas, Texas. This kennel has the distinction of having bred 100 Wire Champions, a record for the breed. *Right*: Ch. Hetherington Pilot, by Ch. Derbyshire Peter ex Ch. Hetherington Model Rhythm, a noted Wire "star" of the early 1940s.

Left: Ch. Hetherington Knight Stormer, an early representative of the Wires bred by Mr. and Mrs. Thomas H. Carruthers, III, who have made a major contribution to Wires in the United States. *Right*: Ch. Hetherington Model Rhythm was Best in Show at Westminster in 1946. Owned and bred by Mr. and Mrs. Thomas H. Carruthers, III, Glendale, Ohio.

eventful occasion, making it obvious that the breed deserved its own classification, which it then received. In fact two classes were provided in which they competed.

James Mortimer joined the ranks of Wire exhibitors in 1888, the first of them having been bred in England, imported from England from W.B. Brumby and Arthur Clear. Under the kennel identification "Suffolk," Mr. Mortimer's dogs chalked up an impressive roster of good wins. Credit is given to his efforts on behalf of his beloved breed; at the Westminster Kennel Club, of whose shows he had become superintendent, the Wire entry had increased to 24 at the 1890 event.

Braxton Virago was the first Wire Haired Fox Terrier registered in the American Kennel Club Stud Book, this in 1887. Virago was a Canadian-bred dog owned by R.W. Dean of Oakville, Ontario, bred by G. Whitaker.

It seems strange that only a Wire or two was registered annually with the American Kennel Club between 1887 and 1891, despite what would seem to have been quite a burst of activity here. Mr. Thomas H. Bellin moved his English breeding kennel of Wires from there to the States; and Mr. G.W.H. Ritchie, long-time New Yorker, became a busy importer of splendid Wires who represented some of Great Britain's finest lines—both events which one would expect to have caused a flurry of excitement; but evidently not so. Perhaps, though, it was delayed reaction that in 1892 Mr. Mayhew came from England, accompanied by his well-known Champion Brittle; and that Major G.M. Carnochan started showing his Suffolk Trazel, purchased from James Mortimer. These events swelled the ranks of Wire exhibitors (if one might put it that way) by two new names, theirs being added to those of Messrs. Bellin, Carnochan, Grainger, Mayhew, Mortimer, Ritchie, and J. Lee Tailor.

In 1894, the importation of Cribbage by Harry M. Smith of Worcester, Massachusetts, along with Sister Patten and Surry Janet created a bit of a stir. Then Oakleigh Bruiser, Endcliffe Banker and Endcliffe Fidget were brought over by a gentleman who became one of the Fancy's most respected dog men, George S. Thomas, along with Richard Toon. Shortly thereafter Mr.

The famed Ch. Hetherington Druid Piper winning the American Fox Terrier Club Specialty at Montgomery County in October 1967. William W. Wimer, III, is the judge; the handler is George Ward. Piper was owned by Mr. and Mrs. Thomas H. Carruthers of the highly prestigious Hetherington Kennel in Ohio. Photo courtesy of Peter Green.

Ch. Flornell Spicy Bit of Halleston, 1934 Westminster Best in Show, owned by Stanley J. Halle, Halleston Kennels, Chappaqua, New York. Spicy Bit was a kennelmate of Ch. Flornell Spicy Piece of Halleston, 1937 Westminster Best in Show. Also owned by J. Halle, and handled by Percy Roberts.

Smith sold Cribbage, Janet, and several other Wires he had owned to Mr. Hunnewill, increasing the strength of his kennel, to which he added still further with the importation of two more Wires from England, thus establishing himself as a Wire owner with whom to reckon.

Whether prompted by this, or just by coincidence, Major Carnochan stepped up his own kennel activities by buying lavishly from England, largely from George Raper, thus setting the groundwork for what became the famed Cairnsmuir Wires. By 1896 competition was tense between the Hunnewill and Carnochan competitors, closely pressed by a Canadian kennel, Norfolk, owned by Charles Lyndon, which already was highly respected in Smooths. However, by 1898 Cairnsmuir Kennels were leading the Wires handily, even prior to the very exciting and important purchase of a dog called Go Bang, who swept the boards wherever he was shown, and was noted as a dog of tremendous quality.

Go Bang's talents as a sire evidently equalled his qualities as a show dog. Thus it was that he retired in 1900, leaving the way clear for his stunning son Heads Up, owned and bred by Mr. Mayhew. Heads Up had the winning situation well in paw until the arrival of Humberstone Bristles, whom Mr. Raper personally delivered to the dog's new owner, Irving C. Ackerman. At the same time, Mr. Raper brought over Raby Match Box for Mr. Wallace Waken in Chicago. We understand that Wire competition set-

51

Santa Barbara K.C., July 1959. Judge John Marvin awards Best of Breed to Ch. Mitre Miss Adorable, Jimmy Butler handling. Best of Opposite Sex, (*left*) Ch. Trucote Tradition, Peter Green handling. Photo courtesy of Peter Green.

tled into a three-way battle between Heads Up, Bristles, and Match Box, enlivening the situation to a startling degree as all three dogs were exceptionally outstanding, making their work exciting and challenging for the judges. When the smoke of battle had cleared, all three of these worthy dogs were about on equal grounds. Meanwhile, Major Carnochan, with Hot Stuff, was cleaning up among the bitches.

Then came "Ben" to Major Carnochan, officially Barkby Ben, and between him and the bitch Hot Stuff many more honors came home again to this kennel. Ben was retired in 1903, clearing the boards for his son, Bulls Eye, whose career here was so exciting that his owner could not resist the temptation to "take coals to Newcastle" and try him out in the show rings of Great Britain. A decision with sad results, as Bull's Eye was lost due to illness in quarantine while awaiting admission to that country.

With all the resources being gathered among Wire breeders, it is not in the least surprising that the breed soon started making itself felt in the keen competition of the Westminster Best in Show ring. Champion Matford Vic started the ball rolling for George Quintard in 1915, repeating the following year; 1917 saw it become three in a row for Wires. Mrs. Roy A. Rainey's Champion Conejo Wycollar Boy took Best in Show that year, then repeated the victory in 1920. Mr. Quintard had started in Wires in 1906, dropped out temporarily in 1910, then returned on an even larger scale five years later. Mrs. Rainey, too, had been a Wire breeder for awhile, and Wycollar Boy had enjoyed a good career as "head dog" at her kennel. It speaks well of this dog's quality and lasting ability that he returned to the shows after a three year interval to take, at that time, his *second* Westminster Best in Show.

The 1920's and onward have seen a whole galaxy of superior Wire kennels here in the United States. From them came some of the biggest "name dogs" of breed history. For example, Champion Signal Circuit of Halleston took the 1926 Westminster Best in Show for owner Stanley J. Halle, Halleston Kennels, Chappaqua, New York. Two years later Reginald M. Lewis, Warily Kennels, New York, received similar honors with his lovely bitch Champion Talavera Margaret. And in 1930 it was John G. Bates with his Champion Pendley Calling of Blarney who became another "two-time winner" by repeating in 1931. Stanley J. Halle had his second Westminster Best in Show when Champion Flornell Spicy Piece of Halleston took the honor in 1937.

Mr. and Mrs. Thomas H. Carruthers III saw their Champion Heatherington Model Rhythm hit the high spot at the Garden in 1946. And Marion G. Bunker's Champion Mooremaide's Magic did so in 1966. Since then no Wire has taken the Westminster Best in Show. We would say that based on past performance, the breed now is overdue.

There have been a number of big and important Wire kennels in the United States during the period of the breed's greatest development here who will never be forgotten. Heading this list (as I knew the owners and the dogs almost from the earliest of them) with utmost admiration in my opinion, was Wildoaks, the fabulous establishment at Goldens Bridge, New York, owned by Mr. and Mrs. R. C. Bondy. Here were owned and bred some of the most memorable Wires of all time.

English and American Champion Gallant Fox of Wildoaks was born in December 1929, by Champion Crackley Supreme of Wildoaks from Mrs. Bondy's renowned imported bitch Champion Gains Great Surprise, the latter also the dam of Champion Beau Brummel of Wildoaks. Champion Striking Emblem of Wildoaks was by Champion Crackley Striking of Wildoaks ex Gay Emblem of Wildoaks. The esteemed Champion Gallant Fox of Wildoaks

Ch. Chief Barmaid, outstanding winner owned by Benrook Kennels, taking Best in Show at Windham County K.C. in May 1949. Tom Gately handling. A fabulous bitch whose career was a great one.

Ch. Travella Superman of Harham, outstanding record holder owned by Harham Kennels, H.N. Florsheim, Chicago, Illinois. Handled here by Tom Gately to Best in Show under judge A.K.N. at Rockland County K.C., September 1955.

and his son Champion Fox Hunter of Wildoaks were a memorable pair, Fox Hunter from the imported bitch Champion Crackley Sunray of Wildoaks. Champion Crackley Striking of Wildoaks was by Champion Crackley Supreme Again ex Champion Crackley Social. And we could continue on through a very impressively long list. Mrs. Bondy was a breeder of the old school, interested in raising superior Wires. She used her importations well towards this goal, and with the assistance of her marvelous kennel manager-handler for a number of years, Mac Silver (until arthritis forced his retirement), and later with Pete Snodgrass handling for her, Wildoaks became truly a legend in its own time. One of the later dogs who was a favorite of mine was the imported Champion Crackley Startrite of Wildoaks. Time passes so quickly that one sometimes misses on dates, but I believe that the kennel was still active until well into the 1960s, and Bessie Bondy never lost one jot of her love and enthusiasm for her Wires. Her son and daughter-in-law, Mr. and Mrs. Philip Bondy, also shared an interest in the dogs, and were to be seen with his mother at ringside very frequently at important Eastern shows.

Right at the top of the list of prestigious kennels breeding superior Wires for more than several decades is Hetherington, only recently disbanded following a long and admirable history. Mr. and Mrs. Thomas H. Carruthers III at Glendale, Ohio, were the owners here, and noted for their homebreds. Among the latter were: Champion Hetherington Knight Stormer, Champion Hetherington Surprise Model, Champion Hetherington Surprise Trust, and the fantastic Champion Hetherington Model Rhythm, the latter completing her title at the National Specialty in 1939.

From the late 1930s, Mr. and Mrs. W.B. Reis, owners of Battlehill and Brentnut Fox Terriers, were making records on the Pacific Coast from their kennel at Brentwood, California. Among the familiar names from here are: Champion Battlehill Dancer of Loynita, Champion Brentnut Letty Geste, Champion Brentnut Wiggie, and Champion Headliner of Florenda. An especially handsome bitch was Champion Battlehill Bernadette.

Forrest N. Hall made Halleston Wires legendary, placing them in all parts of the United States where they won well for their owners.

Mr. and Mrs. Harold Florsheim's Harham Wires have been among America's most outstanding. Among them are: Champion

Foxbank Entertainer of Harham, Champion Travella Superman of Harham, Champion Travella Starstud of Harham—to barely scratch the surface.

Many other folks with truly *good* Wires come to mind from the first half of the 1900s who left their mark upon the breed. Nell Smit of Trucote Kennels, for one, who came here during World War II from Belgium (I had the pleasure of meeting her when she first arrived in New York) as Mrs. Leonard J.A. Smit; then later married Joseph Urmstom in California. Nell was a charming and dedicated terrier person, who helped to get Lakelands popular here, and had a very special love for the Wires. The success she attained was well deserved.

The Fred Dutchers had Champion Copper Beech Storm, a handsome dog who did some good winning under Steve Shaw's handling. He was a son of Champion Wyretex Wyn's Jupiter of Glynhir ex Champion Denbeigh Dream Girl.

Mrs. Munro W. Lanier had some lovely Wires. For her, I recall Jimmy Butler handling Champion Emprise Sensational and Champion Mac's Revelation.

Mrs. Franklin Kroehler always had some good ones. And it may come as a surprise to some of our readers to know that Mr. and Mrs. James A. Farrell, Jr. owned the outstanding *Wire* bitch, Champion Flornell Spicy Morsel.

When English Champion Sunnybrook Spot On came to the United States, where he was handled by Peter Green for Mrs. Robert Clark of Springfield Farms Kennels, knowledgeable Wire people realized that this was an event of importance. What may not quite have been realized back at the time was that Spot On would found a dynasty in the American Wire Haired Fox Terrier world, which is exactly what he did. Spot On, who was by English Champion Townville Tally'O from Sunnybrook Gosmore Photogenic, had, while still in England, sired a dog whose dam was his half sister, being also by English Champion Townville Tally'O (who was by the noted English Champion Winter Statesman) from Viscum Vera (who was a Statesman daughter). This dog was born in February 1972, bred by Miss Hall, and owned by Michael Weissman and his mother of Yonkers, New York. He was Champion Aryee Dominator who, in the capable hands of handler George Ward over a period of five years' campaigning, became the Top Winning Wire Fox Terrier of all time, with a record of 78

The ringside fairly held their breath at Westminster and at the American Fox Terrier Club Specialty Show as the competition narrowed to Ch. Sunnybrook Spot On (*left*), Peter Green handling; and Ch. Ayree Dominator (*right*) with George Ward handling. The only two times these great Wires met in competition, and Spot On was the winner both days. Photo courtesy of Peter Green. Spot On sired Dominator.

Ch. Crackley Striking of Wildoaks, a highly important Wire of the 1939–40 period, was imported from England for the Wildoaks Kennels owned by Mr. and Mrs. Richard C. Bondy, Goldens Bridge, New York.

Bests in Show, 163 Group Firsts; and 22 additional placements made this dog the third among all Terriers, where show records are concerned. Like his sire, Spot On, Dominator also proved himself outstanding as a sire, numbering among his sons the breed's two top winning American-breds of all time, Champion Terrikane's Tulliver (45 times Best in Show) and Champion Bev-Wyr's Sovereign Escort (43 times Best in Show). The impact of this family on Wire Fox Terriers very clearly speaks for itself.

No discussion of Wires would be complete without paying tribute to Mrs. Paul M. Silvernail of Crack-Dale fame who over many years, at Madison, Connecticut, maintained a kennel known far and wide for the quality of its dogs. The Crack-Dale dogs produced many generations of champions, and Mrs. Silvernail herself was dearly loved in the Fancy. She was an extremely popular multi-breed judge and the author of the book, *The Complete Fox Terrier*, which has gone through numerous editions. During the 1970s, the Silvernails moved to Thousand Oaks, California. Now both have passed away and are truly missed. But the family Wire interest carries on through Evelyn and Paul's granddaughter, Chris Wornall, who is a breeder as well as the wife of Wood Wornall, so highly successful a professional handler specializing in the rough-coated terriers.

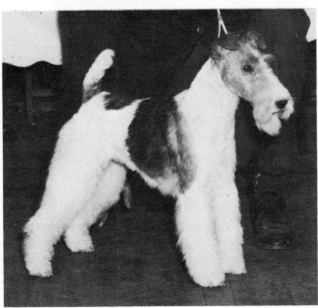

Ch. Real Jay, import, at National Capital in April 1967. Owned by Mrs. Munro Lanier, Jay won the American Fox Terrier Club Specialty in 1968. Photo courtesy of Peter Green.

Wire history in the making at Santa Barbara K.C. in about 1957. Judge Tom Keator, making his selection between two great Wires owned by Mrs. Joseph W. Urmston. Ernie Sharpe handling to Best of Variety the bitch, Ch. Mitre Miss Adorable as Roland Muller (*left*) handled the dog, Eng. and Am. Ch. Caradoc House Spruce, to Best of Opposite Sex. Photo courtesy of Peter Green.

A very long time Wire fancier who owned the breed from 1933 until late 1969, is the popular judge Nick Calicura. It was a bitch bred and sold by Mr. Calicura to Evelyn Silvernail who became "brood bitch of the year" for her as the dam of five champions bred to one of the Crack-Dale dogs. Nick finished some half dozen Wire champions for his kennel, but was quite heavily involved with professional handling which, of course, limited the showing he was able to do for himself. His Wires were based on Dustynight/Emperor bloodlines.

As with the Smooths, we could continue talking endlessly about people and dogs who have helped bring the breed to its present excellence. But we have some very interesting kennel stories which we feel do a splendid job continuing the story of Fox Terriers in the United States.

CRIZWOOD

Crizwood Kennels are owned by Chris and Wood Wornall at Sun Valley, California. Chris, living up to her heritage as granddaughter of Evelyn (Mrs. Paul) Silvernail of Crack-Dale fame, is a dedicated breeder. Woody is one of the leading terrier men in the United States and was an assistant to Ric Chashoudian. Then, when Ric retired to judging, he went out on his own with very notable success.

The foundation bitch at Crizwood was a very lovely one, Champion Bexleydale Mighty Mite, whose ownership went from Bea Turtle (Bexleydale) to Donna Perdue and then to the Wornalls. "Mighty" was "Woody's first 'girl', who came along too early in his career." This splendid bitch was truly electric in the ring, loved showing, and gained her championship on a Montgomery weekend with three 5-point majors. Her career as a special was limited; but she had some good wins, such as two Specialty Bests in Show and some Groups, which included defeating some of the best known Wires of her day.

Mighty was six years old when her first litter was born—six puppies (four males and two females). Her best puppy, and the one of whom Chris says "best I have bred up until this year" was Champion Crizwood's High 'N Mighty.

There were also two girls in that litter from Mighty who became Champion Crizwood's Mighty Bea and Champion Crizwood's Mighty Minnie.

When Bea was ready for breeding, the stud selected for her was English and American Champion Trucote Admiral, which resulted in Champion Crizwood Done To The Nines. The latter, in her turn, was bred to Champion Libwyre The Grand and which produced Crizwood Celebration, who is four generations down from Mighty.

Mighty's other daughter, Mighty Minnie, has produced Sweepstakes winners and Specialty point winners.

Bred for a second litter, Mighty Mite produced Champion Crizwood's Too Hot To Handle, who was Best of Winners at the Southern California Specialty, then sold to Carol Beatie in Florida for whom she completed title and became a brood bitch.

Chris and Woody, on one of their trips to England following the death of Mrs. Nell Urmston, so famous in the terrier world as owner of Trucote Kennels, called on Herbert and Peggy Atkin-

Steve Shaw casts a judicial eye over the lovely Ch. Bexleydale Mighty Mite on whom Crizwood Kennels were founded. Co-owner Wood Wornall handling. Mighty belonged to Bea Turtle of Bexleydale Kennels, then to Donna Perdue and later to the Wornalls. She has proven her worth many times over through her progeny. A perfectly balanced, elegant, very outstanding Wire.

son, who had all of Nell's dogs after she died. Champion Trucote Admiral was then a six year old, and the Wornalls loved him on sight. After much persuasion, and the promise that he would continue to be a house dog, the Atkinsons agreed to let the Wornalls have him, which made it a fantastic trip for them, since they also found Champion Dynamic Super Sensation during this trip.

Upon their return to the States, Woody got Admiral into show shape, and he, despite being seven years of age, went out and won Best in Show at Sacramento. Chris Wornall says of this dog, "he was best known for his incredible head and neck, which even at ten years' age he still excelled in—the cleanest, narrowest head of any Wire I have ever seen."

Following his show career, Admiral retired to become a "couch dog," the house-pet of Mari Morrison, where he remained until his death in February 1986. He also spent a year in Connecticut with Bob Fisher and Casey Crothers in order to be easily available for Eastern stud work. He was remarkable and memorable dog.

At the present time, Chris Wornall is watching with keen anticipation some puppies she has by Champion Wyrecrest Wait and See, who was bred in Holland by William Josse, imported by Frank and Barbara Swigart, then leased to Carol Beatie. He was handled by Woody, then later by Gary Dorge, and was a half brother to Champion Dynamic Super Sensation, having also been sired by Bengal Cripsey Brigadier. He won ten Terrier Groups here, then was sent back to Holland, which turned out to be a considerable loss to the breed in the United States as his get are turning out to be pure dynamite. Two of them, owned by Chris Wornall, were sent East for the 1986 Associated Terrier, one taking Best in Sweepstakes and the other Winners Dog from the 6-9 months puppy class. Chris says they may well turn out to be the best she has ever bred.

One of the best known Wires to have been campaigned thus far by Woody is Frank and Barbara Swigart's Champion Dynamic Super Sensation, who was bred by Mr. and Mrs. Kilsdonk in Holland. This fantastic dog won 17 consecutive Specialty Shows, 24 all-breed Bests in Show, and 66 Terriers Groups. Her first win in the United States was Best of Breed at the New York Specialty under judge Ed Jenner. Her first all-breed Best in Show was at Devon on Montgomery weekend under Anne Clark; then she went Best in Show at Montgomery itself under Anne Marie Moore. "Snooty" is now a couch dog.

Smooths are also bred at Crizwood. For her first attempt with Smooths, Chris leased a bitch from Bob Fisher, Champion Deception, whom she bred to Champion Karnilo Chieftain of Foxden. The litter included Champion Crizwood's Telstar Neil D, who was later sold to Gene Simmonds. Woody showed him to the title, then Bobby Fisher specialed him to some good wins, including two Bests in Show.

The Wornalls imported a most gorgeous Smooth in Champion Newmaidley Gladiator from Linda Beak. A superb dog in every way except temperament, he was shown to his title, then went to a pet home.

Ch. Newmaidley Gladiator is a truly magnificent example of what a correct Smooth should be. He was imported by Chris and Wood Wornall, Sun Valley, California, and is the epitome of correct type and balance. A truly outstanding example of what to look for in the breed.

One of the first dogs Woody campaigned after leaving Ric was the Smooth, Champion Royal Irish Reigning Baronet, owned by Betty Morton and bred by Albert Baron. A show-dog-and-a-half back in the days, a decade or so in age, when this was by no means true of all Smooths, he became a Best in Show winner with numerous Groups to his credit.

Champion High Desert Holiday, Smooth, was bred by the Wornalls, sold to Elsie Simmons, then re-purchased by Chris. She is a "Brat" daughter and was bred back to her sire, which proved a smashing success, resulting in Crizwood's Rhapscallion and three other gorgeous puppies, one a Montgomery Sweepstakes winner.

FOXBOW

Foxbow Smooth Fox Terriers, at Palouse, Washington, are owned by Sue Akin, whose love of terriers began early in childhood. Sue grew up with a most wonderful Airedale. When, in 1971, as a young married woman with twin sons, she was able to again own a dog, a Wire Fox Terrier seemed a good choice for a family pet. As luck would have it, the breeder whose newspaper ad Sue answered turned out to be the late Mae Lemm-Marugg of Spokane. She, along with Mrs. Eve Ballich, co-bred the multi-Best in Show winning Champion Lemmwyre Magic Evening, whose record as the Top Winning American-bred Wire Bitch still stands, as far as Mrs. Akin knows.

From Mae Lemm-Marugg, the Akins purchased a nice Wire dog whom they called Sam and whom they enjoyed until 1985, when he died at age 15.

It was Mae Lemm-Marugg who introduced Sue Akin to the world of dog shows. In 1974, Sue bought a Wire puppy bitch from her. "Hattie" became Sue Akin's first show dog and foundation bitch. She struggled to learn the art of conditioning a Wire, and is proud to say that her little white tornado became Champion Lemm-Wyre's Magic Mayhem in 1977, owner-handled and conditioned. Hattie was bred later that year and produced two champions in her first litter. At nearly 12 years of age, Hattie is still a well-loved member of the Akins' household.

Gradually the Smooths were taking over the Akins' interest. Sue began making plans for phasing out the Wires for Smooths, eventually setting out to find a really exciting Smooth she could buy. In 1980 she learned of a very likely male puppy in Canada who was being offered for sale by his breeder, Mae Cameron. Arrangements were formalized and soon "Digger" arrived at his new home. Sue's heart was lost immediately upon sight of the new addition to her family. Digger proved to be a very special puppy. When he was old enough to be shown, he quickly became American and Canadian Champion Dragoon of Foxbow, going on to enjoy a highly successful career in "specials," handled by Denis Springer.

The first Smooth litter at Foxbow was born in 1982, sired by Digger, by Canadian Champion Strathrobin's Chaud Frambois ex Canadian Champion Charming Cherub ; the dam of the puppies was Champion Foxbow Donna, the bitch whom Sue co-owned

Am. and Can. Ch. Dragoon of Foxbow as a young dog in 1981 winning a Group 1st judged by the late Vincent Perry. Handled by Dennis Springer for Susan Akin, Palouse, Washington.

with Jim Smith. About this same time, Jim Smith and Sue Akin became business partners, and he added his knowledge and talents to Foxbow. In 1983 they were able to lease a lovely bitch from the Raybill Kennels, Champion Raybill's Half Fast Waltz. This bitch they bred to Digger, and in the resultant litter were two outstanding puppies who became Specialty winners, Champion Foxbow Exchequer and Champion Foxbow Evening Star.

Jim and Sue are also pleased with the next Foxbow litter. Born in 1985, this litter has American and Canadian Champion Dragoon of Foxbow on both sides. These "Double Digger" grandkids will, hopefully, be making their mark in the ring soon.

In total, Sue Akin has finished three Wire champions (one co-owned with Jim Smith) and bred three Wire champions. She has finished one Smooth and bred one champion Smooth (co-bred with her son) and co-bred two other Smooth champions with Jim Smith. Others also are on their way towards their titles. A total of ten Foxbow champions have finished so far.

Although really quite a small kennel, Sue prefers to work with just a few dogs, thus affording each more personal attention. Jim generally keeps one or two at his home, and Sue keeps four or five at hers. Although not actually "doggy," Sue's husband has been willing to share their home with the terriers. As Sue comments, "Breeding and showing is certainly a demanding and fascinating avocation. There is always more to learn, a new challenge to be met. I can't imagine what life would be like without my Fox Terriers—maybe a bit dull!"

To summarize the Foxbow story: In 1974 the first show dog was acquired, a Wire bitch bred by Mae Lemm-Marugg and Eve Ballich. Three years later he became Champion Lemmwyre's Magic Mayhem, and was by Champion Duneryne Telstar ex Champion Lemmwyres Magic Evening.

The "A" litter of Wires arrived, also, in 1977, by Champion Evewire Explorer ex Champion Lemmwyre Magic Mayhem. Bred by Susan Akin, it included Champion Foxbow Alexis and Champion Foxbow Apache of Calico.

In 1978, Champion Lemmwyre's Evening Magic, by Champion Mutiny Mainstay of Glenarden ex Champion Lemmwyre's Magic Evening arrived, followed by two other litters, one of which included Champion Foxbow Coquette.

It was in 1980 that the Smooth interest took over with American and Canadian Champion Dragoon of Foxbow. A Best in Show and multi-Group winner in both the United States and Canada, Digger was No. 6 Smooth in the United States for 1982; No.1 Smooth in Canada for 1981, and No.2 in Canada for 1982. He is the sire, to date, of four who have gained championship titles: Champion Foxbow Donna, Champion Raybill's The Shimmering, Champion Foxbow Exchequer, and Champion Foxbow's Evening Star.

The "D" litter, Smooth, was born in 1982 by Digger, which produced Champion Foxbow Donna. Then in 1983 came the "E" litter, star of which was Champion Foxboro Exchequer. This dog was Best of Breed at the Fox Terrier Club of Chicago Specialty in

June 1985; Best of Breed at the Western Fox Terrier Breeders Association Specialty one week later; sold to Les Wheaton in Canada, and has become a multi-Group winner, handled by Dennis Springer.

Champion Foxbow Evening Star, littermate to Exchequer, was Best Smooth in Sweepstakes, Western Fox Terrier Breeders Association Specialty, June 1984; Winners Bitch and Best of Opposite Sex at Hatboro in 1984; Winners Bitch and Best of Winners at Devon in 1984; and Winners Bitch and Best of Winners at Montgomery County 1984; all part of the East's big, prestigious "Montgomery weekend" each October. She was Best of Breed in 1985 at the Fox Terrier Fanciers of Puget Sound Specialty in November 1985.

The "F" litter, Smooths, arrived in 1985 by Digger, from which Foxbow Feather, a lovely bitch puppy has been kept.

Already, there is a new champion at Foxbow, Champion Loriden Foxbow Bogart, a Wire (by Champion Townville Tristanian ex Snowtaire Fanno Seawyre) and Grand Sweepstakes Winner at the Fox Terrier Fanciers of Puget Sound Specialty, November 1985.

FOXMOOR

Foxmoor Smooth Fox Terriers are located at Richmond, Texas, where they are owned by Mr. and Mrs. Harold Nedell. This kennel is the culmination of a life-long ambition of a "dog show groupie" in the forties. Harold Nedell spent his late teens and early twenties in the company of leading Eastern fanciers and professional handlers of many breeds, prior to, in 1948, beginning full time employment with Len Brumby Jr., traveling to dog shows with him and with Phil Prentice.

Marriage and three children kept Harold's dog show activities to a minimum during the 1960's and 1970's, but in partnership with Harry Murphy he did manage to raise and show some Westies and some Cairns. Later in the 1970's Lakelands took his interest. As he comments, "The eclectic nature of my breed selection had to do with the tastes of our three daughters more than my own, because working with Len, I became convinced that the Fox Terrier was perfection itself—truly the doggiest of dogs." So when the last pet died and the family resources improved, Harold's thoughtful wife suggested that he should now get the breed he al-

Somebody brand new at Foxmoor! The noted English Wire, Ch. Maltman Country Life of Whinlatter, is a champion in both the U.K. and the U.S. Purchased as a foundation stud dog for a Wire line at Foxmoor.

ways had wanted. Harold comments, "I do not think she had finished the sentence before I had Winnie Stout on the phone."

The upshot of that phone call was the arrival of Champion Quissex Upsadaisy as the foundation bitch for Foxmoor. Daisy was just under four months' age when the Nedells purchased her, and while her productive career was limited to just three litters and 11 surviving puppies, she made the most of her opportunities. She is the dam of eight champions. Again quoting Harold, "those statistics are for the people who are impressed by numbers. For myself, good, successful breeding programs are measured by the long term impact on the breed. Daisy's sons and daughters are bound to have such an impact."

Champion Foxmoor's Macho Macho Man has been an outstanding show dog, ending his ring career by winning Best of Breed at the American Fox Terrier's Centenary Show in June 1985. His stud career will undoubtedly attain spectacular heights, as the 25 champions presently to his credit are prior to his reaching four years of age; thus there is a long siring period still ahead for him.

Another son of Daisy's, Champion Foxmoor Field Marshall, was sold to Vera Goold in England and has two Challenge Certificates including Crufts for 1986. His offspring are also starting to make their presence felt at the English shows.

A third Daisy son, Champion Foxmoor Five Star General, was sold to Farkash Weiland in France. He is close to his French title (undoubtedly finished by the time you are reading this), and has a Terrier Group and a Best of Breed in Belgium among his credits.

Still another young dog from Daisy, Champion Foxmoor Chief of Staff, sired the Best of Opposite Sex Smooth at the Centenary and has a number of champion offspring. The productive careers of bitches take longer to assess, but it looks as though Daisy's two daughters will follow in her paw prints. The oldest, Macho's litter sister, Champion Foxmoor One Tough Cookie, is the dam of Champion Foxmoor Forever Amber, Winners Bitch at Westminster in 1984. And Champion Foxmoor Gavotte, Champion Foxmoor Graham Cracker, and the latest youngster who earned three majors from the puppy class at age six months, Foxmoor Dick Tracy, are other progeny of this outstanding bitch.

But, as Harold Nedell comments, "Foxmoor and Daisy could not do it alone. There are two great stud dogs who have helped Foxmoor immeasurably." These are Ed Dalton's famous Champion Ttarb The Brat, whose union with Daisy was pure magic; and another outstanding Fox Terrier, Mrs. James A. Farrell's marvelous homebred, Champion Foxden Warspite.

About two years ago, Foxmoor ventured into Wires, and it is hoped that they will soon have some decent young homebreds in the ring. The foundation sire, English and American Champion Maltman Country Life of Whinlatter, was purchased and imported precisely for this purpose. He soon was followed by several bitches, including the Nedell's second Wire champion, Elmridge Sweet Harmony, bred in Wales by Lynn Snow.

69

BUCKLEIGH

Buckleigh Smooth Fox Terriers are owned by Mr. and Mrs. Michael Buckley at Lowell, Massachusetts.

Mike Buckley purchased his first Smooth from Winnie Stout in 1966, and was active in showing both in Junior Handling and a breed competition through 1973. After getting divorced from his first wife who was not at all interested in dogs, and then re-marrying, Mike and his new wife decided to have a family before getting back into Smooths.

As a child, Mike won the Junior Handling competition at the big, important Westchester Kennel Club Dog Show in 1968, and was judging five or six match shows annually throughout his middle teens.

Now the Buckleys are again really involved in Smooths, being active with 11 adults and two litters. They are having a lot of fun, win or lose, really enjoying the dogs and the people they meet.

Probably due to Mike's earlier activity in the breed, they have been able to re-establish themselves and purchase excellent foundation stock that might not have been possible for someone starting from scratch. Their goal is to breed and show the best Smooths possible, always keeping the standard in mind.

The Buckleys are members of the American Fox Terrier Club, the Fox Terrier Club of New England, the Smooth Fox Terrier Breeders Association (U.K.), the Fox Terrier Club (U.K.), and the New England Terrier Club.

It was Champion Quissex Matilda with whom Mike Buckley was winning Groups, owner-handled, back in 1970. Bred and co-owned by Mrs. Winifred Stout, Matilda was by Quissex Vladimir ex Foxformee Charlotte.

Now at Buckleigh Kennels one finds Champion Quissex Insolence, daughter of Champion Foxmoor Macho Macho Man ex Quissex Wise Crack, who finished her title at Elmira Kennel Club in December 1985 and is awaiting a litter by Champion Toofox the Colonel. Her sister, Quissex Little Black Wren, is also close to the title.

Champion Quissex Quicksilver is another of the Buckley Smooths, by Champion Battle Cry Brimstone ex Foxmoor Two Step.

The handsome dog Champion Foxmoor Double Diamond is entirely of Australian breeding, being by Champion Ttarb the Brat

Ch. Quissex Matilda pictured with Mrs. John Marvin in June 1970. A Group-winning Smooth, owner-handled by Michael D. Buckley, bred by and co-owned with Mrs. Winifred Stout. This was an early Smooth by Quissex Vladimer ex Foxformee Charlotte when Mr. Buckley was first becoming interested in the breed.

ex Champion Farleton Fine Finish. He had an exciting show career, already with numerous Bests of Breed and Group placements to his credit. His contribution to Buckleigh should be considerable.

The hot young show prospect would seem to be the latest champion, Buccaneer's Max, who completed title by taking Best of Winners at the American Fox Terrier Club Specialty in February 1986. This was his fifth major, although previous to the Specialty he had been shown only on three weekends.

His first time out as a special, Max went 2nd in the Terrier Group at Tallahassee, Florida, under judge Bob Graham. He is a son of American and Canadian Champion Watteau Bridegroom ex Champion Dalriada's Buccaneer Ballad; bred by Canadian fanciers Ken and Pat Reinke.

CARIBE

Caribe Smooth Fox Terriers are owned by Joe and Murrel Purkhiser and located at Wylie, Texas. Its informal beginning dates back into the 1930's, Joe having received his first Smooth when he was too young to remember; his Dad raised them. Caribe had its official start in the dog world during 1965 when Joe and Murrel started seriously raising and showing Shelties and Collies, which was not an easy task for a professional military family. Despite this fact, they did manage to breed and show some good ones. In 1978, the kennel was dispersed due to Joe's assignment as Defense Attaché in Belgrade, Yugoslavia. Only two old Sheltie champions went there with them.

Murrel Purkhiser is a teacher of the first grade and Joe is now a retired Air Force Colonel who is at present doing social work with the state. Nearly all of their non-working time is spent on dog-related activities, one way or the other. Murrel is secretary of the local all-breed club, and the Purkhisers jointly edit a National Breed Club magazine. They are also co-chairpersons for the Lone Star Fox Terrier Club's Specialties.

It was during their three years in Yugoslavia that the Purkhisers decided that they would again start breeding Smooth Fox Terriers upon their return home, which is what they did. Thus since 1983 Caribe again has become a Fox Terrier kennel specializing in Smooths. Although small, Caribe has quickly become one of the most successful breeding and exhibiting kennels of Smooths in the

Ch. Toofox The Caribe Chief Spy taking Best in Show at Salina K.C. in 1985, one of four such victories already earned by this outstanding young dog. Owned by Caribe Kennels, Joe and Murrel Purkhiser, Wylie, Texas.

country.

Much study and thought went into the stock on which Caribe would re-assemble. Finally the dog was found who was exactly what Murrel and Joe wanted—Champion Toofox Tantrum owned by Priscilla Wells. There was just one small problem. Priscilla refused to part with him. So the Purkhisers tracked down the dog's breeders, Bill and Betsy Dossett, purchasing a bitch from them. It was during a subsequent visit to the Dossetts that they fell in love with a two-month-old white puppy with a black head. In order to get rid of Joe, the Dossetts finally allowed themselves to be persuaded to let him take the pup home. His call name is "Burt"; his registered name Toofox The Caribe Chief Spy, and at eight months of age he had earned the title Champion. At two years old he had a total record of six Specialty Bests of Breed, four All-Breed Bests in Show, 60 Group placements including 19 Firsts, and 105 times Best of Breed. Included among these wins are Best of Breed at the Westminster Kennel Club in both 1985 and 1986; Best of Breed at Montgomery County kennel Club in 1985; and during 1984 and 1985 three consecutive Bests of Breed at the Lone Star Fox Terrier Club's Specialties.

Burt's abilities as a sire are also becoming impressive. At only two-and-a-half-years old he had a daughter, Champion Toofox Agent Ninety-Nine, bred and co-owned by Caribe. Champion Toofox Agent Ninety-Nine was Best of Opposite Sex to him at the Fall 1985 Lone Star Specialty, Montgomery County Kennel Club and at the 1986 Westminster.

Burt is and always has been a house dog. Joe says of him, "he is probably the sanest Smooth yet to come along, as anyone who knows him will agree." He is jointly handled by Joe Purkhiser and Priscilla Wells, and has been for most of his career.

Caribe Kennels are based upon two outstanding pillars of the breed; the Purkhisers feeling that the basis of their success has been that of the blending of Champion Kevrayno Sabre Jet and Champion Ttarb The Brat, pointing with pride to their two foundation bitches, who are out of "the top producing Smooth bitch in history," Champion Toofox Lady Evelyn.

Ch. Nimrod's Jewel of Pandora, one of the earliest Smooth winners owned by Charbonne Kennels. By Ch. Nimrod's Jolly Zan ex Chiron's Lucky Fox of the Bastion, was part of the foundation for this now so very famous kennel.

Ch. Sugarland Fox Trot, bred by Merna Miller, owned by Charlotte Le Vecque and Marion Clayman. Littermate to Ch. Nimrod's Jeqel of Pandora. These two were foundation bitches at Charbonne Kennels, Highland, California.

CHARBONNE

Charbonne Smooth Fox Terriers really started out under the kennel prefix Sugarland with the purchase of two Smooth bitches. These two girls rather quickly became Champion Sugarland Fox Trot and Champion Nimrod's Jewel of Pandora. The former finished with three 5-point majors and the latter went Winners Bitch at the Western Fox Terrier Specialty in 1972 when her puppies were eight weeks old. They were co-owned by Charlotte Le Veque and another lady, who, in 1975, stopped her activities in dogs.

Charlotte Le Vecque retained her interest in the Smooths, and, at Highland, California, Charbonne Kennels are building some fine and exciting records.

Champion Sugarland Fox Trot went on to produce four champions in two breedings. The first, an inbreeding to her sire Champion Nimrod's Jollyzan, produced Champion Sugarland Syncopation and Champion Sugarland Sirius, C.D. Next she was bred to the English import, Champion Newmaidley Pennywise, from which came Champion Sugarland Samba and Champion Sugarland Smooth Sailing.

Samba became Ms. Le Vecque's top producing bitch to date. She was bred twice for two litters by the same sire, American,

Mexican, and Canadian Champion Lizabethan Buckingham Bard; and produced five champions, namely Champion Charbonne Bon Vivant, Champion Charbonne Cotillion, Champion Charbonne Savoir Faire, Champion Charbonne Fandango, and Champion Charbonne Gendarme. There were three Best in Match winners in this litter with a total of five Best in Match wins, entries for these matches each running several hundred. Bon Vivant was Best Smooth in Sweepstakes at Western Fox Terrier Breeders Association in 1980.

Two dogs of this breeding went on to become the foundation stock for other Smooth breeders. Cotillion has produced three champions for Vince and Kathy Grosso (Winsom Smooths), and has other puppies currently in competition.

Bon Vivant sired a litter for Sue and Steve Lytwynec (Foxfield), and their current stock is from that line.

Samba had an interesting second career in Junior Handling. She was co-owned with Kirstie Lytwynec, and working together they went on to multiple Best Junior Handler in Show awards, qualifying twice for Westminster.

Ms. Le Veque continued her own breeding program with Fandango. She was bred to Champion Foxhills Cash and Carry, which produced Champion Charbonne Enfant Terrible, who was one of the Top Winning Smooths for 1984 with multiple Best of Breed and Group placements, including a Group 1st. A sidelight on this dog is that he finished his championship from the Bred-by Exhibitor Class. Fandango's second champion is Champion Charbonne Habanera, who finished with three champions, including Winners Bitch at the Fox Terrier Club of Northern California.

Habanera was bred to her grandsire, Champion Ttarb the Brat, and it is her youngsters who are the current crop at Charbonne.. Her daughter, Champion Charbonne Waltzing Matilda, was Best Smooth in Sweepstakes at the Fox Terrier Club of Northern California in 1985. Her son, Charbonne A La Mode, was Best of Winners at Orange Empire in January 1986, a 3-point major.

Charbonne is proud of its 13 champions, especially as Charlotte is able to do only limited breeding. She breeds a litter every two or sometimes every three years, doing so only when she is looking for something to show; she does not have the facilities for large numbers of dogs. Her dogs are house dogs, and she feels, very sensibly, that with more than five she is not able to give each the time and individual attention they are entitled to receive. With these limitations she cannot use her bitches as frequently as she would otherwise.

Charbonne puppies reign supreme, receiving great time and attention from both their owner and from the other dogs. Much care is also taken in naming them: the girls all having some form of dance in their names while the boys, reflecting their owner's French heritage, are named with French words.

CRAG CREST

Crag Crest Kennels are owned by Mr. and Mrs. Fred Kuska (Fred and Jane to their friends), and located at Colfax, California. The Kuskas have been active in Smooths without interruption from the early 1960s onwards, during which period they have owned many dogs of outstanding quality, type and bloodlines, having purchased judiciously from abroad as well as bred with excellent judgment here at home.

Their earliest Smooths were Jac-Paw Janaan and Champion Jac-Paw Jan-Jac, who were Little Andelys breeding (Mrs. Barbara Lowe Fallas). Also early on were Champion Sandhill Sweet Talk and Champion Sandhill Little Princess, progeny of Champion Downsbragh Nighstick (the William Brainards). Following these were Champion El Auren's of Crag Crest; the imported Newmaidley Black Tulip (with majors); Champion Nornay Navigator, English Champion Newmaidley Joshua; American Champion Watteau Snufsed of Crag Crest; Champion Grambrae Serene and Champion Grambrae Silver Glint (both Specialty Bests of Variety), Champion Watteau Avocet; Champion Quissex Matilda (Group winner), Champion Sandhill Majorette; Champion Albany Watermark; Champion Crag Crest Now Hear This (Foxridge Kennels); Champion Boreham Barrister (48 times Best of Variety); Champion Crag Crest Counselle and her four daughters (Champions Crag Crest Louisiana Belle, Little Lulu, Nancy Davis, and Crag Crest Crown, who lacked just one point); Champion Crag Crest Colonel Kuska, Crag Crest Do Tell (American Foxterrier Club Sweeps finalist), Foxformer Joan; Burmar Bonnet; Burmar Martin, Crag Crest Signal Danger; Crag Crest All Clear; Viscum Violet (Specialty Reserve Winners Bitch); Viscum Vildean (majored); Champion Viscum Vexillum, Champion Crag Crest Violets Are Blue (earned title in four 4-point majors), Sinful Sabra of Crag

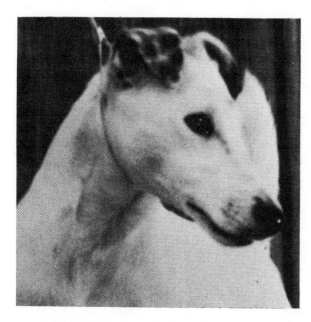

Crag Crest All Clear, by Ch. Boreham Barrister ex Crag Crest Signal Dancer, is considered the most influential and dominant of all the sires at Crag Crest Kennels as to uniformity of type, size, ears, feet, balance—things often hard to get from one sire, comments his owner, Jane Kushka. This stunning dog is representative of the Crag Crest breeding program.

Crest (died lacking one point); American and Canadian Champion Crag Crest Shogun; Champion Foxhill Dingo Lass; Crystal Clear of Crag Crest (Specialty 5-point winner and Best of Winners); Crag Crest Right Royal (majors); Crag Crest To Beechee's Brook (5-point Winners Dog and Best of Winners); Champion Ttarb's Trevallion, Champion Crag Crest Foxhill Shallalla; and Champion Crag Crest Amberwood Tripan (brilliant career in California).

The Wire, Champion Viscum Valente, has also done well for Crag Crest, although the interest here is dominated by the Smooths.

The owners of Crag Crest share their interests in many directions, including horses, cattle and their ranch. Then came the grandchildren, all of which cut back on the time available for showing dogs. However, they did manage to keep some (those who had been purchased for that purpose) out with their handlers. These included Champion Boreham Barrister, who had Best of Variety on more than 40 occasions under Ric Chashoudian's handling, at such shows as "the National," the Garden, Santa Barbara, Golden Gate, Beverly Hills; and in Texas, Louisiana and New Mexico. He scored Group wins and placements; but most of all, he contributed greatly to his kennel and to his breed as an outstanding sire.

Even earlier than Barrister, Champion Watteau Snufsed of Crag Crest was carrying the banner high for his owners during the 1960's. But it is very evident that Crag Crest has never been a "show minded" kennel, the Kuskas' activities in this direction having been kept to a minimum—just enough to prove their breeding theories or to occasionally bring out a retired champion.

Seldom are more than three or four dogs shown annually, and entries made at just a dozen or so shows each year. It is as *breeders* that the Kuskas take their pleasure, experimenting and testing bloodlines, type and temperament.

As comments on the breeding program, Jane Kuska has said, "All Clear has been the most *dominant* for consistency in type, style, and courage of the dogs. He threw the best in the old Watteau line and Hampole through Viscum and Riber." All Clear was sired by Ch. Boreham Barrister.

Crag Crest has bred some utterly magnificent white Smooths, of which Mrs. Kuska says, "We rarely even tried to show the whites in this country due to unexplainable prejudice here in the U.S.A. But oh! what beautiful style and type one got from these great old dogs."

The very best of the Crag Crest dogs, Mrs. Kuska tells us, were never shown or never were finished. She notes "I say *best* because many of the top handlers would stop off here and grade them."

FORTUNE

Fortune Smooth Fox Terriers are owned by Lisa Sachs at Huntington, New York, founded on stock from the Quissex Kennels of Mrs. Winifred Stout in Rhode Island.

A wedding gift to Lisa from Winnie Stout, known as Peter and not originally intended to be a show dog, turned out to become Champion Quissex Proclamation, C.D., C.G., when his animation, love of shows, and general soundness prompted his new owner to try entering him, which she did at a February American Fox Terrier Club Specialty. There he went Reserve Winners Dog, owner-handled in some very keen competition, leading to his being started out the following spring in earnest. Almost before it was realized, he was a champion, having gained four majors and his title owner-handled.

It had been Lisa's original intention to have, as her foundation bitch, Champion Winsome's Wheel of Fortune, and a real disappointment when she proved to be sterile. Lisa had expressed an interest in Winnie Stout's English import bitch, Champion Viscum Vesta, only to find that Vesta was already leased. There was, however, a lovely bitch puppy from her sired by Champion Quissex Deacon whom it was felt might work out well; and she grew up to become Champion Quissex Vestal Virgin, C.D., her successes in the ring including Winners Bitch at Montgomery County, after she had recuperated from her first litter. Despite her unpopular color, white, she gained her championship in 15 shows.

Champion Raybill Quissex Volare is the dam of at least three champions with several major-pointed progeny still being shown. This good bitch was owner-handled to her championship at age six years. Primarily used as a brood bitch, she has produced quality for her present owner with three major-pointed get by Champion Quissex Proclamation C.D., C.G. and one young hopeful by Champion Foleywood Tobias.

Champion Quissex Proclamation, C.D., C.G., is a son of Champion Quissex Deacon. Lisa says of this dog, "He is good at everything he does, and exemplifies the spirit of the Fortune Smooths—all-'round dogs." Peter finished with majors under Ed Jenner, Roger Hartinger, and Wilfred Brumby. He was Tom Partis's choice as Best in Match at the Eastern Smooth Breeders Association Match.

Fortune's Gold Medallist was Winners Bitch at the Fox Terrier Club of Maryland Specialty in April 1985, from the Novice Class her first time out. She was also first in the Novice Class at her only American Working Terrier Trial when four months of age. She shares her human, Catherine Gagen, with a German Shepherd and two cats.

Fortune's Ghostwriter has seven points including one major from the Bred-by Exhibitor Class. She has a young litter by Champion Foxden Warpaint.

Fortune's Time Bandit is a double grandson of the Top Producer, Champion Quissex Deacon, and is hopefully prepotent for some of Deacon's best qualities. He is the only viable male pup out of Champion Quissex Vestal Virgin, C.D., who was Winners at Montgomery County in 1981. Bandit will be test-bred to his mother's half sister and an outcross bitch at Fortune Kennels.

The kennel's principal "young hopeful" is Fortune's Blackjack, who was a Christmas gift from his breeder Winnie Stout. At his

Fortune's Ghostwriter at nine months. A very promising young Smooth bred and owned by Lisa Sachs.

first show he returned home with a 5-point major, owner-handled at the age of ten months. Lisa hopes that he will go well with Quissex bitches at Fortune, and that he may become an eventual replacement for Jack in the modeling profession.

Quissex Wedding Belle C.D., C.G. has been seen in *Bride's* magazine as well as some well-known commercials, most notably chasing bubbles for the Fisher-Price Bubble Lawn Mower. This is a group of dogs enjoyed by their owner in many different ways.

Mrs. James A. Farrell, Jr., *seated*, reaching up to pet her homebred Ch. Foxden War Paint who is in the arms of Mary Davies. *Far right* is Mrs. Davies's husband, Archie, with an unidentified Foxden bitch. The Davieses own the kennel in Southbury, Connecticut, where many of the Foxden Smooths live now that Mrs. Farrell no longer maintains her own kennel.

FOXDEN

Foxden Kennels, at Darien, Connecticut, were established during the early 1930's by Mr. and Mrs. James Farrell, Jr; and this kennel has been continuously active from that time up until the present day when Mrs. Farrell ("Stevie" to her friends) continues the interest she and her late husband shared over more than four decades. Over the years, Greyhounds have been consistent favorites with Mr. and Mrs. Farrell, who have imported, bred, and owned some of the finest. There have been top-winning Beagles, too, in the limelight from this kennel; and Mrs. Farrell loves and has owned some outstanding Pugs. But always the Smooths have been the primary canine interest—the one which has stuck without interruption throughout the years.

Two of the early Foxden dogs who were especially admired and important were Champions Flornell Checkmate and Flornell Sundowner. From the very beginning the Farrells have visited England frequently, visiting important shows and kennels there, always seeking top quality stock with which to enhance their own. This they have done with tremendous success. Many great dogs have come from England to Foxden, where they have both won well and reproduced their quality in future generations. Foxden continues to be a strong influence in the Fox Terrier world today, as it was in the beginning and has remained through the years. Not only is Mrs. Farrell still breeding and showing, and supplying foundation stock for numerous other breeders, too; she is also an active official of the American Fox Terriers Club, of which organization she has served many terms as President.

Among the famous Smooths at Foxden Kennels over the years have been the exquisite bitch Champion Flornell Prestonian Jewel, who was bred in 1947 by W. Fairhurst in England, by Democrat of Sker ex Lesterly Mischief. Champion Foremark Ebony Box of Foxden came to the United States towards the end of the 1960s (he was born October 9, 1963), a son of Watteau Snuff Box from Watteau Gaybird, and he was bred by Mrs. W. Newbury. Under Jane Forsyth's handling, he fast became a Best in Show and multiple Group winner, in addition gaining a wide circle of admirers. He also proved himself as a sire of merit.

Then there was another lovely bitch, Champion Viscum Vanilla of Foxden, born in 1964. Also from England, she was bred by Mr. B. Walker and was by Hampole Tatler.

Champion Watteau Pandora's Box of Foxden came to the Farrells from England in the mid-1960s where she did well in the show ring and as a producer. Champion Watteau Last Word of Foxden (Champion Watteau Snufsed of Crag Crest-Lingrove Linnet) was a successful importation who numbered among his progeny the Farrells' own handsome bitch, Champion Foxden Fairy Godmother and littermate Champion Foxden Leprechaun (who played an important role in the advancement of Madison Weekes's Waybroke Kennels in Florida). These two were bred by the Farrells, from Champion Camphill Golden Fairy, born on April 4, 1968, and were a dog and a bitch respectively.

Champion Ellastone Fireflash, son of Ellastone Firecrest from Eatonwood Sufredon Treat, was bred by F. Dyson and was a Foxden importation of the late 1960's.

Now the Foxden stud force consists of the father-son team of War Paint and Warspite whose aggregate total of champions sired to date comes to about 50; Champion Higrola Horatio of Britlea, sire of 28 champions, and a son of his, Champion Foxden Deck Officer, who is just starting out.

FOXTROT

Foxtrot Smooth Fox Terriers are owned by Jane D. Swanson at Erie, Illinois, whose first litter was born in 1979. Since then Foxtrot has compiled the very noteworthy record of 30 champions either having been bred or shown by them to their titles as owner. This figure should increase dramatically, there being close to 20 dogs who will be in the ring soon.

Champion Kraehollow Katy O'Della was purchased by Jane Swanson as a three-month-old puppy. She became the No. 2 Smooth Fox Terrier Bitch in 1980, Knight System, and was Top Ten rated during three other years. Always owner-handled, she finished as a puppy, consistently beating the special while still in the puppy class. As a brood bitch, she has been bred three times, producing ten pups. So far, five of these have finished, with four others extremely close to their titles. In other words, out of ten puppies born, only one was not of show quality, and that one is working successfully on an obedience career. Katy, although not Jane's first Smooth, is considered to be her foundation bitch. Katy is by Champion Toofox Blazin' Saddler ex Champion Kandihill Digger O'Della and her breeder is Martha Riekenberg.

Katy's first champion from her first litter is Champion Foxtrot Maximillion Laughs, by Champion Roughrider's Bandit. He was Winners Dog at the American Fox Terrier Club Specialty in Dallas at ten months, finishing the next weekend, always breeder-owner-handled from the puppy class. He is now the senior stud dog at Foxtrot, as well as being Jane's "number one bed sleeper house dog." Currently he has sired six champions with another six almost finished, and another ten just waiting to become old enough for the ring. He is stamping his puppies with style and elegance and the true *Foxtrot* look—obviously bred by Jane Swanson.

Champion Foxburo Patent Pending is by Champion Foxburo Chateau of Pathens ex Foxburo Fancy Pants, bred by John and Gayle Moynier of Asti, California. Jane saw "Rufus" in 1983 while on a trip to California, and was so taken with him that she brought him back on her next trip out. He finished his title with a bang, making wins at the International and at Devon for his majors. He is now co-owned by Foxtrot and Foxburo (the Moyniers). His first year at stud was 1984, during which he produced seven champions with several more major-pointed. Two of these pups have been multiple Group-placing, Champion Foxland Quiet Riot

Ch. Foxtrot Maximillion Laughs, by Ch. Roughrider's Bandit ex Ch. Kraehollow Katy O'Della, owned by Jane Swanson, Erie, Illinois.

and Champion Foxtrot Fast Lane, owner-handled. Fast Lane now is a multiple Group winner.

Fast Lane is the offspring of Patent Pending and Katy O'Della. At nine months he went to Montgomery County where he was selected Winners Dog in 1983; since then he has gone on as an owner-handled special to be the 6th Smooth Dog in the United States for 1985. By February 1986 his Group placements stand at five Group 1sts, three 2nds, one 3rd and one 4th—this all in stiff Chicago-land competition.

Jane Swanson places emphasis on the fact that all of her dogs are natural and all are amateur owner-handled. The first litter of the Foxtrot Kennels was whelped at the end of 1979 and the first homebred champions were finished in 1980. Maximillion was from

Jane Swanson's second litter, in 1980.

Since moving in 1984 to her present location, Jane has been able to expand into a more relaxed kennel situation. Foxtrot normally houses between 20-30 Smooths at all times, these being retired show dogs, show dogs on the circuit now, and youngsters in training. The kennel is entirely a one-person operation. All breeding, whelping, training, feeding, grooming, showing and clean-up is Jane's own responsibility with no help or assistance. All decisions to breed and which dogs to show where are also her own. She prefers it that way! Concentrated study and research of dogs and pedigrees helped to lay a very substantial groundwork for the basis of her kennel, and Jane is known for her ability to recite pedigrees on each of her dogs (and many that she does not own) for at least four generations back. She credits doing her homework in this manner with being the backbone of her success.

Foxtrot houses three stud dogs at the present time in addition to the two already discussed: Champion Delta's Chipper, Champion Foxtrot Freestyle, and Champion Sheez Beez Raybill Cajun.

GAIDOUNE

Gaidoune is a very long established kennel identification in the Terrier World, perhaps best known for many superlative Scotties. But Helen Gaither, the owner, at Wheeling, West Virginia, has always been very aware of and interested in Smooth Fox Terriers as well, having followed them through the years; so now she is especially enjoying having a few who are from Waybroke Kennels and being most capably campaigned for her by their breeders Hubert Thomas and Madison Weeks.

The two of these Smooths who have been especially making their presence felt at recent shows are Champion Waybroke Extra Sunshine and Champion Waybroke Bentley.

Extra Sunshine, who completed title going Best of Winners at the St. Louis Specialty under Dr. Deubler, is now a Group winner doing well in keen competition. His championship was finished while still a puppy, so he should have a bright future before him.

Bentley also gained title in an auspicious manner taking Best of Winners at the American Fox Terrier Club Specialty at Montgomery County. With two such excellent young dogs, we are sure that Helen Gaither should have many good times with this breed and we wish her every success.

HY-TIME

Hy-Time Kennels, owned by Sherry and Jim Elliott at Clacka-mas, Oregon, is a small establishment dedicated to breeding from the respected old Watteau and Newmaidley bloodlines.

The top male here is Champion Hy-Time Magnum P.I., who was rated among the Top Ten Smooth Fox Terriers for 1984 and 1985. He is a Best in Show winner, a Specialty winner, and a mul-tiple Group winner, among his successes having been that of being the first winner of the Puget Sound Fox Terrier Specialty. As a sire, he has puppies successfully being shown in both the United States and Canada.

Magnum is a grandson of Champion Ttarb The Brat and of Champion Raybill's Breeze Away, C.D., being by Champion Crag Crest Shogun ex Wellsdome Mitzsey Dancer. He was bred by C. Wells.

The foundation bitch at Hy-Time is the tan and white Salcrest Dancing Anna, daughter of Champion Bengal Fishgate Quadrille, (who is an English import, ex the Canadian import, Butcherboy Captivation). She was bred by Salcrest Kennels, and has proven a valuable asset at Hy-Time.

Magnum has numerous sons and daughters doing well in the rings. One of them is Hy-Time Hot Shot, from Foxbow Diane of Hy-Time, who very likely will be a champion soon.

KARNER

Karner Fox Terriers are owned by Thomas Partis and situated at Craryville, New York. This kennel is the home of a very famous bitch from the 1970s, Champion Stoney Meadows Flavor, who finished title in five straight shows during 1977 and then was bred to Champion Foxden Warpaint, by whom she produced two champions.

Bred by the Potter Wears, Flavor is a daughter of the widely admired Champion Stoney Meadows Nutmeg.

LAURELTON

The Laurelton Smooth Fox Terriers are owned by Richard and Virginia Ashlock, Ontario, California.

This couple has been interested in Smooths since 1979 but were unable to own one until 1981, when they acquired Foxburo's Classy Chassis from John and Gayle Moynier of Foxburo, and

Ch. Foxburo's Brown Derby at age five months. A truly smashing youngster owned by Laurelton Smooths, Richard and Virginia Ashlock, Ontario, California.

took her through to championship. "Cindy" has proven her worth many times over as a constant and loving companion and as a consistent producer. She is the dam of five champions.

Classy Chassis's first litter for the Ashlocks consisted of five puppies by a champion from the Toofox breeding program. Three of these puppies have already become champions, including a Specialty Best of Winners as well as another with Group placements.

Her second litter was by Champion Foxden Warlord, which also produced a Specialty Best of Winners (both of these dogs handled *only* by their owners) and a Champion female for which hopes are high as a producer.

Classy Chassis is a granddaughter of the English imports English and American Champion Karnilo Chieftain of Foxden and Champion Teesford Fanfare. She is heavily linebred on the famous Pathens stock from the family of Mullenteen Miss Nora. With so solid a foundation behind her, it's easier to be successful as a breeder!

The Ashlocks also acquired the Specialty Best of Opposite Sex winning Champion Foxmoor Quissex Fantan from Mr. Harold Nedell. "Polly" combines the import Champion Ttarb The Brat through his son Macho with the well-known Quissex and Foxden lines. Her litter by Champion Toofox the Colonel looks very special.

To date, Laurelton has bred five champions and finished others. Most of their dogs are owner-handled to their titles, only very occasionally going out with handlers. The Ashlocks are proud that two of their most successful champions were shown only by themselves in the Bred-by Exhibitor Class. Virginia Ashlock comments, "Without the help and encouragement of John and Jayle Moynier, who gave us our start in the breed, we would never have come this far. Smooth Fox Terrier people are the greatest!"

Leading influence behind the Laurelton dogs has been Foxden, as well as Champion Ttarb The Brat and Toofox. All of the Laureltons go back to Chieftain at least once. The Warlord puppies have no lines to Brat; but the Colonel pups are three times linebred to him. Again quoting Mrs. Ashford, "It's not surprising that The Brat and Chieftain are presently No. 1 and No. 2 All Time Top Producers among Smooth sires. All Time Top Dams are Mullenteen Miss Florence No. 2; and her daughter Champion Pathens Someone Special No. 1, but there are at least one or two coming on now in contention to pass them."

QUISSEX

Quissex Smooth Fox Terriers are owned by Mrs. Winifred H. Stout, who has just recently moved into her lovely new home at Foster, Rhode Island.

As a child, Winnie Stout was introduced to the sport of showing dogs by her aunt, a Kerry Blue Terrier fancier, and by Mrs. D. Mather Briggs of Rehoboth, Massachusetts, who gave Winnie her first Old English Sheepdog from her noted Cartref Kennels while living in Newport during World War II. As a foxhunter in the Rose Tree country of Pennsylvania, Winnie was an avid reader of horse books, many of which were illustrated by Paul Brown. This gentleman drew Smooth Fox Terriers, on nearly every page, accompanying the riders and in and out of stables. But despite living in the midst of hunt country, Winnie never saw a Smooth Fox Terrier "in person" until Mrs. Stewart Simmons moved onto the next farm.

After graduating from Radcliffe, Winnie took the obligatory job in New York and purchased her first Smooth from Barbara Lowe Fallas of Andely. She remarks on having the most vivid memory of eight litters of tiny puppies in a whelping kennel, Mrs. Fallas's polite but rather intimidating bodyguard, and the two caged nightingales, one of which was kept downstairs and was trained to sing in the daytime!

Champion Climax of Andely was a delightful companion, although he had always been a kennel dog and thus there was a great deal he did not know. On Winnie's first visit with him to her parents' farm, he fell into the pond, but ended up as an accomplished frog-catcher. In those days (1955) dogs were permitted to ride on trains, but only in a private Pullman compartment or in the baggage car. Depending on Winnie's fortunes at the time, she and Climax travelled Pullman or in baggage—with the mail and almost invariably a coffin.

From 1960 onward, while living and teaching at St. Mark's School in Scarborough, Massachusetts, Winnie Stout bred Bloodhounds and Old English Sheepdogs, the Smooth and her Saluki being non grata with her husband. But after their move to Cambridge, the big dogs were gradually phased out and the Smooths were taken up in earnest in 1964. Then it was that Winnie was able to acquire a lovely puppy bitch from the Glovers in England, Champion Hewshott January, who became the first of a series of

Ch. Quissex de Quincey at nine months at the American Fox Terrier Club in October 1959. Here he won Best in Sweepstakes and Reserve Winners Dog from the puppy class. Owned by Mrs. Winifred Stout.

Ch. Viscum Vellum, by Eng. Ch. Viscum Voluntary ex Viscum Valerie, as a youngster in England prior to joining Quissex Kennels.

imports. However, the two who really sparked the Quissex breeding program were Newmaidley Dream, imported in whelp to Champion Watteau Snuff Box; and Champion Viscum Vallum a few years later.

Dream was a litter sister to Champion Newmaidley Destiny, the dam of Champion Newmaidley Vodka and double granddam of Champion Newmaidley Whistling Jeremy. She produced a litter of five of which only one finished, but three of whom bred champions, these having been Champion Quissex Pipe Dream and her sisters, Tinderbox and Bandbox. Their descendants are in the Quissex Kennels today.

Vellum was of the Hampole line and a great-granddaughter of English Champion Herman Parthing's Loyal Lad. She won the American Fox Terrier Club Sweepstakes, was Best of Opposite Sex at Associated Terrier, and became the dam of Champion Quissex Tinsel by the Farrells' English and American Champion Watteau Last Word of Foxden. Another Hampole-bred bitch, Lindow Quissex Forest, was mated to the Wears' imported Snuff Box son, Champion Watteau Snifter, and produced Champion Quissex de Quincey. Bred to Tinsel, he produced Champions Quissex Quintessence and Silver Gilt, both of whom in their turn produced well. Quintessence became the dam of Quissex Furthermore when bred back to Last Word. And Furthermore produced Champions Quissex Marengo and Moreover.

Concurrently, the import Foxmoree Charlotte (by English

Champion Hermon Rebel, a Loyal Lad son) was bred to Quissex Vladimir (a son of the import Champion Watteau Musical Box, a litter brother to Snuff Box, and Battle Cry Vanity Box, by Ebony Box ex Quissex Bandbox). This produced Winnie Stout's first homebred and owner-handled Group winner, Champion Quissex Matilda.

Matilda was bred to De Quincey, producing Champion Quissex Nixie. Mated to the import Champion Viscum Veracity (by English Champion Watteau Snuff Box ex English Champion Hampole Hero, a daughter of Loyal Lad) she produced Champion Quissex Deacon (1971-1985), who became the most successful Quissex Smooth up until that time. A Group and Specialty winner, Deacon sired 32 champions and three Group winners.

Another successful breeding along these lines was the mating of Tinsel to Veracity, producing Champion Quissex Spun Gold Decision. This bitch, Spun Gold, was bred to Mrs. Farrell's Best in Show import Champion Ellastone Fireflash and produced Champion Quissex Seycon Surefire who, when mated to Deacon, produced eight champions, including a Group winner, in two litters bred by Richard and Jan Tretrault.

In 1974, Winnie Stout went to England where she purchased Champion Karnilo Completa. Strong in Watteau bloodlines, she produced many champions, most notably Champion Quissex Upsadaisy, the dam of six Foxmoor Champions by The Brat, and two by Champion Burnaun Rascal of Maryholm. Winnie Stout had many fine imports from the Viscum Kennels of Bevan Walker, who had based his breeding program on Champion Hampole Hero. Most notable was Champion Viscum Vesta, an all-white bitch who won a Group handled by Mrs. Stout's daughter, after only five days in the United States.

Another dog who did much for the Quissex breeding program was Champion Foxden Hercules, sired by the Best in Show Champion Foxden Herbert (an Ebony Box son, and out of the exquisite Champion Watteau Pandora's Box of Foxden). Hercules was an indefatigable Junior's dog for Winnie's daughter Sarah Chatfield, and helped her to qualify for the Garden Junior Showmanship. He later won many Groups for Hugh Thomas and Madison Weeks of Waybroke Kennels and sired more than 20 champions. Of him, Winnie Stout comments, "Herk would certainly have won a versatility award as he went to ground readily and killed dozens of woodchucks at Mary Andregg's farm in the Berkshires."

Over 100 champions down the line, Winnie Stout is still pursuing her original game plan, to develop a successful mixture of the old Hampole and Burmar strains with that of Watteau, which is, of course, the progenitor strain for Karnilo and Newmaidley. Mrs. Farrell's great Chieftain bred Quissex many winners. And today Mrs. Stout is adding the blood of Champion Ttarb The Brat, who has been so enormous a success in this country. She looks forward to another 20 years in Fox Terriers with constant fresh challenges, as the competition is becoming hotter all the time.

Quissex Smooths live in their owner's house, and as an owner-handler for 30 years, she has taken great pleasure in their companionship and that of the great and varied world of dog people. To paraphrase Kipling, Mrs. Stout comments, "if you can keep high standards and a sense of humor, there is no better way to have fun."

TOOFOX

Toofox Smooth Fox Terriers are owned by Bill and Betsy Dossett of Wylie, Texas who began breeding Smooths in 1974. They were given their first bitch, Mini-Echo, who was sired by English and American Champion Teesford Fanfare, who had been an outstanding producer for Hank and Pat Speight of Pathens fame. The Dossetts bred Mini-Echo to Paragon of Gaycliffe, who was sired by another top winner and producer, Champion Price's Crusader.

This first litter produced Champion Miss Me Too Spot who became the foundation bitch for all of the following 50 champions who have to date been bred at Toofox or co-bred by the Dossetts during the past since 1975.

Champion Miss Me Too Spot became the Top Smooth Fox Terrier Bitch in 1976 under the handling and conditioning of John Coghlan, and was the Top Producing Bitch in 1979. She excelled in legs, feet and show disposition, and has passed these qualities on to her progeny. As a brood bitch, she was bred to three of the most outstanding dogs available: Champion Kevrayno Sabre Jet, Champion Karnilo Chieftain of Foxden, and Champion Ttarb The Brat. Through further mixing of these lines, Toofox has been able to develop substance, soundness, movement and disposition as a trademark of their line. Several top competitors in the Smooth ring started with Toofox Smooth Fox Terrier puppies as their foundation stock: Joe Purkhiser, Martha Lenaberg, Martha Reikenburg, Ron Markle, Gina Fontinakes, Nancy Hannaford, and Evelyn Petty, just to name a few.

To talk a bit about the individual Toofox Smooths, the first, of course, at the head of the list is Champion Miss Me Too Spot, No. 1 Bitch 1976; No. 2 Smooth 1976; Top Producer 1979; a Group winner and also Best of Opposite Sex at an American Fox Terrier Club Specialty.

Champion Toofox Tasmanian Devil played movie star in *Superman III*. An outstanding producer with ten champion offspring including four Group winners.

Champion Toofox Black Magic is a multiple Group winner, Best of Winners at Westminster, and an outstanding producer with eight champion offspring.

Champion Toofox Lady Evelyn, a Specialty winner is the dam of 15 A.K.C. Champions. She is tied for All Time Top Producing Smooth Bitch and the dam of four Group winners. She is the only Smooth ever to have defeated Champion Ttarb The Brat in a Specialty Show.

Champion Toofox Tribute To Gaycliffe is a Group winner, was Best of Breed at the 1985 American Fox Terrier Club Specialty Show, Best of Opposite Sex at Montgomery County, and the dam of four A.K.C. Champions, including multi-National Specialty winner "The Colonel."

Champion Toofox The Caribe Chief Spy has four all-breed Bests in Show, Best of Breed at Montgomery County, twice Best of Breed at Westminster, three times Best of Breed at the Lone Star Fox Terrier Club Specialty, No. 1 Smooth, all systems, for 1985. Also during 1985 he was the American Fox Terrier Club Grand Challenge and Homer Gage Trophy winner. He is the sire of Best of Opposite Sex winner at Montgomery County and 1986 Westminster.

Champion Toofox The Colonel is a Best in Show winner, a multiple Group winner, 1984 Montgomery County Best of Breed, 1985 New York Associated Terrier Club Best of Breed, 1985 American Fox Terrier Club Thomas Keator Memorial Trophy winner, 1985 New England Fox Terrier Club Best of Breed, 1984 American Fox Terrier Club and Homer Gage Trophy winner.

Champion Toofox Joyeux Noelle was the 1983 Welwire Memorial Trophy winner.

94

Ch. Toofox The Caribe Chief Spy, by Ch. Ttarb The Brat ex Ch. Toofox Lady Evelyn, Best of Breed at Westminster in 1985, is a splendid example of correct type, balance and quality in Smooths. Owned by Caribe Kennels, Joe and Murrell Purkhiser, Wylie, Texas.

Champion Toofox Joshua was a multiple Group winner, No. 7 Smooth, Knight System, in 1985.

Champion Toofox Blazin Saddler is a multiple Specialty winner and the sire of ten champions.

Champion Atwood's Toofox Blazin Echo was No. 10 Smooth in 1977 and a Lone Star Fox Terrier Club Sweepstakes winner.

Champion Toofox The Welchman in 1980 was winner of the American Fox Terrier Club Welwire Trophy.

Since March of 1984, Toofox has won Best of Breed at five of the six most recent American Fox terrier Club National Specialty Shows. Prior to this, Toofox dogs and bitches had picked up three Homer Gage or Welwire Memorial Trophies as the Best American-bred Dog or Bitch in 1980, 1981 and 1983. Toofox Smooths have truly become a tradition in the mid-80s, and must be contended with at the National level.

Three Toofox dogs were in the Top Ten in 1985; Champion Toofox The Caribe Chief, Champion Toofox The Colonel, and Champion Toofox Joshua, rating No. 1, No. 4 and No. 7 respectively.

WAYBROKE

Waybroke Kennels at Jacksonville, Florida, are owned by Hubert M. Thomas and Madison Weeks, who are the breeders or the owners of more than 100 dogs who have completed their championships. Of these, 80 are Smooth Fox Terriers; Waybroke has also bred Standard Poodles, Scottish Terriers, Norwich Terriers and Whippets.

Under the Waybroke banner there have been Best in Show winning Smooth Fox Terriers, Poodles and Scotties as well as a Group winning Norwich.

The most famed of all the dogs at this kennel is the great Smooth, Champion Waybroke Extra Smooth, the Top Winning American-bred of all time in his breed and the Top Producing American-bred Sire. Extra Smooth's show record includes first 60 times in the Terrier Group, and seven Bests in Show. His champion progeny at this time numbers 45, with many others on the way to their titles. It is especially notable, the authors of this book feel, that not only was Extra Smooth a Waybroke homebred, but so were his sire and dam, Champion Waybroke Red Lobster and Champion Waybroke Smooth As Silk. "Andy" was always owner-handled to his exciting show successes, as have been and are all Waybroke exhibits, with very few exceptions.

The foundation of Waybroke goes back to Foxden Kennels and Champion Foremark Ebony Box of Foxden, she having been Champion Foxden Titania, who was bred by Mr. and Mrs. James A. Farrell, Jr.

An award which is especially valued at Waybroke is that of the Homer Gage Memorial Trophy, offered by the American Fox Terrier Club (won by an American-bred dog). This was accounted for by American and Brazilian Champion Waybroke Smooth Operator, a Top Ten winning dog who enjoyed a highly successful career in the United States, then fared equally well in Brazil by becoming a Group and Best in Show winner, co-owned by Waybroke with Sergio Nerigo.

Waybroke has many exciting young dogs coming along, so should remain in the Smooth Fox Terrier limelight over a bright and lengthy future.

APP'S

App's Wire Haired Fox Terriers started out in 1964, owned by Norma Appleyard at Newton Centre, Massachusetts, with the purchase from Mac Silver of App's Sunny Boy, sired by Champion Gallant Fox of Wildoaks. Sunny Boy was handled by Mac to his championship in 10 shows and he was the sire of one litter.

Champion Revlis Magnet was also purchased from Mr. Silver. A daughter of Champion Deko Druid (grandson of Champion Travella Strike and Champion Burtons Betoken) from Champion

Ch. Waybroke Red Lobster, the sire of famous Ch. Waybroke Extra Smooth and Best of Winners at Montgomery County under Dr. Leon Seligman. Red Lobster won numerous Groups in the U.S. and one in Puerto Rico. Bred and handled by Hubert M. Thomas and Madison M. Weeks, owned by Mr. and Mrs. James T. White.

Gay Venture of Wildoaks (Champion Roundway Lightning of Gayterry-Champion Dancer of Wildoaks), she was bred twice, once to Champion Rigador Right Again (English Champion Zeloy Endeavour-Rathmore Pretty Piece) and on the other occasion to Champion Evewire Exemplar (Champion Evewire David Dynamite-Champion Evewire Evenstart).

Champion Homewire Happiness was purchased from Mrs. Ballich, and with Press Agent produced Champion App's Toryna and Champion App's Masquerade. She was by Champion Win Mor's Christar ex Champion Evewire Druid Flirt. Happiness also was bred to Champion Cucen Critique of Ayer Acres (Champion Evewire Evening Edition-Champion Cucen Countess), this producing Champion App's Reign-Beau, who was used just once.

Champion App's Toryna was bred to Champion Harwire Hetman of Whinlatter and produced Champion App's Victory, Champion App's Star Kist, and Champion App's Ad Lib. The latter was purchased by Flavio Werneck for a client in Brazil; she did some winning there and produced two litters, one of which in-

Ch. App's Press Agent handled by Sheena Garrett for breeder-owner Norma Appleyard, Newton, Massachusetts, during the judging at a dog show.

cluded a Best in Show pup. Toryna's second breeding was to Champion Briartex Tavern, producing Champion App's Prime Time and Champion App's Coquette. App's Accent, same litter, is within one point of finishing.

Champion App's Prime Time has done some splendid winning and sired Champion Betwire Dream Girl. Coquette has been bred twice, to Champion Trucote Admiral and to Champion Esquire's Shiver Me Timbers.

Timbers-Coquette breeding produced two promising youngsters, App's High Tech and App's Topa. High Tech won the Wire Fox Terrier Sweepstakes at Montgomery in 1985, and App's Topa placed in the Sweeps class.

The above represents a modest but well-planned and successful venture in breeding and showing Wire Fox Terriers. Norma Appleyard comments, "Achievements in breeding and showing over the past years would not have been possible without the help of Robert Clyde, App's mentor and friend."

BOWYRE

Bowyre Kennels has been an interest for the Bousek family at Cedar Rapids, Iowa, since about 1960. The kennel established its reputation when the first of its show dogs, Champion Wildwood Cinderella, was owner-handled to Best in Show in 1961. For breeding to this splendid bitch a Champion Crackley Cockspur son was imported, both of them being from Crackley bloodlines. Their first litter produced the Bouseks' first homebred champion, Bowyre Cockney Girl, who was to become a Group and Specialty winner and top rated here in America.

During the next ten years, Wayne and Janie Bousek imported a number of English Champions and other outstanding breeding stock with which to improve their breeding program. The imported English Champion Whitwyre Money Market, a Best in Show, Group and Specialty winner, earned championship in the United States, Canada, and Mexico, also becoming the sire of 11 champions and the foundation of the present breeding program.

Eng., Am., Can., and Mex. Ch. Whitwyre Money Market, by Mitre Advocate ex Eng. Ch. Whitwyre Even Money, bred by Mrs. M. Whitworth. Wayne Bousek owner, Bowyre Kennels, Cedar Rapids, Iowa.

Money Market's leading son, Champion Bowyre Contender, also a Group and Specialty winner, was a highly rated Top Ten Wire in 1973 and 1974, and sire of 19 champions.

In 1975, American and Canadian Champion Cefnbryn Cookie was imported from Wales by the Bouseks. She, too, became a Best in Show winner, Group and Specialty winner and was Top Wire Bitch in 1976. She is one of the very few important show bitches to also have become a Top Producer, which she has done with a total of nine champions, eight of them sired by the Bouseks' Champion Bowyre Contender.

The best of the Contender-Cookie progeny was the bitch Champion Bowyre Biscuit, winner of four consecutive Sweepstakes who completed her title at nine months. She won her first Group at 13 months, and went on to become a Best in Show, Group and Specialty winner and a Top Ten Bitch in 1981. She was the dam of five champions prior to her untimely loss in 1983.

The Bousek Wires have been entirely owner-handled to all wins and titles, including five all-breed Best in Show winners, seven Specialty Show winners, and ten Group winners. To date they have bred or owned an impressive total of 47 champions.

Am. and Can. Ch. Cefnbryn Cookie, by Brigade Major ex Cefnbryn Carassima. Bred by T.V. Williams, owned by Wayne and Janie Bousek, Bowyre Kennels, Cedar Rapids, Iowa.

Ch. Heathcote Enchantress, the foundation bitch at Brownstone Kennels, by Ch. Deko Dragoon ex Ch. Meritor Zeloy Sunflower, became the dam of 10 champions including numerous other outstanding producers. Owned and loved by Ann K. and John M. Brown, Shawnee, Kansas.

BROWNSTONE

Brownstone Wire Haired Fox Terriers belong to Ann K. and John M. Brown at Shawnee, Kansas, who started out in Standard Schnauzers, finishing three champions in that breed, after which their interests turned to the Wires.

It was their meeting with Heathcote Enchantress that brought about this change. After a camping trip in the mountains near Fort Collins, Colorado, they recalled Fred Hiigel having mentioned that he had purchased a real good Wire Fox Terrier bitch, and they decided that they would like to see her. When Ann Brown set eyes on "Penny" it was a case of "love at first sight." The lovely bitch went right through to her championship, winning Groups at only a little over a year. The Browns got to see her win now and again, as she piled up a record that eventually found her with four Bests in Show and 14 Terrier Group 1sts—a showing spitfire all the way!

Meanwhile, Ann had an opportunity to show a Wire in a Terrier Group, enjoying the experience so thoroughly that she longed for more of the same. So she and John decided to call Fred Hiigel, who they knew was retiring to become a judge, about leasing Penny. They ended up owning her, and Penny owning them. She became their constant companion, dear friend, and died peacefully on their bed at the age of 16 years.

When acquired by the Browns, Champion Heathcote Enchantress (Penny) was three-and-a-half years old. Six months later she produced her first litter. Bred to Champion Gosmore Kirkmoor Craftsman for two litters; to Champion Axhaline Jimmy Reppin for two litters; and once to Champion Brownstone's Johnny One Spot she produced a total of ten champions.

Penny's grandparents, English Champion Zeloy Emperor on her sire's side, were a great influence on the breed. The world's greatest Wire Fox Terrier sire was her grandsire on the dam's side, Champion Zeloy Endeavor, and was Emperor's sire. Mrs. Brown speaks of Emperor as "sensible, hound marked, short coupled, nice head, good reach of neck. Had good bone and feet." He produced 31 American champions. Penny's sire, Champion Deko Dragoon, produced 22 champions.

Some of Enchantress's offspring are also noted producers. For instance, Champion Brownstone's Breeze Away, by Champion Gosmore Kirkmoor Craftsman, produced three champions. Champion Brownstorm's MacBroom, by the same sire, produced 13 champions. Champion Brownstone's Hey Dey, by Jimmy Reppin, produced seven champions. And Hey Dey's daughter, Champion Brownstone's Miss Kiss, produced seven champions by MacBroom.

In total, Brownstone Kennels has to its credit the very impressive total of 30 champions bred there.

EVEWIRE

Evewire Kennels has bred close to 100 champions, being at present third in line (behind only Hallwyre and Hetherington) as the outstanding producer of Wire Fox Terriers in the United States. This is a record which may well be broken before the story is fully told, as there are fewer than 10 champions between Evewire and these two, with Evewire still actively involved in breeding which the others are not.

Mrs. Eve Ballich of Stevenson, Maryland, has been breeding Wire Haired Fox Terriers since 1956, when her first homebred to gain the title, Champion Little Bit's Sassy Bit, did so. Sassy was a daughter of the great record-breaking importation, Champion Travella Superman of Harham. A descendant of hers, Champion Evewire Sassy Image, became the 90th homebred champion Eve has produced, this in 1980.

Eve Ballich, although now a resident of the Baltimore area, hails from the Mid-west, her birthplace a little town called Eldora in Iowa. There in farm country, Eve grew up surrounded by farm animals, although she did have a Smooth Fox Terrier as a pet. She involved herself with farm animals by exhibiting them at local 4-H shows, local and state fairs, even then having a keenly competitive spirit.

She had decided, in her youth, that she would like to follow a career of nursing. Thus she attended the University of Iowa School of Nursing, after which she became a Psychiatric Nurse at Johns Hopkins University.

When Eve decided that she wanted a Wire puppy, she contacted Mrs. Richard C. Bondy whose Wildoak Kennels were busily engaged in showing and breeding top ones. Not yet having been "bitten by the dog show bug," Eve wanted this first Wire puppy entirely as a companion. But then came Smart Love of Wirehart, from George Hartman, whom we feel sure promptly realized the enthusiastic Wire breeder and exhibitor Eve could become, and with George's encouragement, she was on her way to many years of pleasure with her kennel.

She credits her success as a breeder to "the influence of outstanding producing bitches and their value in establishing a bloodline, directly and through their descendants." For example, she points out, Champion Little Bit's Sassy Bit, Smart Move of Wirehart, and her later acquisition, Champion Nugrade Nuflame, each themselves produced only two champions, but it is through these offspring and their progeny that Eve has bred successfully down through the generations.

Champion Nugrade Nuflame was the dam of Champion Evewire Little Man and a bitch, Champion Evewire Dynamite. Little Man has sired ten or more champions; Dynamite has produced Champion Evewire Explosive, Champion Evewire Druid Doll (Specialty Show and Terrier Group winner), and Champion Evewire Druid Dynamic, sire of some two dozen champions, setting a record as the Wire sire for producing American-bred champions. Dynamic's famous progeny include Champion Evewire Evening

Ensemble, a Group winner and Champion Evewire Exemplar, multi-Terrier Group winner.

Among the famous dogs at Evewire, Champion Evewire Evening Edition has sired many champions, including the great Best in Show winner whom many of us consider the best of all "Evewires," the aptly named Champion Evewire You Better Believe It. To date You Better Believe It has 17 champions to his credit.

Champion Evewire Echo, Champion Evewire Early Event, and many others have added to the prestige and quality of this kennel.

Currently Champion Evewire Main Event (Champion Evewire Explorer-Champion Evewire Enthusiastic) and Evewire Executive (by You Better Believe It from Evewire Sparkle Plenty) are sharing the stud limelight with You Better Believe It. Executive is a youngster of great potential for whom Eve Ballich has high hopes.

Ch. Foxglen Statesman, by Eng. and Am. Ch. Littleway Haranwal Barrister ex Ch. Penda Townville Tanya, was Winners Dog at Westminster in 1975. Home-bred owned by Irene Rhodes, Foxglen Kennels, Sharpsville, Pennsylvania.

FOXAIRN

Foxairn Kennels, specializing in Cairns and Wire Haired Fox Terriers, are owned by Sanderson and Margaret McIlwaine (Mrs. McIlwaine is the former Peggy Beisel) and located at Whitmore Lake, Michigan. The kennel was established shortly after the McIlwaines' marriage in 1980, when they settled on a cozy ten-acre wooded site just north of Ann Arbor, Michigan.

Sanderson, a Cairn and Scottie breeder, and Peggy, a Wire person who previously had been in Old English Sheepdogs, met while Peggy was an employee of, and Sandy a client, of George Ward's.

Peggy acquired her first Wire in 1978, Champion Reedwyre's Dominate Me, a Dominator daughter, and later the McIlwaines purchased that bitch's litter sister, Champion Reedwyre's Dubonnet, who became the foundation bitch for the Foxairn Wires.

With the acquisition of an import, English and American Champion Sarabel Sailorman, the McIlwaines are successfully producing the quality they admire. Their most outstanding of these to date is Champion Foxairn Ensign, who combines some of the greatest English Wires, going back to Spot On, Dominator, Craftsman, and Superflash. Ensign is a multiple Group winner, and was winner of the 1985 American Fox Terrier Club Homer Gage Award—this at just two years of age.

The McIlwaines have finished ten Wire champions, six carrying the Foxairn prefix, these between 1980 and 1985.

Already some of the Foxairn sires and dams have made the Top Ten Producers List this past year. Although relatively new to the world of Wires, Peggy and Sandy are certainly off on the right track towards becoming one of the leading kennels in the breed.

FOXGLEN

Foxglen Kennels is a small operation owned by Irene Rhodes and located at Sharpsville, Pennsylvania.

Mrs. Rhodes's first puppy, purchased when seven months old, was Hallwyre Happy Candidate who came from the noted kennels of Forrest Hall. Although her grooming at that period left much to be desired, Mrs. Rhodes did show this dog, gaining championship honors with him.

Next to finish was a homebred, a lovely bitch named Champion Foxglen Jill's Summer Love, who was sired by Champion Bengal Ryburn Regent. Then came Zeloy Envoy from Ernie Robinson in

England, this one handled only by Mrs. Rhodes and finishing title in a mere six shows.

During a visit to England, Mrs. Rhodes became acquainted with Elsie Williams, bringing home a bitch who became Champion Penda Townville Tanya when she completed her championship by taking Winners Bitch at Montgomery County She then produced numerous champions including Foxglen Tamora, sired by the Zeloy dog who also gained championship by taking Winners, then going on to Best of Winners at Montgomery. A son of Tanya, Champion Foxglen's Bold Eagle, was also in the spotlight, a winner at the Wire Haired Fox Terrier Club of the Central States.

Tanya, unfortunately, developed mammary tumors which recurred after surgery, so eventually she had to be put down. Mrs. Rhodes still has a daughter of hers, 13-year-old American and Canadian Champion Foxglen Molly O'Mine, who was in the Veteran's Class at Montgomery in October 1985. All told, Tanya produced six champions (three of them American and Canadian) and has more than a dozen titled grandchildren.

Latest to finish is Champion Forchlas Dyna Fi, a little bitch Mrs. Rhodes saw and fell in love with during a visit to Crufts in 1985—another who finished in half a dozen shows, handled exclusively either by Mrs. Rhodes or her daughters. She is presently awaiting her litter by Champion Maltman Country Life of Whinlatter.

Currently there is also a homebred bitch close to title, Foxglen's Dynamite, needing only a few single points with which to finish.

GAYTERRY

Gayterry Wire Haired Fox Terriers, owned by Mr. and Mrs. Thomas M. Gately, are among the world's most renowned kennels of this breed. Tom Gately, since childhood, has counted dogs and horses among the most important factors of his life, and at age 16 years used, as he says, his "hard earned savings" to purchase his first show dog, which was not a Wire but an Irish Terrier puppy, who was to become his first champion.

The success with the Irish made Tom extremely enamored of the dog show world, and he decided practically right then that he wanted to become a top professional handler. To this end he served a period of apprenticeship under renowned breeders, ex-

Kay and Tom Gately with Ch. Boarzell Brightest Star in 1942.

Mr. James A. Farrell, Jr., President of the American Fox Terrier Club, presenting the Baywood Trophy for Best American-bred Wire (won by the same owner three times) to Mr. and Mrs. Thomas Gately in 1971 with Ch. Gayterry's Little Cherry.

hibitors, and professional handlers. While still at a very young age, he launched a professional handling career that was to span a highly successful period of 41 years, during which period many of the world's great Fox Terriers passed through his hands.

In 1931 Tom met Kay, who was to become his wife. After a six week courtship they were married, and have been a "team" ever since. Shortly after their marriage, they settled on "Gayterry" as their lifetime registered kennel name—a combination of their name and that of the Irish who was still with them. Also part of the deal when the Gatelys were married were the several Wires Tom had acquired soon after going on his own as a handler. Throughout the years, and still to this day, the Gatelys have always owned a few Wires themselves.

During their busiest handling and breeding days, Gayterry was located at Wilton, Connecticut. One of the first outstanding Wires they handled was many times Best in Show winner, English and American Champion Boarzell Brilliance, whose breeder-owner, Mrs. H.H. Swann, emigrated from England to the United States. Tom and Kay also handled the excellent full sister, Champion Boarzell Beauty.

Another fabulous historic dog, Ch. Roundway Lightning of Gayterry, from the kennels of Tom and Kay Gately 1937 at Wilton, Connecticut.

Eng. Ch. Boarzell Brilliance also became an American and Canadian Champion with many Bests in Show to his credit. Owned by Mrs. H.H. Swann, born in November 1935, handled by Tom Gately. By Eng. Ch. Stocksmoor Sportsman (Intl. Ch. Gallant Fox of Wildoaks—Lady Ha Ha) ex Boarzell Brightness (Intl. Ch. Gallant Fox of Wildoaks—Dogberry Lady Gay). Bred by owner.

Mrs. Swann had left the dam of these two, Boarzell Brightness, in England for a repeat breeding to Champion Stocksmoor Sportsman. After arriving in this country, Brightness had her third litter; this one included Champion Boarzell Brightest Star. Mrs. Swann found the keeping of many dogs incompatible with her new environment and thus decided to sell some of them. Brightest Star was sent to the Gatelys to be sold while still a puppy; but they fell in love with her on sight, and thus "strained the exchequer" to make the purchase for themselves. This was in 1938 when they were very young, struggling handlers. But "Jinny" was well worth any sacrifices her purchase may have entailed, for not only did she mature into a bitch of outstanding greatness, but one who brought them years of pleasure.

Owing to commitments to clients, the Gatelys often found it necessary to hold "Jinny" back in favor of other people's dogs. Notwithstanding this fact, she had a fabulous record, and Kay and Tom basked in her glory. Tom notes, "Some enormous offers were made for her, but how can you sell something you truly love?"

Jinny's first breeding was not until she had reached six years of age, but her first puppy was one who brought added glory to Gayterry. This was the multiple Best in Show winner and outstanding sire, Champion Sirius of Gayterry. Another of Jinny's progeny was Champion Brightest Star of Gayterry; and as the years passed, there was a continuing flow of top champions from this line.

Jinny's sire, English Champion Stocksmoor Sportsman, and her dam, Boarzell Brightness, were sired by the immortal Champion Gallant Fox of Wildoaks. There is much discussion regarding the merits and vices of inbreeding and linebreeding. It has been the Gatelys' experience that, if done with exceptional specimens who are both mentally and physically sound, such breeding can be a most useful tool. It has been their practice, as breeders, to make a complete outcross about every second or third generation.

In addition to the many champions which Kay and Tom bred and kept for themselves, there were numerous others of equal quality who went to superior homes. In addition to their own superb Wires, the Gatelys had the lead on some of the all-time Top Winning Wires which they handled for others, most of whom they had selected and purchased for their owners during their many trips to England.

The Gatelys have, as very busy and respected judges, an entirely new lifestyle at the present time. They share the year between their two homes, at Pineville, Pennsylvania (May to December) and Orlando, Florida (December to May). And their lives are still shared by Wire Fox Terriers, the present ones being Champion Sadachbia of Gayterry (born in 1972) and her daughter Champion Lone Star of Gayterry, these bitches, of course, being descended from the beloved Champion Boarzell Brightest Star.

Best in Show winners made famous by the Gatelys and owned by them include, in addition to the already mentioned Brightest Star and her son Sirius, such well remembered Wires as English and American Champion Caracas Winter Call Boy, Champion Gila of Gayterry, and Champion Gayterry Little Cherry. Their homebred champions included Champion Arcturus of Gayterry; Champion Celestial of Gayterry; Champion Comette of Gayterry, Champion Brightest Star of Gayterry; Champion Sadalsuud of Gayterry, Champion Jupiter of Gayterry; Champion Dark Star of Gayterry, Champion Cosmo Super Star of Gayterry; Champion Lyra of Gayterry, Champion Gayterry Antares of Harham, Champion

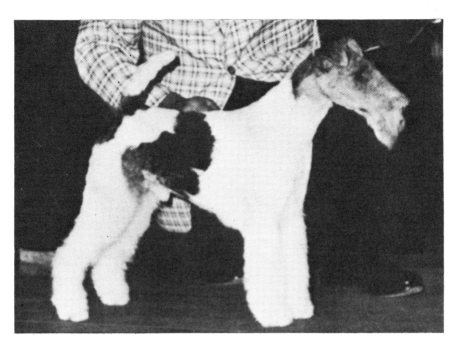

Ch. Libwyre's Legend, by Eng. and Am. Ch. Townville Tobias ex Am. and Can. Ch. Holmwire Vitoka Vanessa (Eng. Ch. Holmwire Tudor Renown ex Vitoka Venturess) winning the Terrier Group at Paper Cities K.C. in July 1978. George Ward handling for the R.R. Libners, Muskegon, Michigan.

Scheatt of Gayterry; Champion Starkist Nyla of Gayterry, Champion Sadal Melik of Gayterry; Champion Enif of Gayterry, Champion Ruc Bah of Gayterry; Champion Lord Alfie Pringle of Chelsea, Champion Gayterry Leo O'Champlain View; Champion Gila of Gayterry; Champion Tula of Gayterry; Champion Zircon of Gayterry; Champion Goldenrod Sunburst, C.D.X.; Champion Sadachbia of Gayterry; and Champion Lone Star of Gayterry, plus, of course, Sirius and Gila and Little Cherry, the Best in Show homebreds.

LIBWYRE

Libwyre Wire Fox Terriers are owned by R. and R. Libner who are residents of Muskegon, Michigan.

The Libners purchased their first Wire Fox Terrier in 1970 as a pet, shortly thereafter becoming interested in showing and developing quality members of the breed. Unfortunately, this first Wire did not meet with their highest hopes. She was a wonderful pet, however, and was subsequently given to a friend who wanted one for that purpose.

Next came a dog sold to the Libners as a show prospect. As they learned more and more about the breed, they soon realized, again, that this one did not measure up either and so was given as a pet to Mr. Libner's secretary.

Based on these two experiences, the Libners contacted professional handler George Ward, through whom they purchased the two dogs who became their first two champions. Later they bred and imported others with considerable success. George, meanwhile, has remained a good friend who has guided the Libners throughout the years in their showing and breeding of some very exciting Wires.

Their first really big break came to the Libners in the purchase of American and Canadian Champion Holmwire Vitoka Vanessa from Charlie Higginson of the famed Holmwire Kennels in England. Vanessa proved to live up to her American owners' highest dreams and expectations. Their daughter, Laura Libner, showed her in Canada during the summer of 1975, winning several Groups and Bests in Show with this lovely bitch, making her the Top Wire Bitch in Canada that year. Thereafter she was bred and became the Top Producing Bitch Producer of Wire Champions over a period of four years. Vanessa is alive and well and lives with the Libners in their home.

Vanessa is a granddaughter of English Champion Winter Statesman and English Champion Zeloy Emperor. These are considered by experts to be two of the greatest Wires ever produced. When it came time to breed her, the Libners imported English Champion Townville Tobias, the last son of Living Statesman, specifically for linebreeding to Vanessa. The litter was, one might say, a smashing success, three of them gaining titles. This trio included the Libners' famed Champion Libwyre Legend who, under George Ward's care and guidance, won many a Best in Show, multiple Groups, and himself produced numerous outstanding champions.

During another trip to England, the Libners saw, at age seven months, the Wire who became English, American, and Canadian Champion Townville Tristanian. They promptly fell in love with this dog, deciding that they must have him for their own. Townville Kennel was not yet ready at that time to sell him, wanting, very understandably, for him to have the opportunity of proving himself in England prior to leaving his homeland. They promised the Libners that when the time came they would contact them,

Eng. and Am. Ch. Townville Tobias, by Eng. Ch. Winter Statesman ex Townville Tamlyn, was the 1974 English Fox Terrier Club Specialty winner and is a Best in Show and Multiple Group Winner in the U.S. A sire of quality, Tobias progeny include Ch. Harwire Hetman of Whinlatter and Ch. Libwyre's Legend. Owned by Robert Libner, Muskegon, Michigan.

which they did. Thus it was that two years after first having seen him they imported Tristanian, again turning him over to George Ward for his show career in America.

Over the years the Libners have bought some other important stock from others of the leading Wire breeders. Among them are Champion Newmaidley Ruby from Linda Beak's famous kennel; Champion Blackdale Elegant Love, a recent acquisition from the Blackdale Kennels in Ireland, she being a daughter of the International Champion Blackdale Aristocrat and Irish Champion Blackdale Playgirl; and, most recently, while attending the Wire Fox Terrier show in England, they saw another stunning young dog whom they were determined to acquire. It took months of negotiation between the Libners, George Ward and the English owner, Harry O'Donoghue, but finally the Libners were successful and Blackdale Stardust came to Libwyre. This outstanding young dog is from a very handsome linebred bitch, daughter of International

Ch. Libwyre's Legend, famous winning and producing Wire Fox Terrier, has been handled to impressive victories by George Ward for owners Mr. and Mrs. R. Libner, Muskegon, Michigan.

FIRST IN GROUP

APER CITIES K.C.

JULY 1. 1978

OLSON PHOTO

Champion Blackdale Starbright, who is generally considered to be Blackdale's most excellent production to date. Starbright's sire is International Champion Galsul Excellence, another highly successful sire. Needless to say, the Libners are expecting big things from this handsome youngster.

When the Libners imported Champion Newmaidley Ruby, a granddaughter of English Champion Harrowhill Huntsman, they had her bred back to her famous grandsire Huntsman. This produced a gorgeous dog whom the Libners named Libwyre's Grand Mufti, to whom was bred the best bitch Vanessa had ever produced. This gave the Libners their splendid bitches Champion Libwyre Brittania and Champion Libwyre Katie Maru. Both of these are slated for breeding to the new Libwyre dog, Blackdale Stardust. Thus the Libners are continuing to look forward to better and brighter events as the produce from these matings hit the show rings.

JOE MOAN

Most of us know Joe Moan of Harrison, Tennessee, as a Scottie enthusiast. Others recognize him instantly for his association with the Pet Foods Division of Quaker Oats. But for those of you who are not aware of the Fox Terrier interest Joe has long held, we are very happy to bring you the story of his very handsome and successful Champion Starwood's Goodie Two Shoes, owner-handled to a smashing good Best of Winners at the Greater St. Louis Fox Terrier Club Specialty, a victory which she repeated at the Atlanta Fox Terrier Specialty, again for five points, under Tom Gately.

Goodie is a daughter of Champion Runwyre Randy Dandy, who was a son of the great English and American Champion Seawire Ellswyre Marksman.

Joe Moan with his very famous Wire Ch. Starrwood's Goodie Two Shoes some time back on the way to her championship. The Moan Kennels, at Harrison, Tennessee, have numerous important winning Terriers who are kennel mates of this very outstanding Wire.

MYSTWYRE

Mystwyre Kennels came into being when a pet owned by Thomas L. and Susanne H. Yates, Hampton, Georgia, was accidentally poisoned. They got a replacement pet from Lynnwyre Kennels (now retired), of whom they were told, "she is much too good not to be shown." Champion Lynnwyre Magic Monica finished in short order, with most of her winning done showing her with a beginner's coat. That, of course, was that. The Yates were by then quite thoroughly "hooked," however, and after about three years they purchased a bitch from the famous Wyrequest Kennels in Spokane, Washington. She was to become Champion Wyrequest's Wildfire, who finished quickly, then went immediately to the whelping box. There, over the years, she has made herself the foundation of Mystwyre Kennels. She herself produced only three champions, but they in their turn have gone on to produce outstanding members of the breed; for instance, Champion Mystwyre Beau-Gentry, who won the Atlanta Fox Terrier Specialty in 1982 and was No. 6 Wire Dog the same year. A daughter, Champion Mystwyre Wingsong, was No. 8 Bitch in 1983.

Over the years, the Yates have used on their bitches such well-known dogs as Champion Harwire Hetman of Whinlatter; his son, Champion Finewire Crusader; Champion Seawire Ellswyre Marksman; and Champion Ana-Dare Emperor.

Mystwyre is a small kennel owned by very enthusiastic fanciers. They have now finished their 15th champion, and like to feel that they will leave their mark on the Wire Fox Terrier breed through better quality with brains as well as beauty.

RAYLU

Raylu Wire Haired Fox Terriers are owned by Gene and Bob Bigelow who are located at Yorktown, Virginia.

Gene Bigelow is a second-generation dog show person, being the daughter of Raymond and Lucile Scaggs, who opened a kennel in Maryland just outside of Washington, D.C. in 1926, the year in which their daughter Gene was born. The Scaggs started with German Shepherds, but Lucile Scaggs fell in love with a Wire puppy on the bench at National Capital and purchased him immediately. He was Tilwall Sun Beau, a son of Champion Crackley Supreme Again. This would have been about in 1929 or 1930.

This lovely and well-known Wire bitch is Ch. Raylu Berlyean Starbrite, by Ch. Deko Druid ex the Group-winning Ch. Raylu Realstar. She was owned and handled to her title by Beryl Pearson, then later belonged to Mr. and Mrs. Dennis Walker. Starbrite is the dam of four champions to date by Ch. Raylu Raconteur, three of them with Specialty wins. Bred by Gene S. Bigelow, Raylu Wires; and Kathryn C. Creech, Kitwyn Wires.

Gene Bigelow cannot remember being without a Wire Fox Terrier at any time during her lifetime. She grew up with an assortment of dogs, but always there were Wires, then later Welsh were added with considerable success. Ray Scaggs' A.K.C. Handler's Card was #100, his daughter Gene's just over #500.

Owing to Lucile Scaggs's asthma, Gene's parents were forced to retire to Arizona in 1947, at which time Gene took over the kennel, having by then met (at the University of Maryland) and married Robert C. Bigelow. She selected Raylu as her kennel name and considers that her "real start" in Fox Terriers was at that time.

Since then the Bigelows have lived in over a dozen homes and locations, due to the Air Force having recalled her husband for the Korean conflict. Hawaii was his first assignment (as Gene says, "what a way to start"), but it was very sad having to part with so many of the "canine friends." She did take two along with her, however. Later it was ROTC for an assignment in West Virginia, then only three dogs, followed by a return to the D.C. area. There were only a couple of litters prior to then. At this period Gene met Eve Ballich, who was just beginning, and Gene might be said to have been doing likewise, as her activities had been so sharply curtailed for so long a period.

Any breeding Gene did at this point was with very careful consideration since unexpected moves made it impossible to keep a number of dogs; thus the Bigelows were limited to "hanging in there" with, at the most, one litter a year. Unfortunately, during that period, many a top quality Wire had to be parted with as a pet. But on the opposite side of the coin, a very satisfying number of people breeding and showing quite successfully now started with a puppy which Gene could not keep for herself, due to the circumstances of so many and unexpected moves.

Bob Bigelow retired some years ago, and Gene has continued to operate with the dogs in much the same manner as formerly. She now keeps at home two bitches and a stud dog, plus her old house pets. She had been able to find fantastic homes for three of her top "gals" (all with Montgomery wins to their credit), all with folks who had lost earlier older dogs of Gene's breeding, which has been very helpful and gratifying as well.

All of the present Wires with the Raylu prefix come from the *one* female line that began with the *one bitch* Gene had selected when the kennel had to be sold and the Air Force became their way of life. She is especially proud, in spite of being so limited in what she could manage, to be the breeder of 31 champions to date (29 Wires and two Min Pins). In addition, she has finished more than that number of her breeding from bitches whom she had finished, who subsequently had gone to new homes where they had been bred. Sometimes a puppy came back to Gene where she was not listed as a breeder, but which actually carried her lines on both sides. Also, some of the titled ones have been co-owned with her husband or with a friend.

The original line at Raylu was very heavy in Talavera Simon breeding, this great dog's last living daughter having been kenneled with Gene's parents. The first bitch was from a combination of Champion Dogberry Rio Grande, Champion Crackley Startrite of Wildoaks, and an addition of the Davishill Little Man line and Champion Talarora Smasher (Simon's grandson).

118

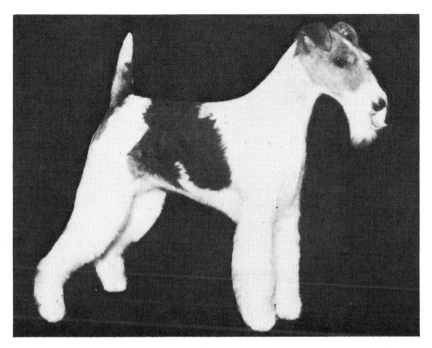

A true "golden oldie" from the 1960s. The famous Ch. Raylu Rendition (1962–1978), by Ch. Derbyshire Dinner Jacket ex Ch. Raylu Resume, was a top terrier with wins including Group 1sts, and dam of the outstanding winner and producer Ch. Raylu Raconteur. Gene S. Bigelow, owner, Yorktown, Virginia.

Studs whom Gene feels have contributed the most to her line moving on successfully have been Champion Glynhir Great Guns and his grandson Champion Evewire Extra Edition; then Champion Derbyshire Dinner Jacket; later came Champion Bev-Wyre's ConBrio Tim (who fortunately became owned by the Bigelows upon his show retirement); and now Tim's son Champion Raylu Recharge, who is the sire of nine champions with more who are pointed. Champion Raylu Raconteur, who went back to Dinner Jacket and the old Guns and Edition lines, also sired well—eight champions to his credit.

Several of the Bigelows' bitches have been Top Producers, which would seem unusual since they retain so few, but at the same time breed them *only* with quality as the goal. The three (at this time all in homes with friends) are spayed, and in their breeding days each had only two litters apiece. Champion Raylu Audi-

119

Ch. Wendywyre Independent, bred and owned by Dick and Laura Forkel, handled by Laura Forkel, taking Best in Show at the Kanadasaga K.C. in 1972. First Best in Show winner bred at this famous kennel.

tion was the dam of the two younger ones Gene has now. Champion Raylu Marsha Music had only males (which the Bigelows can use when and if). And Champion Raylu Reminisce had a marvelous record, including Winners Bitch at a Montgomery County American Foxterrier Specialty, and is the dam of a good dog who has finished, handled by Gene. All three of these bitches come home regularly to be groomed, are adored by their owners, and share their beds—the ideal life for retired champions who thus have the opportunity of enjoying their old age and bringing pleasure throughout their lifetime! Gene has two old timers at home, too: one aged 15 years, the other 16, whom as she notes, she "feels badly at leaving for any reason."

120

WENDYWYRE

Wendywyre Kennels are breeders of outstanding Wire Fox Terriers, owned by Richard and Laura Forkel at Orange, California.

The Forkels purchased their first Wire bitch in 1964, Lively Wendy Lee, who was the foundation bitch and for whom "Wendywyre" was selected for the identification of this kennel. At that time the Forkels were located at Whittier, California.

Wendy was bred just once, to Champion Nemo's Magic of Livewyre, who was owned by John Lasch of Casa Blanca Kennels. The resulting litter produced four puppies, two of whom gained their titles, the bitches Champion Diana of Wendywyre and Champion Snowfire of Wendywyre.

Diana, on her first appearance in the show ring, at the initial event of the Great Western Terrier Specialty in Los Angeles, went Winners Bitch from the Bred-by Exhibitor Class, bringing home a 5-point major, while littermate Snowfire also started off in a notable manner with back-to-back Group 2nds early in her career.

In 1968 the Forkels moved to Syracuse, New York, and in the process of doing so purchased their first stud dog, Champion Rosecliffe To Choice, "Topper," from Rosecliffe Kennels at Rosewood, California. "Topper" became a champion at shows in upstate New York and was the sire of seven of the Wendywyre homebred champions.

In 1970 Champion Top Gunner of Wendywyre became the Forkels' third home-bred champion.

Then in 1972 Champion Wendywyre Independent, as a class dog at that time, homebred, shown and conditioned by Laura Forkel, went Best in Show at Kanadasaga Kennel Club in June. "Indy" was shown by Laura on 11 occasions, during which he amassed one Best in Show, two Group 1sts, a Group 2nd, two Group 3rds and a Group 4th, finishing his title in July 1972. He was sired by American and Canadian Champion Rosecliffe Top Choice ex Wendywyre Surprise Package.

Champion Ana-Dare Endeavor came to Wendywyre in 1973, sent to the Forkels by Daisy Austad, following the death of John Lasch, Casa Blanca Kennels. Laura finished "Pal" the first time she had him out, taking a Group 3rd in the process. He was the sixth to gain title from the famed litter of seven by English Champion Zeloy Emperor ex Champion Holmwire Tudor Radiance, bred by Mr. and Mrs. Jorgensen of Ana-Dare Wire fame. "Pal"

Ch. Warwick Watchman, age 10 months, receiving a few finishing touches on the way to the ring from his owner-handler Laura Forkel.

was the sire of five champions, among them the homebred multiple Best in Show winner, Champion Wendywyre Look Out.

In 1981, back in California, Champion Wendywyre's Look Out went Best in Show at Los Encinos, giving the Forkels their second Best in Show dog. He now has numerous such wins on his record (by Champion Ana-Dare Endeavor ex Champion Wendywyre Free Spirit).

Champion Wendywyre's First Class also came along in 1981. And in 1982 "Tully" was purchased—Champion Warwick Watchman, who finished title in six shows. The following year, when the Forkels traveled to the Wire Fox Terrier Club of Central Ohio Wire Specialty Show in Ohio, held on May 11th, to accept their Hall of Fame Award as breeders of 15 American Kennel Club champions, they took Tully along to show. One hardly can wonder when the lovely dog (owner-handled and conditioned by Laura), went on to gain Best of Variety at this keenly contested and quality-packed event, that Laura and Dick were really on cloud nine throughout the trip home! Actually "Tully" was just carrying on in the tradition of his family, as he is descended from Champion Brownstone's MacBroom, Champion Terrikane's Tullive, and Champion Gosmore Kirmoor Craftsman, all who had preceded him to the honor.

Tully is the sire of the latest homebred champion at Wendywyre, Champion Wendywyre Top Billing.

WYRELEE

Wyrelee Wire Haired Fox Terriers are owned by Nancy Lee Wolf at Scotts Valley, California, who has been a breeder of them since about 1972. To date she has bred the impressive total of 21 champions, and also has eight dogs, six of them Wires, who have earned Companion Dog degrees in obedience.

Nancy Wolf's two foundation bitches, on whom the kennel is primarily bred, were Champion Wyrelee Banned in Boston, C.D., and Champion Halsho Whirlaway of Wyrelee. Banned in Boston is the granddaughter of the "pet" bitch Nancy purchased in 1969. Whirlaway was purchased from Harold Shook in 1972. Most of the current dogs at Wyrelee are a direct line from one or the other of these two. Banned in Boston produced five champions; Whirlaway presented her owner with three.

Nancy is a very active lady in the world of Wire Fox Terriers. She is a member of the Board of Governors of the American Foxterrier Club, a past President of the Fox Terrier Club of Northern California, and belongs to the Great Western Fox Terriers Breeders Association, the Fox Terrier Club of Central States (for both of whom she has judged Specialty Sweepstakes), and the Wire Fox Terrier Association of Great Britain. She enjoys judging.

Among the noted winners in this kennel are Champion Wyrelee Star Bright, by Champion Libwyre Legend ex Champion Wyrelee's First Noel, who on the way to the title gained Best of Breed and a Group 3rd from the classes. Champion Wyrelee's More Ringside Gossip, a Group winner from the classes, was also a Specialty winner in 1985. Champion Wyrelee's the Huntsman had six Best of Breed victories from the classes while making up his title. Champion Wyrelee Double Trouble, C.D. is another outstanding terrier of Nancy Wolf's. Champion Wyrelee's Wondrous and Champion Wyrelee's Cracker Jack, littermates, are champions of the mid-1980s; Wondrous gained title in 1984 at back-to-back weekends including Santa Barbara while Cracker Jack was Winners Dog at the 1984 American Fox Terrier Club National Specialty, Montgomery County, October 1984.

A well-known brace of Wyrelees are the dog Champion Wyrelee's Hot Stuff and the bitch Champion Wyrelee's First Noel. The bitch, Noel is the dam of several of the leading Wyrelee winners. Together these two were Best Brace at a Northern California Specialty.

WYREQUEST

Wyrequest Wire Fox Terriers in Spokane, Washington, owned by Mr. and Mrs. Raymond M. Splawn, are among America's most successful and prestigious, with a record of 31 home-bred champions to their credit in their third decade of breeding.

As their foundation, established breeding stock was imported from the leading English bloodlines. An early import was Champion Nugrade Regent, by English and American Champion Bengal Ryburn Regent ex Nugrade Bridget.

The following year Regent was joined by Champion Nugrade Countess, who was to become one of America's Top Producing Wire Fox Terrier bitches.

Later Henry Sayres imported Champion Tavabob for the Splawns, to bolster their stud force. English Champion Tava Wren was later added to the Wyrequest brood bitches. After earning her American championship she was put to work in the whelping box with very exciting, satisfactory results.

The Splawns' most recent addition to their kennel is Champion Denidale Yer Man, son of Blackdale Aristocrat from Denidale Night Nurse. The Blackdale Kennels of Ireland have made their mark in the world of Wires. These lines were added to Wyrequest with the breeding of Blackdale Confidence to Champion Denidale Yer Man, with the result that there are several youngsters carrying the Wyrequest prefix, and these bloodlines are now ready to go. Their quality is bound to cause considerable excitement in show ring competition.

YELSAM

Yelsam Wire Fox Terriers, owned by Dr. John T. Masley of Charleston, Illinois, and his first wife June, was a small enterprise which brought great pleasure and success to them. Both John and June Masley enjoyed breeding, finishing their good ones, and showing to a limited degree. They seldom specialed a dog, and never campaigned one just for the sake of making a record.

Over the years, the Masleys bred 37 litters, from which 29 champions were finished. They themselves finished 20 champions and three Obedience Title holders, two of which earned U.D. degrees. Of this number 17 were homebred, a record which was recognized by the Masleys' inclusion in the Wire Fox Terrier Club's Hall of Fame.

Outstanding Wire breeders Mr. and Mrs. Raymond M. Splawn, owners of Wyrequest Kennels, Spokane, Washington, with their Am. and Can. Ch.Tavabob by Eng. Ch. Seedfield Meritor Super Flash ex Tavallaire.

John and June Masley purchased their first Wire from Irving C. Ackerman in the 1930's while they were living in the San Francisco area. They had bred one litter when World War II intervened. Following the end of the war, they were impressed by the advertisements and the record of a well-known kennel of the time, and purchased a bred bitch on the installment plan. They were fortunate, since their third litter produced their first champion. However, subsequent breedings and additional bitches with the same bloodlines produced nothing more. This was the first phase of Yelsam Kennels, during which time the Masleys had bred nine litters.

Next they followed the route of breeding their bitches to the top winning dogs. This was an improvement and did tend to upgrade the litters which were produced. However, this was at best a hit-or-miss proposition since they had no definite plan and thus had no established bloodlines which they were following. During this phase in their breeding program, Yelsam bred 12 litters and finished six champions.

Twenty years ago the Masleys realized that if they were to be truly successful, it would be necessary to establish a plan and follow it through. Irving Ackerman, early on, had given them good advice on a breeding program, and the linebreeding theories of George Skelly seemed to fit into it. So, between the two, the Masleys devised a plan which, for them, worked out successfully. However, during this time their breeding activities were severely curtailed for a seven year period, during which Dr. Masley served as an American Kennel Club Field Representative. Even so, they were fortunate during those years, from the mid-60's onward, to have bred 16 litters, from which 22 champions emerged. Now Dr. Masley breeds an occasional litter and exhibits rather sparingly.

Current bloodlines at Yelsam go back to two bitches acquired from George Ward: Champion Albany Trinket and Mooremaides Wonder Girl. Trinket was linebred from the English Champion Travella Strike, while Wonder Girl had English Champion Winter Statesman as her maternal grandsire and paternal great grandsire.

Trinket gave the Masleys two champions, one of which was Champion Yelsam Gentleman Jim, by Champion Caracus Cavalier who was a Statesman son. This was an outcross, but gave Yelsam strong Statesman and Strike genes in their line.

The other was Champion Yelsam G.W. Smythe, a complete outcross with Canadian Champion Tulsemere Tuscan as the sire. This breeding, however, retained the Strike blood of his dam.

An almost perfect "nick" was achieved when the Smythe daughter, Wendy Wyldee of Yelsam, was bred to Jim. This particular combination of Strike and Statesman blood seemed to be the catalyst, and Wyldee produced from it nine champions, making her one of the Top Producing Wire Fox Terrier bitches of all time, this from a total of 18 puppies whelped. The one regret, John Masley notes, is that when he joined A.K.C, they had four or five of her most promising puppies which they placed in what they had been assured would be "show homes," but unfortunately two or three of them (which quite possibly could have finished) never had the opportunity to achieve their titles. Had they done so, Wyldee then would have been *the* Top Producing Wire Bitch. This is one of the disappointments that can occur in showing good show prospects as one never can be certain that the first enthusiasm for showing them by the new owners will remain.

126

Two of Wendy Wyldee's puppies merit special mention. The first of these, Champion Yelsam Tina, had two litters with a total of six puppies, all of which finished, by Champion Yelsam Jum Boe who is a Wonder Girl son by Champion Aryee Dominator thus heavily linebred to Statesman. Here, again, a combination of Strike and Statesman genes seemed to be the answer. Subsequent linebreeding of Tina's offspring to studs carrying Statesman blood have given the Masleys quality puppies. At present, a fourth generation of Tina's, bred to Champion Terrikane's Tulliver, is being shown and should finish easily. This will make the seventh consecutive generation from Champion Albany Trinket to have finished.

The other of Wyldee's pups, and probably the best of them all, was Champion Alpine Ginger Snap of Yelsam. She was born shortly after John went with A.K.C. and had begun to curtail breeding. Lou Auslander was looking for a Wire for his wife's brother, and an agreement was reached that he could have Ginger if he would finish her. They also agreed that she would not be campaigned, since Mr. Auslander was judging a lot and Dr. Masley was with A.K.C. Ginger was turned over to Dick Cooper, who finished her in two weekends at three shows. The first two were 5-point majors at which she went Best of Variety. At the third show there were absentees and only four points; however, winning Best of Variety, Ginger was shown in the Terrier Group, which she won, gaining the five points. For Best in Show she was seriously considered. But, true to the agreement which had been made, she was never again shown and became a beloved house dog. John Masley comments that he saw her the following week and believes her to be one of the best Wire bitches he ever has seen.

Dr. Masley comments, "Any success in our breeding program has to eventually be credited to things we learned from both Irving C. Ackerman and George Skelly. I remember Mr. Ackerman saying, 'don't worry about the size of the bitch. A smaller, typy one will be the better producer.' And, with regard to studs, 'a larger, stallion type is preferred.' Both Wyldee and Tina were small; Jim and Jum Boe large, as were their sires. Skelly's study of linebreeding, showing the percentage of success with various combinations, has also been a valuable guide in selecting prospective studs for our bitches. That, together with a measure of luck, has been our formula for success."

We are indebted to Dr. John Masley for having sent us the following list of Wire Fox Terrier Club Hall of Fame members. Inclusion on this list means that the person named has bred 15 or more Wire champions. Each name is followed by the kennel identification and number of champion Wires bred there.

Mr. and Mrs. Forest N. Hall	**Hallwyre**	100
Mr. and Mrs. T.H. Carruthers,III	**Hetherington**	93
Mrs. Eve Ballich	**Evewire**	91
Mr. and Mrs. R.C. Bondy	**Wildoaks**	50
Mr. and Mrs. Raymond M. Splawn	**Wyrequest**	46
Mr. and Mrs. Wayne Bousek	**Bowyre**	29
Dr. and Mrs. John W. Masley	**Yelsam**	29
Col. and Mrs. Robert Bigelow	**Raylu**	27
Mr. and Mrs. James H. Brown	**Brownstone**	26
Mr. Harold Shook	**Halsho**	26
Mr. and Mrs. Myron J. Hook	**Mountain Ayre**	24
Mr. and Mrs. E.A. Kraft	**Wynwyre**	24
Mrs. Franklin J. Kroehler	**Merrybrook**	21
Mr. and Mrs. Richard J. Forkel	**Wendywyre**	20
Mr. and Mrs. W.L. Lewis	**Glynhir**	20
Ms. Nancy Lee Wolf	**Wyrelee**	19
Mr. and Mrs. Thomas M. Gately	**Gayterry**	17
Dr. Charlotte Jones/Miss E. Stark	**Koshare**	17
Mr. and Mrs. D.E. Jorgensen	**Ana-dare**	17
Mr. and Mrs. Aubrey D. Clay	**Deewyre**	16
Mrs. Virginia S. Simms	**Mountaineer**	16
Mr. and Mrs. Robert H. Fine	**Finewyne**	15
Mr. and Mrs. Robert Libner	**Libwyre**	15
Ms. Mari M. Morrisey	**Brookhaven**	15
Mr. and Mrs. George Ward	**Albany**	15

The Dr. Frank R. Booth Distinguished Service Award, offered for the first time through the Wire Fox Terrier Club in 1980 in memory of Dr. Booth, has been presented to the following:

1980	Dr. and Mrs. John W. Masley, *Yelsam*
1981	Mr. and Mrs. T.H. Carruthers, III, *Hetherington*
1982	Mr. George F. Skelly, *Cordate*
1983	Mrs. Joanellan Wahl, *Showgirl*
1984	Mrs. Virginia S. Simms, *Mountaineer*

← **Overleaf:**

Ch. Raylu Reminisce at 11 months. One of the famous Raylu winners owned by Gene and Bob Bigelow, Yorktown, Virginia.

130

Overleaf: →

1. Fortune's Ghostwriter, owned by Lisa Sachs, taking Best of Winners at Riverhead K.C. under judge Jane Forsyth, Riverhead K.C., 1984.

2. Ch. Foxtrot Fast Lane, by Ch. Foxburo Patent Pending ex Ch. Kraehollow Katy O'Della, is a multiple Group winner with five Terrier Group 1sts already to his credit. Jane Swanson, owner, Foxtrot Kennels, Erie, Illinois.

3. Ch. Viscum Valente, by Eng. Ch. Crispey Camelot ex Viscum Viva, was purchased by Mr. and Mrs. Fred Kuska of Crag Crest Kennels from Mr. Walker of Viscum fame. This group and Best of Breed Wire and Top Ten Dog (all systems) is pictured taking Best of Breed at the Great Western Specialty in the 1970s.

4. Ch. Crizwood Telstar Neil D, multiple Best in Show winner, as a puppy going Best in Match at the Beaters Club event over 800 entries at the beginning of his career. Owned by Gene Simmonds, Handful Kennels, bred by Chris Wornall, handled by Bob Fisher.

5. Ch. Twinfox Jason of Crag Crest is by Ch. Bronwyn Velvet Brass (Am., Mex. Ch. Belle-chien New Addition ex Bronwyn Star Soloist) from Crag Crest Wind Chant (Crag Crest All Clear ex Crag Crest Written on the Wind). Owned by Crag Crest Kennels, Mr. and Mrs. Fred Kuska, Colfax, California.

6. Ch. Foxden Exchequer, Best of Breed at the Great Western Terrier Specialties, handled by James Smith for himself and Susan Akin, Palouse, Washington.

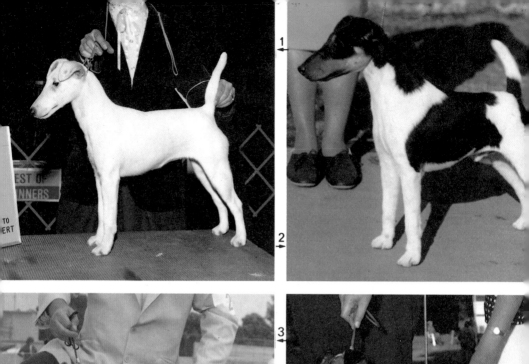

1

2

3

4

5

6

← **Overleaf:**

1. Ch. Karnilo Completa, lovely imported bitch owned by Mrs. Winifred Stout, Foster, Rhode Island.

2. Am. and Can. Ch. Quissex The Pimpernel, by Ch. Quissex Janrich Jackanapes ex Quissex Lorgnon. Winning Best Smooth at Kenilworth in 1984.

3. Ch. Waybroke In A Pickle was Best Smooth in Sweepstakes at the American Fox Terrier Club Specialty under Mrs. James A. Farrell, Jr. Pictured finishing her Championship under Dr. Lee Huggins. "Pickles" is now a Top Producer. Owner-handled by Hubert M. Thomas and Madison M. Weeks, Waybroke Kennels, Jacksonville, Florida.

4. Ch. Toofox the Welchman, by Ch, Toofox Diamond Gem ex Ch. Toofox Farrah Faucet Dossett, taking Winners Dog from the Bred-by-Exhibitor Class, Dallas, 1980. This winner of the Homer Gage Trophy, American Fox Terrier Club 1980, was bred by Mrs. William E. Dossett, owner, Toofox Kennels, Wylie, Texas.

5. Ch. Unicorn's Laurelton Joker, by Ch. Fotinakes Dreadnaught ex Ch. Foxburo's Classy Chassis, has won 20 or more Bests of Breed and several Group placements. Bred by Virginia and Richard Ashlock, Laurelton Kennels, Ontario, California.

6. Ch. Laurelton Please Do, by Ch. Foxden Warlord ex Ch. Foxburo's Classy Chassis, bred by Virginia and Richard Ashlock; owned by Virginia Ashlock and Gayle Moynier, Ontario, California.

134

Overleaf: →

1. Ch. Charbonne Bon Vivant, bred by Charlotte Le Vecque, Highland, California, co-owner with Barbara Lytwynec. Pictured at age six months winning Best Smooth in Sweepstakes, W.F.T.B.A. in 1980. From a 5-champion litter.

2. Foxmoor Two-Step by Ch. Ttarb The Brat ex Ch. Foxmoor One Tuff Cookie, following this win, had 10 points, including both majors. Bred by Mr. and Mrs. Harold Nedell, Foxmoor Kennels, Texas. Owned by Mrs. Winifred Stout, Quissex Kennels, Foster, Rhode Island.

3. Ch. Waybroke Smooth Trick, Winners Bitch for a major at Asheville in 1981. Trixie is a daughter of those great producers Ch. Waybroke Extra Smooth and Ch. Waybroke Sunny Side Up. Handled by Madison M. Weeks for owners Jack Lindsay and Gilbert Aleman.

4. Ch. Quissex Proclamation, C.D., C.G., by Ch. Quissex Deacon ex Raybill Quissex Lace Work, was bred by Winnie Stout and is owned by Lisa Sachs, Huntington, New York.

5. *Left*: Ch. Charbonne Savoir Faire, co-owned by C. Le Vecque (breeder) and Constance Gallagher. *Right*: Ch. Charbonne Fandango bred and owned by Charlotte Le Vecque, Highland, California.

6. *Left*: Ch. Waybroke Box Score (Ch. Watteau Musical Box—Ch. Foxden Tatania, daughter of Ch. Ebony Box). *Right*, Ch. Crag Crest Colonel Kuska (Ch. Boreham Barrister—Ch. Crag Crest Counselle). Both owned by Crag Crest Kennels, Fred and Jane Kuska, Colfax, California.

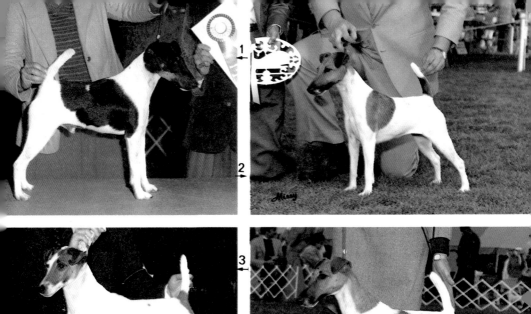

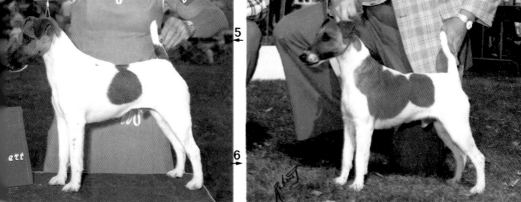

← **Overleaf:**

1. Ch. Foxburo Patent Pending, by Ch. Foxburo Chateau of Pathens ex Fox-buro Fancy Pants, was bred by John and Gayle Moynier, Asti, California. Owned by Jane D. Swanson, Foxtrot Kennels, Erie, Illinois. He is pictured winning Best of Breed at Erie in 1983.

2. Ch. High Desert Holiday was bred by Chris Wornall, sold to Elsie Simmons, then re-purchased by Mrs. Wornall. She is a sister to Ch. High Desert Scout. Pictured as a youngster, handled by Wood Wornall.

3. Ch. Raybill Quissex Volare is by Ch. Buckleigh Avenger of Foxden ex Ch. Viscun Vesta. Breeder, Mrs. Thomas M. Stout. Owner-handler, Lisa Sachs, Huntington, New York.

4. Crizwood's Rapscallion, owned by Rose Richards, bred by Chris and Wood Wornall, Sun Valley, California. Winning Best in Sweepstakes at Montgomery County in 1985. This handsome young dog is from Ch. High Desert Holiday bred back to her sire Ch. Ttarb The Brat.

5. Ch. Buckleigh's Avenger of Foxden taking Best of Variety at Green Mountain K.C. in 1973. Handled by Jane Forsyth for Mr. and Mrs. James A. Farrell, Jr., Darien, Connecticut.

6. Ch. Sugarland Smooth Sailing winning a Best of Breed. Handled by Wood Wornall for Ms. C.R. Le Vecque, Highland, California.

7. Foxbow Evening Star was Best Smooth in Sweepstakes, Great Western, June 1984. Co-owned and co-bred by Susan Akin (handling) and James Smith, Palouse, Washington.

8. Ch. Quissex Insolence, by Ch. Foxmoor Macho Macho Man ex Quissex Wise Crack, completing title in December 1985. Bred by Mrs. Winifred Stout; owned by Mr. and Mrs. Michael Buckley, Lowell, Massachusetts.

Overleaf: ⟶

1. The first weekend out for Foxbow Exchequer took him from the classes to Terrier Group 2nd, May 1984. Handled by James Smith, co-bred and at that time co-owned by James Smith and Susan Akin, Palouse, Washington.

2. Ch. Raybill's Half-Fast Waltz, by Ch. Janrich Jaunty ex Ch. Raybill Quissex Volare. The dam of Ch. Foxbow Exchequer and Ch. Foxbow Evening Star. Leased by Susan Akin and James Smith for Foxbow's "E" litter. Owned by Billie Lou Robison and Shannon Theel, the latter handling.

3. Ch. Quissex Quickstep by Ch. Battle Cry Brimstone ex Foxmoor Two Step, taking Winners at Rockland County in 1985. Bred by Mrs. W.H. Stout; handled by Joyce McComiskey; owned by Mr. and Mrs. Michael D. Buckley, Lowell, Massachusetts.

4. Ch. Foxmoor One Tuff Cookie—an outstanding producer owned by Foxmoor Kennels, Mr. and Mrs. Harold Nedell, Richmond, Texas.

5. Ch. Sugarland Sirius, C.D., bred and owned by Marion Clayman and Charlotte Le Vecque, Highland, California.

6. Ch. Foxmoor Double Double Chief taking Best of Breed at Skokie K.C. in 1985. Foxmoor Kennels are owned by Mr. and Mrs. Harold Nedell, Richmond, Texas.

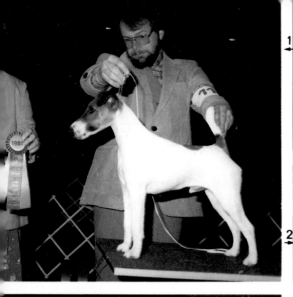

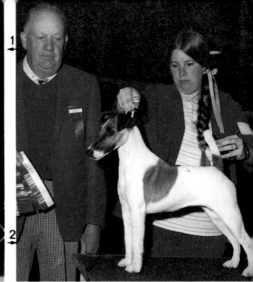

1

2

WINNERS

ROCKLAND COUNTY
KENNEL CLUB INC

KLEIN   SEPT 1985

3

INNERS

N COUNTY
L CLUB
G 1984

L. SOSA

4

5

BEST OF BREED
OR VARIETY

SKOKIE
KENNEL CLUB

6

1

2
BEST OF
BREED

3

4
BEST OF
OPPOSITE
SPRINGFIELD
KENNEL CLUB
1985
ASHBEY

5

6

7

8
ROUP
RST
WINDSOR
EL CLUB
983
ASHBEY

← Overleaf:

1. Ch. Waybroke Bentley completed title with Best of Winners at the American Fox Terrier Specialty, Montgomery County 1983. Handled by Madison Weeks. Owned by Helen B. Gaither, Gaidoune Kennels, Wheeling, West Virginia.

2. Am. and Can Ch. Hy-Tyme Magnum P.I., by Ch. Crag Crest Shogun (by Ch. Ttarb The Brat) ex Wellsdome Mitzsey Dancer (by Ch. Raybill's Breeze Away, C.D.), winning Best of Breed in October 1985. Bred by C. Wells; owned by Sherry and Jim Elliott, Hy-Tyme Kennels, Clackamas, Oregon.

3. Ch. Quissex Spun Gold Decision is an excellent and well-known bitch from Quissex Kennels, Mrs. Winifred Stout, Foster, Rhode Island.

4. Fortune's Gold Medalist, by Ch. Quissex Proclamation, C.D., C.G., ex Ch. Quissex Psaltery. Breeder-owner Lisa Sachs, Huntington, New York; co-owner, Catherine Gagen.

5. Ch. Stoney Meadows Flavor is owned by Karner Kennels, Thomas Partis, Craryville, New York.

6. Paulanna Pilgrim is from Ch. Riber Reality who was imported by Bill and Betsey Dossett, for their Toofox Kennels, Wylie, Texas.

7. Ch. Foxden Warspite is one of many generations of famed winners owned by Mrs. James A. Farrell, Jr., at Foxden Kennels, Darien, Connecticut. Handled by Mark Threlfall who has gained Multiple Best in Show and Group awards with this splendid dog.

8. Ch. Waybroke Extra Sunshine, Group winning Smooth owned by Helen B. Gaither, Gaidoune Kennels, Wheeling, West Virginia. Finishing his title by going Best of Winners under Dr. M.J. Deubler at the Greater St. Louis Fox Terrier Club Specialty from the six to nine months Puppy Class. Handled by M. Thomas, co-breeder with Madison M. Weeks, Waybroke Kennels.

Overleaf: ⟶

1. Ch. Foxden Hercules with Sarah Chatfield winning Open Senior in Junior Showmanship at Montgomery County K.C. Mrs. Winifred Stout is the mother of Sarah and the owner of Hercules, Quissex Smooths, Foster, Rhode Island.

2. Ch. Sugarland Smooth Sailing, Smooth bitch by Ch. Newmaidley Pennywise ex Ch. Sugarland Foxtrot, was born June 1976. This model Smooth for Junior Showmanship bred by owner, Ms. C.R. Le Vecque, and M. Clayman; co-owned with Kirstie Lytwynec. "Samba" and Kirstie went on to multiple Best Junior Handler in Show award and twice qualified for Westminster.

3. Ch. Foxairn Ensign with Peggy Beisel McIlwaine. This handsome and successful young dog was bred by the McIlwaines and Dr. Alan Riga and is on lease to Mr. Roger O'Toole, Bloomfield Hills, Michigan.

4. Your show prospect should be taught to "bait" alertly in the ring for a tasty snack as Ch. Foxairn Ensign is doing here, at Montgomery County Terrier Show in 1985 where he was winner of Best of Opposite Sex. Handled by Peggy Beisel McIlwaine, Foxairn Kennels, Whitmore Lake, Michigan.

Ventura County Dog Fanciers As

BEST JR SHOMAN

BEST OF BREED
or VARIETY
GR. MURFREESBORO
KENNEL CLUB
SEPTEMBER 1985
PHOTO BY SABRINA

← **Overleaf:**

1. Ch. Raylu Marsha Music, by Ch. Raylu Recharge ex Ch. Raylu Recital Piece, finished with five majors, plus two good American Fox Terrier Club wins in Pennsylvania. Bred, owned, and handled by Gene Rayburn, Raylu Kennels, Yorktown, Virginia. Pictured here at Charlottesville in 1980.

2. Ch. Brownstone's MacBroom at 10 years of age taking Best of Opposite Sex for the Veterans Class at Great Lakes Terrier Association, June 1984. Owned by Ann K. and John M. Brown, Shawnee, Kansas.

3. Ch. Brownstone's MacBroom winning Best of Opposite Sex at age 11 years at Greenwich Kennel Club in June 1985, day after the American Fox Terrier Club Specialty. A very proud and special time for his owner-handler Ann K. Brown, Shawnee, Kansas.

4. Ch. Mystwyre Inherit the Wind winning Best of Variety in 1985. Owned by Thomas L. and Susanne H. Yates, Hampton, Georgia. This is the 15th champion at Mystwyre Kennels.

5. Ch. Yelsam Craze, by Ch. Yelsam Jum Boe ex Wendy Wyldee of Yelsam, was bred by John W. and June L. Masley and is owned by Mrs. Kay Guimond in Canada. After completing his title in the United States, he gained his Canadian title, placing consistently in the Group. He is proving himself the sire of excellent progeny. Pictured making points toward U.S.A. championship. Handled by George Ward.

6. Ch. Libwyre The Grand Mufti, by Harrowhill Huntsman ex New Maidley Ruby, was imported *in utero*. A magnificent dog who hated showing. Owned by the Libners; handled by Wood Wornall.

1. This is Ch. Raylu Reminisce, by Intl. C. Bev-Wyre's Conbrio Tim ex Ch. Raylu Reality. One of four champions in her litter, she is a Top Ten bitch who in 1979 was Winners to complete her title at the American Fox Terrier Club Specialty in conjunction with Montgomery County. As a special during 1980, shown 18 times she won eight Bests of Variety and six Bests of Opposite Sex. However, she was defeated by her kennelmate and niece, Raylu Marsha Music, on two occasions. Owned by Raylu Wire Fox Terriers, Gene and Bob Bigelow, Yorktown, Virginia.

2. Ch. Wyrequest's Leader of The Bunch, by Am. and Can Ch. Wyrequest's Leader of the Pack ex Can. Ch. Wyrequest's Liberty Bell. Owned by Mr. and Mrs. Raymond M. Splawn, Wyrequest, Spokane, Washington. Winning the Terrier Group at Five Valley K.C. in 1983.

3. Eng. and Am. Ch. Taua Wren, by Eng. and Am. Ch. Trucote Admiral ex Taua Sisan, was bred by A.R. Davison. Owned by Mr. and Mrs. Raymond M. Splawn, Spokane, Washington.

4. Ch. Foxairn Ensign, by Eng. and Am. Ch. Sailorman ex Ch. Reedwyre's Dubonnet (thus a grandson of Eng. and Am. Ch. Townville Tristanian and Ch. Aryee Dominator), is pictured winning the Terrier Group at Oakland County K.C. in November 1985. Owned by Foxairn Kennels, this splendid dog at one time was on lease to Mr. Roger O'Toole, Bloomfield Hills, Michigan.

5. Am. and Can Ch. Wyrequest's Pay Dirt, by Am. and Can Ch. Nugrade Regent ex Am. and Can Ch. Nugrade Countess, winning the Terrier Group. Handled by Raymond M. Splawn, breeder-owner, Wyrequest Kennels, Spokane, Washington, at San Mateo, California.

6. Raylu Born A Star, by Ch. Raylu Recharge ex Ch. Raylu Audition, going through from the Bred-by-Exhibitor Class to Best of Winners at Wire Fox Terrier Club of the Central States in May 1985. Owner-handled by breeder Gene Bigelow, Raylu Wire Fox Terriers, Yorktown, Virginia.

7. Ch. Wyrelee's Wondrous, litter sister to Ch. Wyrelee's Cracker Jack, finished in 1984, Santa Barbara back to back weekends. She is by Ch. Wendywyre One and Only ex Ch. Wyrelee's First Noel.

8. Ch. Terrikane Tulliver, by Ch. Aryee Dominator, was bred by Mr. and Mrs. John F. Kane, later owned by Mr. and Mrs. T.N. Carruthers III, and is now owned by George Ward, Albany Kennels, Constantine, Michigan. The Top Winning American-bred Wire Fox Terrier, Tulliver has to his credit 49 Bests in Show, 111 Group 1sts. Pictured winning one of his Bests in Show in 1978.

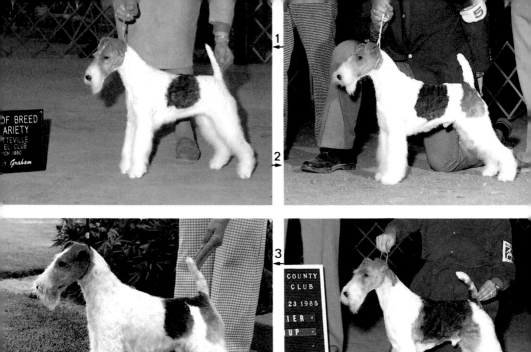

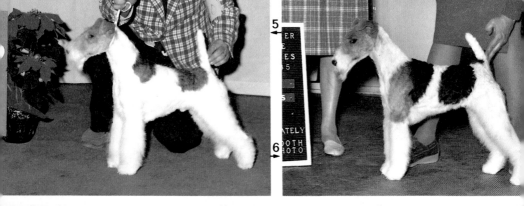

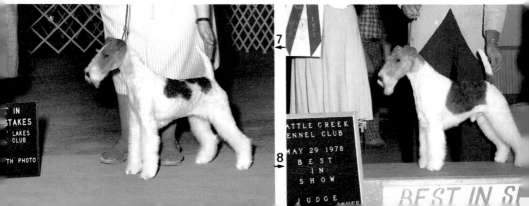

1 →

2 →

3 →

4 →

5 →

6 →

7 →

8 →

← Overleaf:

1. Ch. Ana-Dare Endeavor came to Richard and Laura Forkel in 1973, reaching them with 13 points toward his title which was finished first time out with Laura. A son of Ch. Zeloy Emperor ex Ch. Holmwire Tudor Radiance, bred by Mr. and Mrs. Jorgenson of Ana-Dare Wires, "Pal" was one of seven to finish from this famous litter; and himself was the sire of five champions. Owned by the Forkels, Wendywyre Fox Terriers.

2. Ch. Raglan Bertice handled by Ric Chashoudian winning a Terrier Group for owners Jim and Helen Hook, Mountain Ayre Kennels. This great bitch produced numerous champions, including the successful and admired Ch. Mountain Ayre Shady Lady.

3. Eng. and Am. Ch. Townville Tristanian, winner of multiple All-Breed Bests in Show in the U.S. and Great Britain, with three Specialty Shows abroad, plus eight Challenge Certificates and two reserve Challenge Certificates. Owned by Libwyre Fox Terriers, Muskegon, Michigan.

4. Another Specialty winner for Wyrelee. This is Ch. Wyrelee's More Ringside Gossip, a Group winner from the classes, the Specialty location having been Chain O'Lakes. Nancy Lee Wolf, owner, Scotts Valley, California.

5. Ch. Crizwood's Done To The Nines, by Ch. Trucote Admiral ex Ch. Crizwood's Might Bea, is a granddaughter of the foundation bitch Ch. Bexleydale Mighty Mite. Pictured winning Best Wire, co-owned by Chris and Wood Wornall of Crizwood Kennels, Sun Valley, California.

6. Ch. Foxglen's Witch's Brew by Can. Ch. Foxglen Man in Command ex Foxglen's Patrician Air, taking First Prize in the Sweepstakes, Montgomery County Kennel Club 1982. Bred and owned by Irene Rhodes.

7. A lovely young bitch with a great family tradition. Ch. Crizwood Celebration is the great-granddaughter of Ch. Bexleydale Mighty Mite, foundation bitch at Crizwood Kennels, Chris and Wood Wornall, Sun Valley, California. Pictured taking Best of Winners at Westminster 1986.

8. Ch. Albany Cyclone, homebred Wire dog owned and handled by George Ward, taking Best of Breed at the Wire Fox Terrier Club of the Central States Specialty on May 11, 1985. An outstanding young dog with a bright future!

Overleaf: →

1. Best Brace at Northern California Specialty: Ch. Wyrelee's Hot Stuff (dog) and Ch. Wyrelee's First Noel (bitch) owned by Nancy Lee Wolf, Scotts Valley, California.

2. Foxglen's Dynamite, by Vimy Ridge Flashback ex Ch. The Little Witch of Foxglen, taking Reserve Winners at the American Fox Terrier Club 1985 Centenary at ten months of age from the Bred-by-Exhibitor Class. Bred, owned, and handled by Irene Rhodes, Foxglen Kennels, Sharpsville, Pennsylvania.

3. Ch. Wyrelee's the Huntsman had six Bests of Breed from the classes en route to his title. Owned by Nancy Lee Wolf, Wyrelee Kennels, Scotts Valley, California.

4. Ch. Libwyre's Grand Mufti, by Eng. Ch. Harrowhill Huntsman ex Ch. Newmaidly Ruby, is famous winning Wire owned by Libwyre Kennels, Robert, Ruth and Laura Libner, in Michigan.

5. Evewire Black Magic taking Winners Bitch at Berks County in 1985 for co-owners Casey Crothers and Mrs. Eve Ballich. Handled by Casey Crothers.

6. Eng. and Am. Ch. Sarabel Sailorman, by Eng. Ch. Townville Tristanian ex Sarabel Sweet Talk, owned by Sanderson and Margaret McIlwaine, Foxairn Kennels, Whitmore Lake, Michigan. Here winning Best of Breed under judge Jane Forsyth at Steel City in November, 1983.

7. Ch. App's Prime Time handled by Bob Clyde to Best Terrier at Rubber City K.C. in January 1984 for breeder-owner Norma Appleyard, Newton, Massachusetts.

8. Ch. Wyrelee Cracker Jack, a fifth generation homebred, was Winners Dog at the National Specialty, Montgomery County 1984. By Ch. Wendywyre One and Only ex Champion Wyrelee First Noel. Owned by Nancy Lee Wolf, Wyrelee Wire Fox Terriers, Scotts Valley, California.

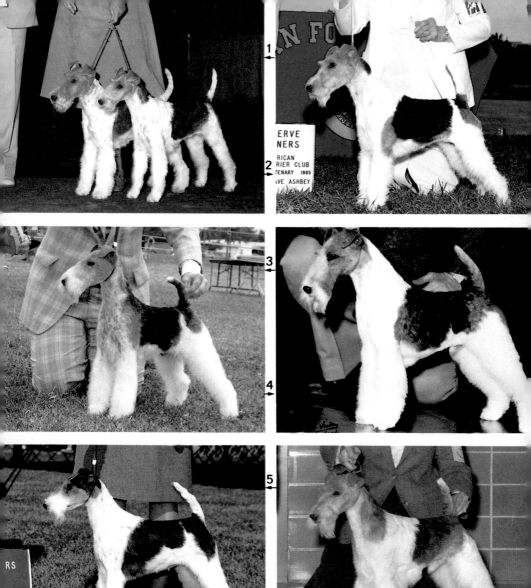

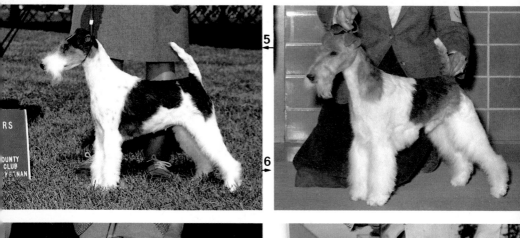

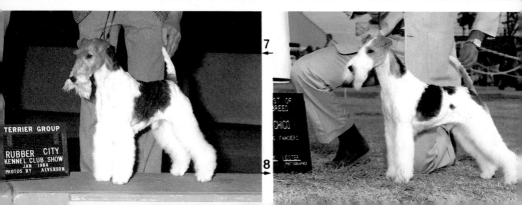

← **Overleaf:**

1. These adorable 8-week-old babies by Wirehill Duskee Gingerman ex Wirehill Clever Huntress are typical of Wirehill puppies. Owned by the Guimonds, Mississauga, Canada.

2. The great and famous Eng. and Am. Ch. Trucote Admiral, owned by Chris and Wood Wornall and later co-owned with Mari Morrisey. Bred by Nell Urmston, Admiral was handled in England by Herbert Atkinson and in America by Wood Wornall. This son of Eng. and Am. Ch. Sandwyre Mr. Softy of Jokyn (Eng. Ch. Talisman fe la Noe aux Loups–Eng. Ch. Sandwyre Lulu of Wilwyre) ex Eng. Ch. Helenstowe Pearly Queen of Jokyl (Eng. and Am. Ch. Sunnybrook Spot On–Helenstone Parasol) was Top Wire in England and Top Wire Sire, and a Best in Show winner in America.

154

Overleaf: →

1. Snapped informally following the big Best in Show win at Ventura County, Ch. Evewire You Better Believe It with his handler Peter Green and the Best in Show judge A.K. Nicholas. One of the many famed Wires bred and/or owned by Mrs. Eve Ballich, Evewire Kennels, Baltimore, Maryland.

2. Ch. Brownstone's Hey Day, by Ch. Axholme Jimmy Reppin ex Ch. Heathcote Enchantress, produced seven champions during the early 1970s. Owned by Brownstone Kennels, Ann K. and John M. Brown, Shawnee, Kansas.

3. Brownstone's Merry Perry, by Ch. Brownstone's MacBroom ex Ch. Brownstone's Jennifer, winning back-to-back majors on a Specialty weekend. Owned by Brownstone Kennels, Ann K. and John M. Brown, Shawnee, Kansas.

4. Ch. App's Toryna winning Best of Opposite Sex, Bob Clyde handling for Norma Appleyard, Newton, Massachusetts.

5. Ch. Raylu Audition wound up a whirlwind Cherry Blossom Circuit by finishing her title with a 5-point major at Old Dominion K.C. By Ch. Besscott's Peter Panic ex Ch. Ray Musical Revue, this lovely bitch is dam of the 1985 Central States Specialty Show Best of Winners, Raylu Born A Star. Bred, owned and handled by Gene Bigelow, Yorktown, Virginia.

6. The newest young "star" of Raylu Kennels heritage. Crystcrack My Sin, at seven months of age in February 1986, is by Ch. Penda Precision (imported by Peter Green, now sold to Europe) ex Crystcrack Chantilly (by Ch. Raylu Recharge). Handled by Peter Green for breeders-owners Gloria Snellings and Kim Harris.

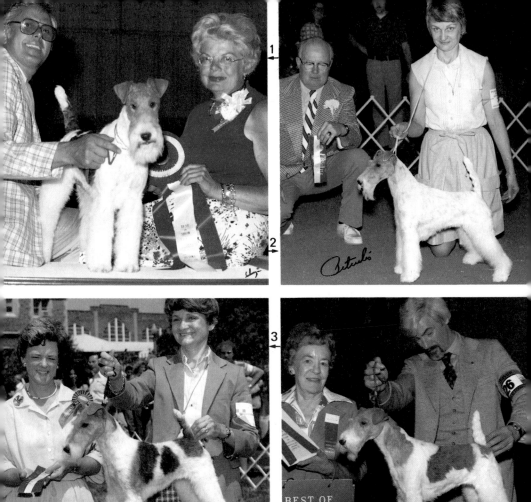

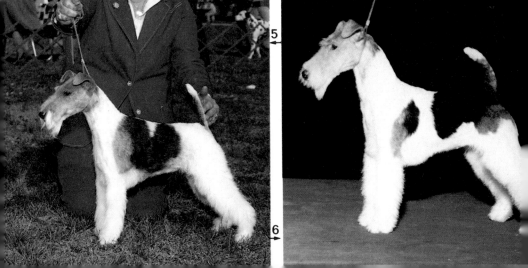

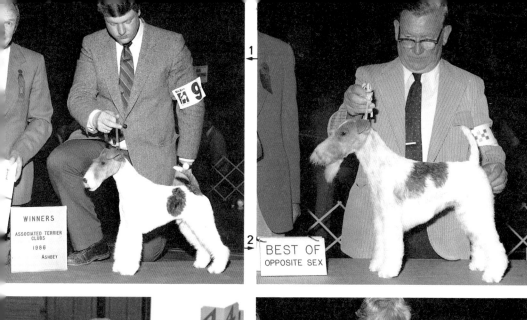

WINNERS
ASSOCIATED TERRIER CLUBS
1986
ASHBEY

BEST OF
OPPOSITE SEX

BEST OF
OPPOSITE
ALBANY
KENNEL CLUB
1980
ASHBEY

Photo by Ritter

← **Overleaf:**

1. Crizwood's Flag Is Up, by Ch. Wyredrest Wait and See ex Amwire's Innocent Imp, is owned by Chris and Wood Wornall. Pictured, handled by Woody, taking winners at Associated Terrier Club in 1986. His litter-brother, also owned by the Wornalls of Sun Valley, California, went Best in Sweepstakes there from the 6–9 months class.

2. Ch. Yelsam Tina, by Ch. Yelsam Gentleman Jim ex Wendy Wyldee of Yelsam, was bred by John W. and June L. Masley and owner-handled by Dr. Masley. This dam of two litters with a total of six puppies, all of which finished, produced a line in which there are champions in four consecutive generations.

3. Ch. Yelsam Jum Boe, by Ch. Aryee Dominator ex Mooremaiden Wonder Girl, bred by John W. and June L. Masley, owned by Nancy McGowan. The Masleys used him at stud three times, getting seven puppies all of which completed their titles. Dora Lee Wilson is handling him here.

4. Ch. App's Star-Kist, bred and owned by Norma Appleyard, App's Wire Fox Terriers, Newton, Massachusetts. Handled by Bob Clyde, here taking Best of Opposite Sex, Albany K.C. 1980.

5. Ch. Yelsam Gentleman Jim, by Ch. Caracus Cavalier ex Ch. Albany Trinket, was bred by John W. and June L. Masley and is owned by Landis A. Hirstein. Finished in seven shows with three Group 1sts and other placements along the way, Gentleman Jim was Winners Dog at the Fox Terrier Club of Chicago in 1971. Sire of nine champions, he qualified and was shown twice in Junior Showmanship at Westminster by Tammy Hirstein.

6. Ch. Albany Trinket, by Can. Ch. Deko Defiant ex Can. Ch. Tuxdene Tango, was bred by Ted Ward in Canada and is owned by John W. and June L. Masley. She had Group placements and produced two champions. A line of breeding starting with this bitch has produced seven consecutive generations of champions. Dr. Masley says of her "she was a small, hard-bitten bitch of good type and as mean as they come." Owner-handled here by Dr. Masley.

158

Overleaf: ⟶

1. Ch. Wyrelee Star Bright, by Ch. Libwyre Legend ex Ch. Wyrelee's First Noel, is one of the outstandingly successful Wires from Wyrelee Kennels, Nancy Lee Wolf, Scotts Valley, California.

2. The background of Nancy Lee Wolf's Wyrelee Wire Fox Terriers. Her first three of the breed: *top,* Trixie Lee Tiburtie, C.D.; *left,* Wyrelee Foxfyre Prince, C.D.; *right,* Wyrelee Volponi Poco, C.D. Trixie was the dam of the other two. All of the present Wyrelee winners descended directly from her. Wyerlee Kennels, Scotts Valley, California.

← Overleaf:

Fortune's Kid Smoothie, C.D. The famous "Jack" of *Breakstone's* TV commercials, has also appeared in one Broadway show, three movies, four kennel spots, once for *Sleepy's Bedding Centers*, and one *Whatchamacallit* candy bar commercial. This in addition to 13 *Breakstone* commercials, not to mention print work and personal appearances. This intelligent and talented Smooth is also the personal pet of his owner and trainer, Lisa Sachs. Jack is one of the most popular models on the East Coast.

Overleaf: →

1. Aust. Ch. Dnalwon Beau Spartacus, by Ch. Rama Smooth Rehearsal ex Ch. Boscottie Edwina, as a youngster. Handled by John Nowland for Mrs. G.M. Nowland winning Best Baby Puppy.

2. Aust. Ch. Emohruo Spring Dreamer at 18 months. The dam of Aust. Ch. Springbox Nimbus Gem, she is a daughter of Aust. Ch. Mirolinda Meldon ex Emohruo Pipers Dream. Owned by Mr. and Mrs. R. Black, St. Ives, Sydney, New South Wales, Australia.

3. Braz. Ch. Wildwood's Up To Date is by Braz. Ch. Harvey v.d. Bismarsquelle ex Braz. Ch. Princess For'ard Dell'Ilva. Bred by Flavio Werneck and Marcelo Chagas and owned by Fair Hair Kennels. Up To Date started his show career in late 1985, finished his title in two weekends by winning three Group 1sts and two Group 2nds. A most outstanding representative of Wire quality in Brazil!

4. Aust. Ch. Dnalwon Beau Bianca, born August 1984, by Ch. Rama Smooth Rehearsal ex Ch. Farleton Princess Meg, an elegant English bitch owned by Mrs. G.M. Nowland, U-Elver, Curlewis, New South Wales, Australia.

5. Aust. Ch. Springfox Nimbus Gem, age 14 months, taking Best Puppy in Show, S.F.T.A. of New South Wales. Owned by Olive Black, Springfox Kennels, Sydney, New South Wales, Australia.

6. Aust. Ch. Worsbro Wink (U.K. import) sister of Penda Worsbro Whistler, by Worsbro's Betoken Again ex Eng. Ch. Worsbro's Oladar Royal Maid, is the dam of Aust. Ch. Canbury Chianti, (U.K. import). Owned by Barbara A. Withers, Canbury Kennels, Ebenezer, Australia.

7. "Let's see what we can turn up here" is obviously on the minds of these two handsome Smooths owned by Mr. and Mrs. R. Black, St. Ives, New South Wales, Australia. They are Aust. Ch. Emohruo Spring Dreamer (*left*) and Erinclair White Guard.

8. Erinclair White Guard at the age 8 months in this photo. This dog is now the sire of Ch. Springfox Nimbus Gem. Owned by Olive Black, Springfox Kennels, Sydney, New South Wales, Australia.

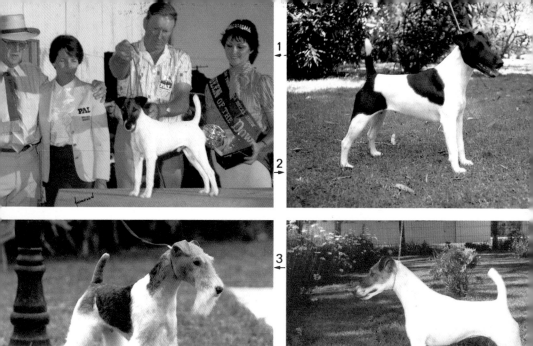

1

2

3

4

5

6

7

8

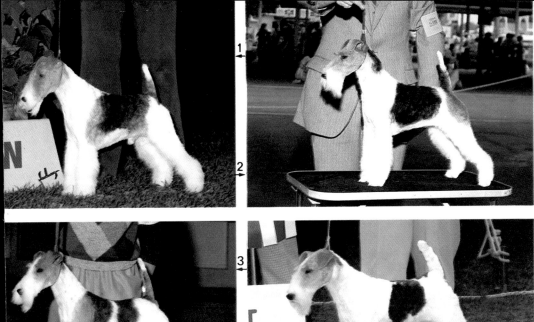

1

2

3

4

5

6

7

8

UMPQUA KENNEL CLUB

OF BREED
OR —
ARIETY

← **Overleaf:**

1. Ch. Wendywyre Look Out, born April 3, 1980, winning Best in Show at Los Encinos in December 1981. Handled by Eddie Boyes for owners Richard and Laura Forkel, Wendywyre Kennels, Orange, California.

2. Ch. Wendywyre First Class, "Maggie," daughter of Am. and Can Ch. Rose-cliffe Top Choice, handled by Wood Wornall for owners Richard and Laura Forkel, Orange, California.

3. Ch. Wendywyre Top Billing, by Ch. Warwick Watchman ex Ch. Wendywyre Jennifer Jones, latest homebred champion owned by Richard and Laura Forkel. Handled by Laura.

4. Ch. Wirehill Duskie Revelation, winning Best in Show at Oxford County K.C. Owned by Lou and Kay Guimond, Mississauga, Ontario, Canada.

5. Ch. Warwick Watchman, by Ch. Brownstone's MacBroom, is owned by Richard and Laura Forkel of Wendywyre Kennels, Orange, California. "Tully" was Best of Variety at the 1983 Wire Fox Terrier Club of Central States Specialty, handled and conditioned by Laura. Frosting on the cake that day for the Forkels was the acceptance of the Hall of Fame Award as the breeders of 15 or more Wire-haired Fox Terrier champions.

6. Am. and Can Ch. Yelsame Craze, owned by Lou and Kay Guimond, Mississauga, Ontario, Canada. Owner-handled by Kay Guimond to Group Placement.

7. Winning Terrier Group placement on the California-Oregon Circuit, Am. and Can Ch. Foxbow Exchequer owned by Leslie Wheaton, Wyndfyre Kennels, Saskatoon, Saskatchewan, Canada.

8. Ch. Snow Fire of Wendywyre, handled here by co-owner Laura Forkel, from the first homebred litter whelped at Wendywyre Kennels following its beginning. Richard and Laura Forkel started in 1964 with the purchase of this bitch's dam.

166

Overleaf: →

1. Eng., Am. and Can Ch. Littleway McTavish, handled by Gary MacDonald, taking Best in Show at Belleville K.C. for owners Kay and Lou Guimond, Wirehill Kennels, Mississauga, Ontario, Canada.

2. Am. and Can Ch. Foxmoor Quissex Mah Jong, owned by Judy Leonard, Foxlinton Kennels, Kanata, Ontario, Canada, taking Winners Bitch and Best of Opposite Sex in Smooths at the American Fox Terrier Club Centenary Show in 1985 while still in the puppy class. Ric Chashoudian was the judge; Mrs. James A. Farrell, President of the American Fox Terrier Club, presents the trophy.

3. Battle Cry Annie Get Your Gun, Smooth Fox Terrier winning the Terrier Group at Lady's Slipper K.C., July 14, 1985. Owner-handled by Emily Gratton. This daughter of Am. Ch. Foxden Dead Eye Dick ex Battle Cry Laser Beam was bred by William Forman and is the dam of the sensational Best in Show winning youngster Can. Ch. Trollhattan's Dack Rambo.

4. Dick Forkel and Nipper. The presence of Ch. Unicorn Excel of Wendywyre, a Smooth, among all the exciting Wires at Wendywyre Kennels is the result of Dick's long association with the Radio Corporation of America. The famous Smooth insignia/emblem of RCA generated his interest in Smooths as well as Wires.

167

1

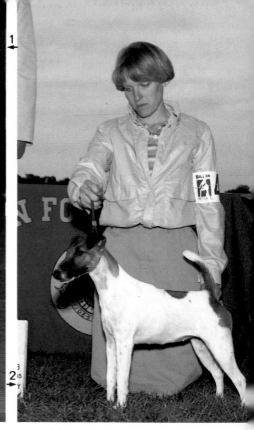

2

3

4

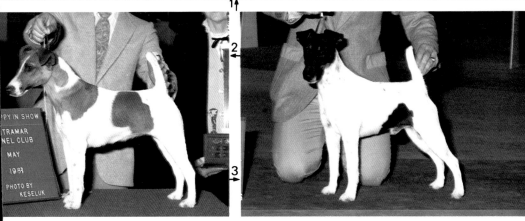

← **Overleaf:**

1. Eng., Am., and Can. Ch. Littleway McTavish, by Intl. Ch. Talisman De La Noe Aux Loups from Eng. Ch. Weltona What A Girl was bred by J.A. Abbott of Littleway Kennels in England. Owned by Kay and Lou Guimond, Wirehill Kennels, Mississauga, Ontario, Canada.

2. Can. Ch. Trollhattan Quissex Jenifer, daughter of Higrola Horatio of Britlea, took Best Puppy in Show at Tantramar K.C. in May 1983. Handled by John Heartz. Bred by Winifred Stout, owned by E.M. Gratton, Truro, Nova Scotia, Canada.

3. Am. and Can. Ch. Buccaneer's Best Man, well known Canadian winning Smooth dog owned by Garrett Lambert, Halfmoon Smooth Fox Terriers, Nobleton, Ontario, Canada.

4. Can. and Am. Ch. Foxbow Exchequer was bred by Sue Akin and Jim Smith, Foxbow Kennels, and is owned by Les Wheaton, Wyndfyre Smooths, Saskatoon, Saskatchewan, Canada. A multiple Specialty winner and a multiple Group winner as well as a champion producer.

170

Overleaf: →

1. A lovely study of English Smooths! Ch. Eng. Ch. Rarity of Riber, by Eng. Ch. Riber Ricochet ex Eng. Ch. Canterway Cavalette, with two of the Riber puppies. Peter and Frances Winfield, owners, Mapperly, Derby, England.

2. Riber Rusty in the garden during 1985. A future "young hopeful" at this famous kennel belonging to Mr. and Mrs. Peter Winfield, Mapperly, Derby, England.

3. The noted British Smooth dog Eng. Ch. Riber Ricochet, by Ch. Watteau Ploughman ex Champion Boreham Briar Rose (Ramsey daughter), was born in 1979. This dog is the sire of Ch. Canterway Cavalette and Ch. Rarity of Riker, F.T.C. Gold Cup winner. Owned by Peter and Frances Winfield, Mapperly, Derby, England.

4. Eng. Ch. Boreham Briar Rose, by Ch. Riber Ramsay ex Ch. Boreham Ballerina, is a splendid representative of the quality Smooths for which Boreham has become world famous. Owned by Mrs. J.T. Winstanley, Fording Bridge, Hants, England.

5. Eng. Ch. Canterway's Cavalette is from Ch. Riber Reality who was imported by Bill and Betsey Dossett, Toofox Kennels.

6. Intl. Ch. Boreham Bellissima, by Astona Georgie ex Ch. Boreham Ballet Star, is a granddaughter of the bitch line from Mrs. J.T. Winstanley's Boreham Kennels in England through Champion Gedstar Petronella.

1

2

3

4

5

6

← **Overleaf:**

1. Head study of the Wire, Ch. Wyrelee Double Trouble, C.D., talented member of the Wyrelee Kennels, Nancy Lee Wolf, Scotts Valley, California.

2. Fortune's Hickory Daiquiri Doc, C.D., by Ch. Quissex Proclamation C.D., C.G. ex Ch. Raybill Quissex Volare, is owner-trained and shown in obedience by Lynne Bockelman. "Daq" was Highest Scoring Dog In Trial at the American Fox Terrier Club Centenary Show in June 1985, which event is pictured. Breeder Lisa Sachs shows Daq on her appearances in the conformation ring.

3. Fortune's Hickory Daquiri Doc, C.D., awaiting a "recall." Owned and trained by Lynne Bockelman.

4. Adult Smooths at play. Quissex Wedding Belle, C.D., and Fortune's Ghostwriter are two of the handsome Smooth Fox Terriers owned by Lisa Sachs, Huntington, New York.

5. Fortune's Remington Steele and his sister Fortune's Hickory Daiquiri Doc, C.D., play "keep away" with a stick. A favorite game of Daq's who learned it from the Shelties she lives with and taught it to several of Lisa Sach's Smooths.

6. Many of the Fox Terrier fanciers are working their dogs in the Terrier earth-trials. Among them Mrs. James A. Farrell, Jr., whose Ch. Jonwyr's Galore of Foxden (dam of Ch. Foxden Gallivant and granddam of Ch. Foxden Warspite) is seen here "going to ground." Mary Davies takes the dogs to these events, and has been meeting with considerable success. The Connecticut Terrier Club's Super Earth is the occasion pictured here.

174

Overleaf: ⟶

1. Ch. Foxburo's Brown Derby on the table in the show ring. Owned by Laurelton Smooths, Ontario, California.

2. What a very pretty head on this bitch owned by Winnie Stout who is putting last minute touches on her grooming the morning of a local dog show. Mrs. Winifred Stout, owner, Quissex Kennels, Foster, Rhode Island.

3. Quissex Wedding Belle, C.D. "at work" on location for *Brides Magazine*. Lisa Sachs, owner, Huntington, New York.

4. Ch. Toofox The Colonel standing at attention in the ring. Handled by Don Sackos for Mr. and Mrs. William Dossett, Toofox Kennels, Wylie, Texas. Note the quality, silhouette and balance of this exciting dog.

5. Foxglen Dynamite relaxing at the Centenary. Breeder-owner, Irene Rhodes, Foxglen Kennels, Sharpsville, Pennsylvania.

6. An informal photo of the great Ch. Evewire Exemplar standing on the grooming table. Bred and owned by Eve Ballich. Photo courtesy of Norma Appleyard.

1 →

2 →

3 →

4 →

5 →

6 →

← Overleaf:

1. Ch. Wyredrest Wait and See, bred by William Josse in Holland, owned by Frank and Barbara Swigart then leased to Carol Beatie. This son of Bengal Crispey (also sire of Ch. Dynamic Super Sensation) from a Zeloy-bred dam, won ten Groups in the United States then was sent back to Holland. A great loss to the breed here as it turns out, for we understand that the five litters he sired while in the States are really of superb quality. Photo courtesy of Chris and Woody Wornall, Sun Valley, California.

2. Ch. Grambrae Serene, by Eng. Ch. Watteau Snuff Box ex Quiet Girl Laurel of Din, was bred in Ireland and imported by the late Henry J. Sayres, coming to Crag Crest Kennels in 1969. A top terrier in every sense of the word, "Irish," scored instantly as a show dog here. Mr. and Mrs. Fred Kuska, owners, Crag Crest Kennels, Colfax, California.

3. Jack, the old pro, with his new friend, 3½-month-old Royal Rock Tri N'Choose, demonstrating their steadiness during a photographic session. Lisa Sachs, owner, Huntington, New York.

4. Ch. Reedwyres Dubonnet, by Ch. Aryee Dominator ex Reedwyre's Bourbon Baby, is one of the outstanding Wires owned by Sanderson and Margaret McIlwaine, Whitmore Lake, Michigan.

5. Ch. Bowyre Biscuit, by Ch. Bowyre Contender ex Am. and Can. Ch. Cefnbryn Cookie, was bred by Wayne Bousek. Owned by Wayne and Janie Bousek, Bowyre Kennels, Cedar Rapids, Iowa.

6. Eng. and Am. Ch. Jonwyre Galore of Foxden imported by Mrs. James A. Farrell, Jr., Foxden Kennels, Darien, Connecticut. "Gal" was purchased from Frank Jones of Jonwyre Terrier Kennels who sent this photo to us.

Overleaf: →

1. Hy-Tyme Hot Shot, son of Ch. Hy-Tyme Magnum P.I. ex Foxbow Diane of Hy-Tyme, was bred by Jim and Sherry Elliott. Owned by Hy-Tyme Kennels and Terry Inlow.

2. Ch. Greenfield's Music Mist at K.C. of Northern New Jersey in 1978. Peter Green handling for Carlotta Howard.

3. This lovely photograph of Ch. Foxglen Envoy's Tamora was selected by *Purina* to appear in their calendar; and is also on the 1985 American Fox Terrier Club Calendar. Tamora has also appeared in several issues of *Pure-Bred Dogs/American Kennel Gazette*. A beautiful presentation of breed character. Tamara is owned and was bred by Irene Rhodes, Foxglen, Sharpsville, Pennsylvania.

4. "Joe and Burt"—a lovely informal photo of Joe Purkhiser with the great Smooth Ch. Toofox The Caribe Chief Spy at Caribe Kennels in Wylie, Texas.

5. More than just a pretty face, but isn't *that* something special? This is multiple Best in Show and Terrier Group winning Eng. and Am. Ch. Forchlas Cariad owned by Ruth Cooper. This successful and widely admired winner is handled by Peter Green.

6. The great "Deano." Eng. and Am. Ch. Jonwyre Galaxy of Foxden owned by Mrs. James A. Farrell, Jr., Foxden Kennels, Darien, Connecticut. This gorgeous head study courtesy of Frank Jones, Jonwyre Kennels, England.

179

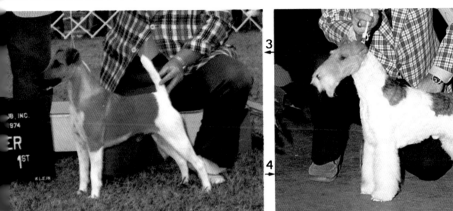

← **Overleaf:**

1. Ch. Bryan Wanda The Witch, Best in Show Smooth Fox Terrier bitch, winning a Terrier Group at Monticello, 1982. Born March 1980, Wanda is by Ch. Ttarb The Brat ex Bryan Steppin' High. Owned by Mary and Joe Vaudo, Sandwich, Massachusetts.

2. Ch. Wyrequest's Wildfire, foundation bitch at Mystwyre Kennels, owned by Thomas L. and Susanne H. Yates, Hampton, Georgia.

3. Ch. Boreham Bonanza was a multiple winner of the American Fox Terrier Club Grand Challenge Cup, the only dog to win it four times. Owned by Carlotta Howard, Rosemont, Pennsylvania, Bonanza is handled by Tom Glassford. Shown taking 1st in the Terrier Group at Erie K.C. in 1974. Photo courtesy of Peter Green.

4. Am. and Can. Ch. Wyrequest's Pay Dirt, by Am. and Can. Ch. Nugrade Regent ex Am. and Can. Ch. Nugrade Countess, winning Best in Show for the Raymond M. Splawns, Spokane, Washington.

5. Ch. Deko Dryad, a widely admired winning bitch owned by Harold Shook of Burbank, California and handled by Ric Chashoudian. Although never extensively campaigned she gained for herself many admirers. A product of the Deko Kennels in Wales, which prefix identified those Fox Terriers owned or bred by Mr. John Coghlin. Pictured winning a Best in Show here in the United States. She is by Zeloy Emperor ex Boko Diadem.

6. Ch. App's Victory, winning Best Wire at Somerset Hills in 1980. Bred and owned by Norma Appleyard, handled by Bob Clyde.

7. New Ch. Riber Reality finishing with Winners at Montgomery County at age one year; a new addition to Toofox Kennels from Peter and Francis Winfield's kennel in England.

8. Ch. High Desert Trapper, Smooth Fox Terrier dog owned by Samuel R. Whittaker, Jr., was handled by Denny Mounce to Best in Show at Grand Forks Kennel Club, June 1, 1985.

182

1. Ch. Crag Crest Foxhill Shallalla, by Ch. Ttarb The Brat ex Ttarb Tessa, was among the top winners at Crag Crest. This high ranking Smooth, all systems, is a Best in Show Terrier with groups and Specialties to his credit. Owned by Mr. and Mrs. Fred Kuska, Colfax, California. Pictured winning Best Smooth at Greenwich in June of 1985. Retired in late 1985.

2. Ch. Charbonne Gendarme, bred by Charlotte Le Vecque and owned by Kathy Poe came from a litter of five champions by Am., Can., and Mex. Ch. Lizabethan Buckingham Bard (grandson of Eng. and Am. Ch. Karnilo Chieftain of Foxden) ex Ch. Sugarland Samba (by Ch. Newmaidley Pennywise ex Ch. Sugarland Foxtrot).

3. Ch. Foxglen Alicia is owned by Cathy and John Moore, Houston, Texas. Bred by Irene Rhodes, Foxglen Kennels, and sired by Vimy Ridge Flashback. Pictured taking Best of Opposite Sex at Nolan River K.C. in 1984.

4. Ch. Forchlas Dyna Fi, by Harrowhill Concorde ex Forchlas Tania was bred in Wales by Mr. R. Roderick prior to purchase by Irene Rhodes for her Foxglen Kennels, Sharpsville, Pennsylvania. This U.K. import is here taking Winners en route to U.S.A. title at the prestigious Western Reserve K.C. event in August, 1985.

5. Eng. and Am. Ch. Townville Tarka, owned by Mrs. Carol Damico, winning the breed, Peter Green handling.

6. Ch. Roughrider's Cowboy taking Best of Variety in an entry of 37 Smooths of which 15 were specials at the prestigious Devon Dog Show at Montgomery in 1978. George Ward handling this outstanding Smooth for Dr. Svend E. Melgard and Mrs. Lloyd B. Evans.

7. Ch. Evewire's You Better Believe It, famous winning Wire owned and bred by Eve Ballich, Baltimore, Maryland, winning Best in Show at Ventura County under the author during the 1970s. A multiple Best in Show and Group dog handled by Peter Green.

8. After going Best in Show under judge Vince Perry, Ch. Wyrequest's One More Time is congratulated by his happy co-owner, Virginia Splawn. Pay Dirt, by Eng. and Am. Ch. Harwire Hetman of Whinlatter ex Ch. Wyrequests Devil May Care, is the only Best in Show winning youngster sired by Hetman. Owned by Mr. and Mrs. Raymond M. Splawn, Wyrequest Kennels, Spokane, Washington.

1

2

3

4

5

6

7

8

1 →

2 →

3 ←

GROUP
FIRST
BOARDWALK
KENNEL CLUB
1985
ASHBEY

GROUP
T
ILLE
CLUB
1982
BONNIE

4 →

5 ←

6 ←

Y
C
83

T OF
EED
SUR
CLUB
R 1985
SY PHOTO

7 ←

VALLEY K.C.

IN SHOW

8 →

← **Overleaf:**

1. Ch. Glanrob Crimson Velvet of Purston winning Best in Show at the Eastern Dog Club in 1986. This stunning young bitch, handled by Robert Fisher for Don Bronillette. Velvet is a daughter of Louline Lord Founteroy ex Glanrob Sanko Marino, and is already a multiple Best in Show winner although just at the start of her career.

2. Ch. Viscum Vesta, owner-handled by Mrs. Winifred Stout, Quissex Smooth Fox Terriers, is a Smooth of true importance and influence on the breed.

3. Ch. Bryan's Wanda The Witch making one of her frequent Group wins for Joe and Mary Vaudo, Sandwich, Massachusetts, Greenville K.C., February 1982. Handled by Peter Green.

4. Boardwalk K.C in December 1984 was the first show in the U.S.A. for Eng. and Am. Ch. Galsul Excellence who celebrated the occasion with style for his American owners, Ruth Cooper and the William McKays. Already a multiple Best in Show winner after less than two months in competition in the States.

5. Ch. Foxglen's Witch's Brew Is by Can. Ch. Foxglen Man in Command ex Foxglen Patrician Air. Bred and owned by Irene Rhodes, Foxglen Kennels, Sharpsville, Pennsylvania.

6. Ch. Unicorn's Cashier's Check, a son of Ch. Foxhill's Cash N' Carry, is one of the top current Smooths on the West Coast. Handled by Wood Wornall for owner Dee Berger, Orange, California.

7. Ch. Foxhill's Cash'N Carry handled by Wood Wornall for Dee Berger, Unicorn Kennels. A Brat son, Cash 'N Carry is an all-breed Best in Show winner, a Specialty winner, and a multi-Group winner.

8. Eng. and Am. Ch. Forchlas Cariad, owned by Ruth Cooper, adding to her impressive list of Best in Show at Chester Valley in 1985. Handled by Peter Green.

186

Overleaf: →

1. Ch. Robwyre Sparkler, an imported Best in Show winner and a Westminster Best of Breed winner, gains the nod of approval for Best in Show at Fox Terrier Club of Southern California Specialty judged by Terrier expert Grace Brewin. Owned by Max Gilberg, New York. Handled by Peter Green.

2. Ch. App's Coquette winning Best Wire at Westchester in 1983, judged by Mrs. John Patterson. Bob Clyde handled for breeder-owner Norma Appleyard, Newton, Massachusetts.

3. Ch. Dynamic Super Sensation, born May 19, 1979 by Bengal Crispey Brigadier ex Dynamic Super Special, was bred by Mr. and Mrs. Kilsdonk in Holland. Handled by Wood Wornall for Frank and Barbara Swigart, Riverside, California. This gorgeous and outstanding Wire bitch was the winner of 17 consecutive Specialty Bests in Show; 24 all-breed Bests in Show, and 66 Terrier Groups.

4. The dog who broke the record to become all-time Top Winning Smooth Fox Terrier, Ch. Ttarb the Brat was bred by Mr. and Mrs. D.C. Brat, owned by Dr. John Van Zandt and Ed Dalton during his show career, and handled by Ric and Sandy Chashoudian. Now in retirement, owned by Mr. Dalton. The Brat is a son of Farleton Captain Sandy ex Ttarb Tuppence. A highly successful stud as well as a show dog, the Brat has outstanding winning progeny wherever Smooth Fox Terriers are shown.

5. Winning her first Terrier Group, Ch. Dynamic Super Sensation was handled by Wood Wornall for Frank and Barbara Swigart, Riverside, California. She chalked up a formidable record during her career in the early 1980's.

6. Ch. Halcar Top Drawer, owned by Carlotta Howard, shown at the Southern California Fox Terrier Club in June 1979. Peter Green handled for Mrs. Howard. The judge was Mrs. Wm. Wimer, III, of Pool Forge Kennels fame.

7. Ch. Turbo Charge just starting his career as a special wins the breed at Rockland County, March 1986. Beth Swiegert handled this splendid young dog for owner, Kathleen Ditmar, Lindenhurst, New York. Born October 1984, Turbo Charge was bred by Mrs. William Dossett, and was sired by Ch. Toofox The Caribe Chief Spy ex Ch. Toofox Tribute to Gaycliff (both parents sired by Ch. Ttarb The Brat).

8. Ch. Pool Forge Maximum Effort, owned by Dee Burdick, takes the Onandaga Terrier Group in the late 1970s. Handled by Peter Green.

187

1

BEST OF
VARIETY
WESTCHESTER
KENNEL CLUB
1983
ASHBEY

2

3

HOW
JB
BRINA

4

5

6

IETY
COUNTY
CLUB
ARCH 1986

7

ONONDAGA K.C.
TERRIER

8

← Overleaf:

1. Three-day-old Smooth puppies by Ch. Mardic Talisman of Quissex ex Ch. Raybill Quissex Volare. Bred by Lisa Sachs, Fortune's Kennels, Huntington, New York.

2. Game time! Three-week-old Smooth pups foreshadowing adult play modes. Owned by Lisa Sachs, Huntington, New York.

3. Puppies, age five weeks, by Ch. Unicorn's Laurelton Joker ex Ch. Firefox Laurelton Spice. Laurelton Kennels, owners, Richard and Virginia Ashlock, Ontario, California.

4. Charbonne Smooth puppies at about three weeks learning to eat. Charlotte Le Vecque, owner, Highland, California.

5. Ch. Foxmoor Quissex Fantan with her 3- to 4-week-old puppies by Ch. Toofox the Colonel. Fantan was Best of Opposite Sex at a Fox Terrier Club of Northern California Specialty and is by Ch. Foxmoor Macho Macho Man ex Ch. Foxden Flavia. Owned by Laurelton Kennels, Richard and Virginia Ashlock, Ontario, California.

6. This is Gene Bigelow's favorite Wire puppy picture and we appreciate her sharing it with us. Bred by Gloria and Kim (Harris) Snellings and sired by Ch. Raylu Recharge, two have become champions; another has more than half the points needed; two have earned C.D. degrees; and two have become champion producers. Puppies with a future as well as adorable babies!

7. Ch. Wyrelee's Hot Stuff at 3½ months relaxing with a bone. Here one notes the very special charm that makes Wire puppies such heart stealers. Nancy Lee Wolf owns this one at Wyrelee Kennels, Scotts Valley, California.

8. Tug-of-war is a good game to play with your Fox Terrier puppy, as is demonstrated by future Ch. Wyrelee Delightful Demon at eight weeks old. Nancy Lee Wolf, owner, Scotts Valley, California.

190

Overleaf: →

1. Winning the Brood Bitch Class at the American Fox Terrier Club Centenary in 1985: *Left*, the foundation bitch from Foxmoor Kennels, Ch. Quissex Upsedaisy, with her offspring by Ch. Ttarb The Brat. Ch. Foxmoor Macho Macho Man (*center*) and Ch. Foxmoor Manorette. Owned by Foxmoor Kennels, Mr. and Mrs. Harold Nedell, Richmond, Texas. Ric Chashoudian is the judge (*left*). Mrs. James A. Farrell, Jr., President of the American Fox Terrier Club standing on the *right*.

2. Westminster Kennel Club 1979. A "clean sweep" for Foxden Kennels, Mrs. James A. Farrell, Jr., Darien, Connecticut. *Left to right*: Ch. Jonwyre's Galaxy of Foxden, Foxden Bon Bon, and Ch. Foxden Painted Lady, handled by the Forsyths, to bring home all the top awards in the breed. Photo courtesy of Frank Jones, Jonwyre, England.

BROOD
BITCH
AMERICAN
FOX TERRIER CLUB
CENTENARY · 1985
DAVE ASHBEY

1↑   2↓

BEST OF
VARIETY
THE WESTMINSTER
KENNEL CLUB
FEBRUARY 12-13, 1979
ASHBEY

Chapter 4

Fox Terriers in Canada

Canadian dog fanciers have long appreciated Fox Terriers. In fact, points of special interest about them include that the first Wire ever registered with the American Kennel Club was not a dog from the United States, but one from Canada! This was Broxton Virago, in the 1887 stud book; the breeder was G. Whitaker of Ontario, and the owner R.W. Dean, Oakville, Ontario.

A gentleman with a long, distinguished history as a Fox Terrier breeder, owner, exhibitor in Canada was the famous James D. Strachan from Montreal. His was the Ormsby Kennel, founded in 1919, whose well-known residents included that lovely Wire, Champion Ormsby Lightning, described in the breed histories as being "a replica of the famed and magnificent Champion Matford Vic." The kennel here was managed by Harry Armistead, who was widely esteemed and to whom a share of credit must go for the success and quality of the Ormsbys.

Some of the early breeders we have found mentioned with respect include Mrs. Irene Webster, from Ottawa; her By Town Kennels were based on British stock, principally from the Pargntons owned by Miss Lewis.

George H. Gooderham was known as the owner of Champion Norfolk Fidget, Charles Lyndon owned Champion Johnny Cannuck, both of them in Ontario. Mr. and Mrs. Frank Beer, again from Toronto, were into Smooths in a big way, making many shows in the States as well as in their own country. The Beers must have started breeding right at the beginning of the 1930's, and continued over at least a couple of decades.

Ted Ward with Ch. Drakehall Duncan, a famous early winner.

S.W. Scarpa, from Quebec, was an exhibitor of the 1930's; among his dogs was the Wire, Starting Event of Wild-oaks, purchased from the Richard C. Bondys, a son of Champion Crackley Startler of Wildoaks ex Champion Gains Great Surprise of Wild-oaks, born in 1933.

Numerous other fanciers also were making their presence felt on the Canadian show front with Fox Terriers. And of course there is little question that the most renowned of all was Ted Ward, Sr., whose kennel prefix "Albany" is carried on to this day by another outstanding terrier man, Ted's son, George Ward. What can one possibly say about these two that has not already been repeated many times? Ted, Sr. instilled in his sons, George and Ted, Jr., not only a love of terriers but a knowledge of them second to none. When George came to the United States and established his kennel in Michigan, he brought with him one of the keenest pair of eyes and soundest discrimination, on what is correct in Fox Terriers of anyone we've ever known. The Wards have started many outstanding fanciers on the road to success and have taken countless dogs to success. Canada can be proud, indeed, of such knowledgeable, talented people, and of the esteem in which they are held wherever terriers are known.

At the present time, there are some very notable Fox Terrier Breeders raising splendid dogs in Canadian kennels. They represent a combination of the best bloodlines from Canada itself, Great Britain, and the United States. Long may they prosper!

FOXLINTON

Foxlinton Kennels, Smooth Fox Terriers, are owned by Judith L. Leonard, Kanata, Ontario, who is working with the breeding from Quissex Kennels and with Foxmoor, both from the United States, in her breeding program.

American and Canadian Champion Foxmoor Quissex Mah Jong is a well-known young bitch from here, a daughter of Champion Foxmoor Chief of Staff ex Champion Quissex Rebel Hill Meringue. As a puppy, she was Winners Bitch and Best of Opposite Sex at the American Fox Terrier Club Centenary Show, bringing her total points at that time to ten; and she completed both her American and her Canadian titles while still a puppy, handled by agent Liz Tobin.

Now a daughter of hers, Foxlinton Foresight, sired by Champion Ttarb The Brat, five months old at time of writing, is showing the promise of a bright future. He is presently co-owned by Brabant Kennels and Foxlinton Kennels, and all concerned are eagerly anticipating his show career.

HALFMOON

Halfmoon Smooth Fox Terriers are owned by the noted professional handler L. Garrett Lambert at Nobleton, Ontario, who is a Smooth fancier with some very excellent members of the breed.

American and Canadian Champion Buccaneer's Best Man was bred by Ken and Pat Reinke and has had an exciting show career in both the United States and Canada. He is a Specialty Show winner, a Sweepstakes winner, and an all-breed Best in Show winner, plus many other honors along the way.

American and Canadian Champion Foxden King Wenceslas, who was bred by Foxden Kennels at Darien, Connecticut, finished his American Championship at Westminster under David Merriman—a very handsome dog. Both of these fine Smooths have much to offer the breed, and it is not surprising that they have done so well.

TROLLHATTAN

Trollhattan Smooth Fox Terriers are owned by Phyllis and Emily Gratton at Truro in Nova Scotia. Phyllis had started her career in dogs with the purchase of a Collie in the 1940's, with her first showing and breeding experience gained with Pekingese. Always

Can. and Am. Ch. Trollhattan's Top Skipper, the first important Smooth winner at Trollhattan Kennels, was a Group winner in both Canada and the United States and sire of several champions. This was Emily Gratton's favorite playmate as a youngster.

Can. and Am. Ch. Hewshot January (purchased from Winifred Stout for Canada's Trollhattan Kennels in 1965) finished her Canadian title with a Group 1st, then produced champions in every litter she whelped. Phyllis and Emily Gratton, owners, Truro, Nova Scotia, Canada.

fascinated by the spirit and form of Terriers, she acquired her fist Smooth, a bitch puppy, in 1959. This was Breakeyton Katrina, bred by Ian Breakey in Quebec; she was a daughter of Champion Heathside Heads Up. Katrina finished her Canadian title as a puppy at a time when shows and entries weren't as plentiful as they are today.

During the 1950s Phyllis started handling professionally. Among the dogs she campaigned were Mr. Breakey's English and Canadian Champion Lavish Warpaint, a son of Laurel Wreath, as well as showing the same owner's Champion Breakeyton Kip (a brother to Katrina) to Best in Show.

In 1955, Phyllis married Harvey Gratton, owner of Trollhattan Dobermans, at Ontario. They moved to a rural, 32-acre location just outside Phyllis's home town, Truro, in central Nova Scotia.

In the years that followed, they were active in training, breeding, grooming, boarding, local dog clubs, Canadian Kennel Club affairs, and judging.

The first big winning Smooth under the Trollhattan banner was Canadian and American Champion Trollhattan's Top Skipper, a son of Canadian and English Champion Brocklands Royal Tan ex a daughter of Champion Solus Zezebel. Skipper was a Group winner in both the United States and Canada, as well as the sire of several champions.

The Grattons had many opportunities to sell Skipper to show homes in America, but he was the playmate of their young daughter, Emily.

During the 1940s, the Grattons integrated some of Britain's best bloodlines into their breeding program; these included Ellastone, Hiya, Viscum, Watteau and Newmaidley.

The acquisition of American Champion Hewshott January, in 1965 from Winifred Stout, was the beginning of a friendship that continues with great rapport. January quickly finished her Canadian title with a 5-point win and a Group 1st under Percy Roberts. She was equally adept in the whelping box, producing champions by every sire to whom she was bred.

Owing to some mix-ups at the time of the Canadian Kennel Club's switch to computerization in the late 1960s, several home-breds were registered without the Trollhattan prefix. Some of these dogs went on to become impressive international winners, most noteworthy among them perhaps having been American Champion Quissex Marc, a January son, who did a lot of winning in the United States out west. He was to have been registered *Trollhattan* Quissex Marc, but came out Quissex Marc.

In the 1970s Harvey Gratton began to devote a good portion of his time to his judging assignments across Canada and in Bermuda. It was at this point that the Grattons' daughter, Emily, took over management of the kennel and planned the breedings. Emily had spent many hours choosing and conditioning prospective show puppies, junior handling, and operating a small pet supply business at the kennel.

Although Harvey passed away in 1977, Phyllis and Emily have continued to breed and show Smooths and Dobes.

Some exciting puppy winners from Trollhattan so far in the 1980s have been Canadian Champion Gleam's Smash Hit, bred by

Phyllis, Best Terrier Puppy at the Atlantic Terrier Association Specialty under judge Barbara Keenan. The puppy was later acquired by Patti Keenan, by whom she was shown to her championship in the States, points for which included a Winners Bitch award at Westminster. Patti then bred this bitch to American and Canadian Champion Foxbow Exchequer, and has done some nice winning with the offspring. Smash Hit has now returned to the Grattons to be part of their breeding program.

The year 1983 saw Canadian Champion Trollhattan Quissex Jenifer, bred by Winnie Stout and owned by Emily Gratton, launch an impressive puppy career, finishing her title with ease and winning a Best Puppy in Show under Terrier breeder and judge Knut Egeberg.

In 1984, Canadian Champion Quissex Winterra Wild Rumor won a Best Puppy in Show.

Battle Cry Annie Get Your Gun was acquired by Emily in 1983, to become the foundation bitch of her own breeding program. "Lulu's" first litter was sired by Canadian and American Champion Horatio of Quissex (owned by Phyllis) and it included the exciting Canadian Champion Trollhattan's Dack Rambo, a Best in Show and Best Puppy in Show winner at just over seven months' age. All of Dack's showing has been before he reached a year old. He has never been defeated by another male Smooth, and has several Best Puppy in Group and Group placements to his credit. His sister, Trollhattan's Dolly Daydream, needs just three points to finish. The breeding was repeated, and in 1986 four show puppies entered the ring: two in the United States, two in Canada.

Both Phyllis and Emily handle their own Smooths, but the serious conditioning, training and campaigning is put in the capable hands of John Heartz of Truro, Nova Scotia.

Phyllis is now a Canadian Kennel Club approved judge of Terriers and is working on her Working and Herding breeds. Always a follower of Wires as well as Smooths (owned Champion Roundway Parasol, bred by Gladys Creasy) Phyllis has recently renewed her interest in breeding them.

Emily, as involved as ever in Dobes, plans to continue and expand her Smooth breeding program. Her greatest frustration is that the Doberman Pinscher Club of America National and Montgomery County usually fall on the same weekend—and at opposite ends of the United States!

This famous Smooth winner of the 1960s was a homebred from the Trollhattan Kennels in Nova Scotia, Canada, bred, owned, and handled by Phyllis A. Gratton to win the Terrier Group at Lewiston-Auburn K.C. in the U.S. in 1965 under noted authority William L. Kendrick. Skipper was by Can. and Eng. Ch. Brooklands Royal Tan ex Trollhattan's Rosabelle, and he was the first big winning Smooth carrying the Trollhattan Kennel identification.

200

WYNDFYRE

Leslie Wheaton at Saskatoon, Saskatchewan, Canada, is the owner of Canadian and American Champion Foxbow Exchequer, son of American and Canadian Champion Dragoon of Foxbow ex American Champion Raybill's Half Fast Waltz. A multiple Specialty winner, "Buddy" has as well multiple Group wins. As a sire he is rapidly proving his worth, having champions to his credit.

Exchequer is the first venture into Fox Terriers for Les Wheaton, who is a professional harness horse driver, presently attending university. Since the purchase of Buddy in June 1985, Les has added a bitch for breeding to him, with the plan in mind of raising and continuing to show Smooths. We note that Lakelands are already owned at Wyndfyre, and we wish Les Wheaton much success with the newly acquired breed.

WIREHILL

Wirehill Fox Terriers were established in 1965 by Kay and Lou Guimond at Mississauga, Canada, becoming permanently registered with the Canadian Kennel Club in 1984. The foundation bitch line here was from Irish breeding, such as Baros and Dunwyre, and from the United States, Wildoaks and Evewire. The male line was Emperor, Statesman, and Super Flash. The "Ginger" line goes back to Gallant Fox.

In addition to the Wires, Wirehill is a famous name in Sealyhams, as the Guimonds owned the great Champion Roderick of Jenmist, who spent his years of retirement with them, and the famous son of this dog, Champion Wirehill Roddy's Fella, Top Sealyham in the United States for 1985.

But returning to the Wires, top dog here is English, American, and Canadian Champion Littleway McTavish, famous Best in Show dog. Also there is American and Canadian Champion Yelsam Craze, descended from Champion Aryee Dominator and Canadian Champion Deko Defiant (brother to Champion Deko Druid). Both Defiant and Druid were imported from England by Ted Ward, famous Canadian Terrier expert and the father of George Ward.

Canadian Champion Duskie Revelation is a homebred Best in Show bitch, in whom Wirehill Kennels take enormous pride. She is by Champion Dimminsdale Fergus ex Champion Frolic, who is of Evewire breeding.

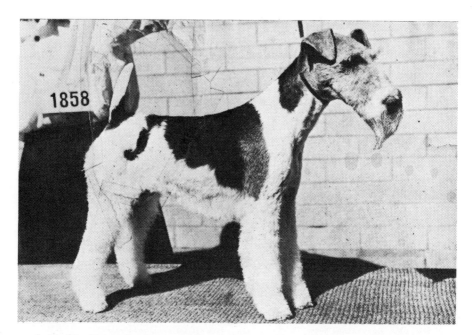

Aust. Ch. Townville Tana, U.K. import, by Eng. Ch. Winter Statesman ex Townville Tamlyn. Photo taken at Brisbane Royal Show where Tana won Best Terrier in Show. Owned by Barbara A. Withers, Ebenezer, Australia.

Two puppies: Canbury Cumup Trumps (bitch) and Canbury Corker (dog) by Penda Pepo, U.K. import, ex Canbury Miss Chief, who is linebred to Worsbro Betoken Again and incorporates all imported stock. She is the dam of four champions. Owned by Canbury Kennels, Barbara A. Withers, Ebenezer, Australia.

Chapter 5

Fox Terriers in Australia

The Australian Fox Terrier Club was founded in Melbourne, Victoria, in 1878, only two short years after the first of all Fox Terrier Clubs, the English one, had come into being. Thus the longevity of Fox Terrier interest "down under" eloquently speaks for itself! The Australian Fox Terrier Club was soon followed by the Southern Fox Terrier Club, also headquartered at Melbourne. Both of these early clubs have been out of existence for many years now, however.

The Fox Terrier Club of New South Wales was formed in 1910, and has been continuously active since that time. Therefore it holds the distinction of being the oldest continually existent club in Australia today. The very distinguished Mr. W. Hamilton was the founding President of the Fox Terrier Club of New South Wales, an office which he filled for about 28 years. Interestingly, it is this club which was first to introduce Judges Training Classes and Examinations for those wishing to become judges, a system which has been widely accepted and used since that introduction. All the way back in 1928 W. R. Polley sat for and passed such an examination before the Fox Terrier Club of New South Wales.

It was in 1868 that the first Smooth Fox Terrier was imported from England into Australia by Mr. I. Fosbery. This was Careless, a bitch who had been born the previous year. She was bred to a white English Terrier, producing the first known Fox Terrier litter in Sydney, and she won several prizes at the Sydney Royal Agricultural Shows. This bitch was the foundation of the breed in Australia.

It was not until eight years later, 1876, that the first Wire Fox Terrier appeared in Australia, having been imported to Sydney from England. This was Nell, who had been bred by the famous Parson Jack Russell. She won at the Sydney Royal Shows in 1878 and 1879 and died in 1885.

It was quite usual in those days to cross the Smooths and Wires in breeding, the progeny then being shown as either Smooths or Wires, depending on the amount and quality of their coats. Interest in these dogs really flourished, and by 1900 Fox Terriers were firmly established throughout Australia.

There was a period during which Fox Terrier entries were really huge, and we have read that in 1937 the Sydney Royal drew 369 Smooths and 169 Wires for a total Fox Terrier entry of 538, which we understand was a world record for the breed at that period.

Although entries in the breed have declined from those days, it would seem that quality very definitely has not. Australian Fox Terriers do a notable amount of winning in the inter-breed competition at the shows there. In addition Australia has been quite "put on the map" by the success of a homebred from there, the Smooth Champion Ttarb The Brat, who came, saw and conquered the United States, breaking all records for Smooths here as well as providing stock for many successful kennels to use here. We salute the Fox Terriers "down under," and are sure that you will find the following kennel stories on some of them of interest.

SPRINGFOX

Springfox Smooth Fox Terriers belong to Mr. and Mrs. R. Black at St. Ives, New South Wales, Australia, who started breeding and showing them early in the 1980's. With careful selection, they are started on what promises to be a successful breeding program; and there could not possibly be greater Smooth enthusiasts than this family.

Pride of place at this young kennel is held by a bitch of tremendous quality who, at only 14 months' age, already has gained her Australian Championship and an imposing list of honors. Starting right off with a Best Baby Puppy in Show early in 1985, at the A.B.S. Blacktown and District A.H. & I. Society, she next gained Minor Puppy in Show at A.B.S. New South Wales Womens Dog Club under Canadian judge Mrs. Stella Loftus. From there it was several times Best Puppy in Show (on one of these occasions, at a

Smooth Specialty in New South Wales, becoming Runner Up To Best In Show); then Best Terrier in Group; and on to Best Junior in Show at A.B.S. Manly District and Dog Training Club.

Australian Champion Nimbus Gem has 12 Champion Certificates and four Bests of Breed, handled to these honors by Matthew Black, 16-year-old son of her owners. A littermate of Nimbus Gem, Springfox Silver Rain, has two Club Challenges, so is also nicely started on her way.

The parents of Gem and Silver Rain are Erinclair White Guard (Australian Champion Maralya Bojangles-Australian Champion Erinclair Jewel Box) and Australian Champion Emohrud Spring Dreamer (Australian Champion Mirolinda Meldon-Emohrud Pipers Dream).

U-ELVER

U-Elver Smooth Fox Terriers are owned by Mrs. G.M. Nowland, located at Curlewis in New South Wales, Australia. It was on towards 1969-1970 when Mrs. Nowland purchased her first Smooth as a house pet, and she was much amazed when he came registered as Tressa Talkative and accompanied by a very old bloodline in his excellent pedigree. It was under the persuasion of a friend that the puppy was entered in his first two dog shows, and a tremendous, but pleasant, surprise to Mrs. Nowland when he came home having won Best of Breed Best Minor Puppy in Show.

With so auspicious a beginning, it is little wonder that Mrs. Nowland was sold on dog shows almost instantly! Tressa Talkative became a multiple Group, Class in Show, and Best in Show winner, having more than 1,000 points to his credit when he retired at seven years of age, after having taken Best in Group at the Brisbane Royal under the noted Canadian judge Thomas A. Quilley.

Having become thus involved in dog showing and interested now in breeding, Mrs. Nowland next purchased two bitches of compatible bloodlines for Talkative, who then went on to become the sire of numerous champions.

Newmaidley Rowena was imported later on from the famed English kennel. Rowena's bloodlines strengthened those Mrs. Nowland already was working with. Since then she has also added Australian Champion Rama Smooth Rehearsal, whose sire was the English import Newmaidley Pennyworth. Rama has been in Mrs.

Nowland's kennels since the early 1980s, and when combined with her breeding bitches has produced another batch of Australian Champions.

Currently, Mrs. Nowland is showing Australian Champions Dnalwon Beau Spartacus, Beau Monarch and Beau Bianca, three outstanding youngsters who all gained their titles with ease.

It is unfortunate, so far as showing dogs is concerned, that Mrs. Nowland lives on a 4,000 acre farm some 300 miles from Sydney and slightly further than that from Brisbane, for distance and traveling do restrict her showing to some extent. She manages to make the Royals, however, her dogs usually giving a good account of themselves.

CANBURY

Canbury Wire Fox Terriers are owned by Barbara A. Withers at Ebenezer, Australia, who started with the breed during 1966,

Eng. and Aust. Ch. Penda Pied Piper, U.K. import, shown 72 times, gained 54 times Best in Show; 68 times Best Terrier. Owned by Barbara A. Withers, Canbury Kennels, Ebenezer, Australia. 1968—1983, by Eng. Ch. Penda Worsbro Whistler ex Wyrecroft War Paint (dam of two champions).

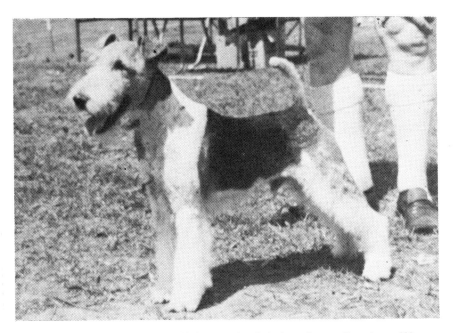

Aust. Ch. Canbury Chianti, U.K. import, by Axholme Jimmy Reppin ex Worsbro Wink, U.K. import. Numerous Bests in Group and Bests in Show. Photo winning British Terrier Show in 1978. Owned and bred by Barbara A. Withers, Ebenezer, Australia.

at which time she saw and selected her first Wire, English Champion Penda Pied Piper, while over there. It had been her intention to take her new purchase with her on her return home, but Australian quarantine laws intervened and so Piper had to stay an allotted time under quarantine there prior to his departure for his new home. When that time had elapsed, Barbara returned for Piper; and also for a lovely bitch, Worsbro Wink. Barbara set off for home by ship with her two new additions; and somewhere off the coast of Africa the family grew, as Wink presented her with three handsome puppy dogs. The story had a happy ending (once the puppies' citizenship had been straightened out, as they had been born of British stock on a ship of Italian origin flying a Liberian flag) as the Royal Agricultural Society sorted things out, and following a further stint in Australian quarantine, all five Wires started off on very creditable careers at home and in the show ring for their new owner.

Piper gained his Australian Championship Certificates in five shows over a time span of 16 days. At these first five events in Australia, he started off with third in his class at the Wire Haired Fox Terrier event. But his fortunes promptly changed for the better, and from there he swept on through with Best Terrier at the Sydney Royal; Best in Show at the Fox Terrier Club; Best in Show All Breeds at Hawkesbury; and Best in Show at the British Terrier Show.

All Australian champions owned by Canbury Kennels have won Best Terrier in Group either once or on numerous occasions. And all have won an All-Breed Best in Show award. Additionally, all have won their class in Specialty Shows or gone Best in Show.

Winners from this kennel of Best in Show awards include Australian Champions Canbury Kismit, Kaprego, The Gamecock, Chianti (U.K. import); Leica Comet; Pretty Perfect (bred at Cantebury then later sold); Katherine; Gold-N-Metior; Miss Dementia; Worsbro Wink; International Champion Penda Polly Perkind (U.K. import); Townville Tana; and, of course, Penda Pied Piper.

During his show career, English and Australian Penda Pied Piper, in 72 ring appearances, won 70 Firsts, 70 Challenges and Bests of Breed, 68 times Best in Terrier, and 54 Best in Show awards!

Canbury has sent numerous Wires to the United States who have gained their titles there. These include American Champions Canbury Kaprego; Canbury Code-O-Arms; Canbury Kapaneus; Canbury Polly Perkins; Canbury Mary Poppins; and Canbury Can Do. This kennel also produced New Zealand Champions Super Sally and Canbury Lady Luck, while other Canbury-bred who have gained championship for new owners in Australia number among them Australian Champions Canbury Gay Charmer; Canbury Miss Fashion, Canbury You Listen; Canbury The Captain; Canbury Chariah; and Canbury Pretty Perfect.

The latest importation to Barbara Withers is as yet unshown in Australia. English Champion Penda Pepo is by Champion Townville Tradition ex English Champion Penda Pretty Perfect. We predict that this is another who will go down in the history of Australian Wires as a major contributor to quality and good type in the breed.

Chapter 6

The Breed Standard

The Standard of the Breed, to which one sees and hears such frequent reference whenever and wherever purebred dogs are written of or discussed, is the word picture of what is considered to be the ideal specimen of the breed. It outlines, in minute detail, each and every feature of the breed, both in physical characteristics and in temperament, accurately describing the dog from whisker to tail, creating a clear picture of what is to be considered correct (or incorrect); the features comprising "breed type" (i.e., those which set it apart from other breeds making it distinctive and unique); and the probable temperament and behavior pattern to expect in various members of that breed.

The Standard is the guide for breeders endeavoring to produce quality dogs and for fanciers wishing to learn what is considered beautiful and typical within the individual breed. It is the tool with which judges evaluate and reach their decisions in the ring. The dog it describes as correct is the one in our mind's eye as we compare dogs and make our evaluations. It is the result of endless hours spent in consideration and study of the breed, its history, its reasons for being; and of its description and previous Standards in our own country and the countries of the breed's origin and development from earliest days up until modern times. All such factors have been studied most carefully by your breed's parent specialty clubs; usually by a special committee selected for this task; then by the board of directors, and later by the general membership. When all are in agreement to that point, the results are turned in to the American Kennel Club for *their* further study and possible comments and suggestions; followed by publication, with the invitation to comment to interested parties, in the official American Kennel Club publication, *Pure-Bred Dogs/American Kennel Gazette.* Following the satisfactory completion of all these steps, the Standard, or any changes in it which may have been under consideration, are approved and become official.

A similar routine is followed in other countries, too, for the drawing-up of breed standards.

In 1985 a significant change was made in the status of the Fox Terrier in the United States. Over almost a full century Fox Terriers here had been regarded as two varieties of the same breed. Thus, although not practiced in many generations, it was permissible under the rules and regulations for them to be interbred, then the offspring registered according to coat (which I am sure has long been forgotten as the lines of each have been kept pure to that variety for many decades). Smooth fanciers and Wire fanciers seem to take an interest in their own variety only; very few if any, in the United States breed both varieties much less interbreed them.

Prior to the early 1940s, the two varieties of Fox Terriers competed against one another at the "specials," or Best of Breed, level; thus only one, the winner of that class, was afforded the opportunity of competing in the Terrier Group. Fox Terrier owners realized that this was a handicap to *both* varieties; and it was a happy day for them, and other breeds of which these circumstances were also true, when the A.K.C. ruling was changed permitting *both* to be judged straight through to Best of Variety. Thus the Best Smooth and the Best Wire *both* became eligible to compete against each other and the other Terrier breeds in the Terrier Group.

Everything went along on an even keel until 1984, when serious consideration by A.K.C. was given to again throwing all varieties in breeds thus separated into one "specials" class, from which just one, in our case Fox Terrier, would be the winner to represent the breed in the Terrier Group. Fox Terrier breeders were not about to let this happen, so immediately the American Fox Terrier Club took steps to separate the Smooths and the Wires into *two separate breeds* rather than two varieties of the same breed as they had been; and to do so fast, before any decision had been reached on

Ch. Watteau Madrigal, one of the many outstanding Smooths from Watteau Kennels, Mrs. A. Blake, West Scrafton, Leyburn, England.

the A.K.C. change of the motion under consideration.

The American Fox Terrier Club, by autumn 1984, had taken all necessary steps, including a new, slightly different standard (now that Fox Terriers would become a separate *breed*) in order to avoid the chance of their becoming one breed rather than two varieties in show classification.

This, and the new standard for Smooth Fox Terriers and the new standard for Wire Fox Terriers were drawn up, approved by the American Kennel Club on December 11, 1984, and became effective June, 1985.

As it turned out, these steps were unnecessary, as the change proposed by the American Kennel Club was defeated by a wide, and loud, majority; thus all the ten or so breeds which would have been affected remained status quo—except for the Fox Terriers which now, after nearly a century of sharing, had become two separate breeds, each with a separate breed standard, at the request and action of the American Fox Terrier Club.

Thus ended the long period of "mutual identity" and Fox Terriers now are two distinct breeds of dog.

STANDARD FOR THE SMOOTH FOX TERRIER

Head—The skull should be flat and moderately narrow, gradually decreasing in width to the eyes. Not much "stop" should be apparent, but there should be more dip in the profile between the forehead and the top jaw than is seen in the case of a Greyhound. The *cheeks* must not be full. The *ears* should be V-shaped and small, of moderate thickness, and drooping forward close to the cheek, not hanging by the side of the head like a Foxhound. The top line of the folded ear should be well above the level of the skull. The *jaws,* upper and lower, should be strong and muscular and of fair punishing strength, but not so as in any way to resemble the Greyhound or modern English Terrier. There should not be much falling away below the eyes. This part of the head should, however, be moderately chiseled out, so as not to go down in a straight slope like a wedge. The *nose,* towards which the muzzle must gradually taper, should be black. It should be noticed that although the foreface should gradually taper from eye to muzzle and should tip slightly at its junction with the forehead, it should not "dish" or fall away quickly below the eyes, where it should be full and well made up, but relieved from "wedginess" by a little delicate chiseling. The *eyes* and the *rims* should be dark in color, moderately small and rather deep set, full of fire, life and intelligence and as nearly as possible circular in shape. Anything approaching a yellow eye is most objectionable. The *teeth* should be as nearly as possible together, i.e., the points of the upper (incisors) teeth on the outside of or slightly over-lapping the lower teeth. There should be apparent little difference in length between the skull and foreface of a well balanced head.

Neck—Should be clean and muscular, without throatiness, of fair length, and gradually widening to the shoulders. *Shoulders* should be long and sloping, well laid back, fine at the points, and clearly cut at the withers.

Chest—Deep and not broad.

Back—Should be short, straight, (i.e., level), and strong, with no appearance of slackness. *Brisket* should be deep, yet not exaggerated. *Loin* should be very powerful, muscular and very slightly arched. The fore ribs should be moderately arched, the back ribs deep and well sprung, and the dog should be well ribbed up.

212

Hindquarters—Should be strong and muscular, quite free from droop or crouch; the thighs long and powerful, stifles well curved and turned neither in nor out; hocks well bent and near the ground should be perfectly upright and parallel each with the other when viewed from behind, the dog standing well up on them like a foxhound, and not straight in the stifle. The worst possible form of hindquarters consists of a short second thigh and a straight stifle.

Stern—Should be set on rather high, and carried gaily, but not over the back or curled. It should be of good strength, anything approaching a "Pipestopper" tail being especially objectionable.

Legs—The forelegs viewed from any direction must be straight with bone strong right down to the feet, showing little or no appearance of ankle in front, and being short and straight in pastern. Both fore and hind legs should be carried straight forward in traveling, the stifles not turning outward. The elbows should hang perpendicular to the body, working free of the sides. *Feet* should be round, compact, and not large; the soles hard and tough; the toes moderately arched, and turned neither in nor out.

Coat—Should be smooth, flat, but hard, dense and abundant. The belly and underside of the thighs should not be bare.

Color—White should predominate; brindle, red or liver markings are objectionable. Otherwise this point is of little or no importance.

Symmetry, Size and Character—The dog must present a generally gay, lively and active appearance; bone and strength in a small compass are essentials; but this must not be taken to mean that a Fox Terrier should be cloddy, or in any way coarse—speed and endurance must be looked to as well as power, and the symmetry of the Foxhoud taken as a model. The Terrier, like the Hound, must on no account be leggy, nor must be too short in the leg. He should stand like a cleverly-made hunter, covering a lot of ground, yet with a short back, as before stated. He will then attain the highest degree of propelling power, together with the greatest length of stride that is compatible with the length of his body. Weight is not a certain criterion of a Terrier's fitness for his work—general shape, size and contour are the main points; and if a dog can gallop and stay, and follow his fox up a drain, it matters little what his weight is to a pound or so. According to present-day requirements, a full-sized, well-balanced dog should not exceed 15½ inches at the withers—the bitch being proportionately lower—nor should the length of back from withers to root of tail exceed 12 inches, while to maintain the relative proportions, the head should not exceed 7¼ inches or be less than 7 inches. A dog with these measurements should scale 18 pounds in show condition—a bitch weighing some 2 pounds less—with a margin of 1 pound either way.

Balance—This may be defined as the correct proportions of a certain point, or points, when considered in relation to a certain other point or points. It is the keystone of the Terrier's anatomy. The chief points for consideration are the relative proportions of skull and foreface; head and back; height at withers and length of body from shoulder-point to buttock—the ideal of proportion being reached when the last two measurements are the same. It should be added that, although the head measurements can be taken with absolute accuracy, the height at withers and length of back and coat are approximate, and are inserted for the information of breeders and exhibitors rather than as a hard and fast rule.

Movement—Movement, or action, is the crucial test of conformation. The Terrier's legs should be carried straight forward while traveling, the forelegs hanging perpendicular and swinging parallel with the sides, like the pendulum of a clock. The principal propulsive power is furnished by the hind legs, perfection of action being found in the Terrier possessing long thighs and muscular second-thighs well bent at the stifles which admit of a strong forward thrust or "snatch" of the hocks. When approaching, the forelegs should form a continuation of the straight line of the front, the feet being the same distance apart as the elbows. When stationary it is often difficult to determine whether a dog is slightly out at shoulder, but, directly he moves, the defect—if it exists—becomes more apparent, the forefeet having a tendency to cross, "weave," or "dish." When, on the contrary, the dog is tied at the shoulder, the tendency of the feet is to move wider apart, with a sort of paddling action. When the hocks are turned in—

214

cowhocks—the stifles and feet are turned outwards, resulting in a serious loss of propulsive power. When the hocks are turned outwards the tendency of the hind feet is to cross, resulting in an ungainly waddle.

N.B.—Old scars or injuries, the result of work or accident, should not be allowed to prejudice a Terrier's chance in the showring, unless they interfere with its movement or with its utility for work or stud.

Scale of Points

Head and Ears	15	Stern	5
Neck	5	Legs and Feet	15
Shoulder and Chest	10	Coat	15
Back and Loin	10	Symmetry, Size and	
Hind Quarters	15	Character	10
			100

Disqualifying Points

Nose—White, cherry or spotted to a considerable extent with either of these colors. *Ears*—Prick, tulip or rose. *Mouth*—Much undershot, or much overshot.

Approved December 11, 1984
Effective June 1, 1985

STANDARD FOR THE WIRE FOX TERRIER
Characteristics—The Terrier should be alert, quick of movement, keen of expression, on the tip-toe of expectation at the slightest provocation. Character is imparted by the expression of the eyes and by the carriage of ears and tail.
General Appearance—The dog should be balanced and this may be defined as the correct proportions of a certain point or points, when considered in relation to a certain other point or points. It is the keystone of the Terrier's anatomy. The chief points for con-

The American Fox Terrier Club Specialty in 1975. Eng. and Am. Ch. Sunnybrook Spot On owned by Mrs. Robert V. Clark, Jr., Middleburg, Virginia, taking Best of Breed, handled by Peter Green.

216

sideration are the relative proportions of skull and foreface; head and back; height at withers; and length of body from shoulder-point to buttock—the ideal of proportion being reached when the last two measurements are the same. It should be added that, although the head measurements can be taken with absolute accuracy, the height at withers and length of back are approximate, and are inserted for the information of breeders and exhibitors rather than as a hard-and-fast rule. The movement or action is the crucial test of conformation. The Terrier's legs should be carried straight forward while traveling, the forelegs hanging perpendicular and swinging parallel to the sides, like the pendulum of a clock. The principal propulsive power is furnished by the hind legs, perfection of action being found in the Terrier possessing long thighs and muscular second-thighs well bent at the stifles, which admit of a strong forward thrust or "snatch" of the hocks. When approaching, the forelegs should form a continuation of the straight of the front, the feet being the same distance apart as the elbows. When stationary it is often difficult to determine whether a dog is slightly out at shoulder but directly he moves the defect—if it exists—becomes more apparent, the fore-feet having a tendency to cross, "weave" or "dish." When, on the contrary, the dog is tied at the shoulder, the tendency of the feet is to move wider apart, with a sort of paddling action. When the hocks are turned in—cowhocks—the stifles and feet are turned outwards, resulting in a serious loss of propulsive power. When the hocks are turned outwards the tendency of the hind feet is to cross, resulting in an ungainly waddle.

Head and Skull—The top line of the skull should be almost flat, sloping slightly and gradually decreasing in width towards the eyes, and should not exceed 3½ inches in diameter at the widest part—measuring with the calipers—in the full-grown dog of correct size, the bitch's skull being proportionately narrower. If this measurement is exceeded the skull is termed "coarse," while a full-grown dog with a much narrower skull is termed "bitchy" in head. The length of the head of a full-grown well-developed dog of correct size—measured with calipers—from the back of the occipital bone to the nostrils—should be from 7-7¼ inches, the bitch's head being proportionately shorter. Any measurement in excess of this usually indicates an over-sized or long-backed specimen, although occasionally—so rarely as to partake of the nature of a freak—a Terrier of correct size may boast a head 7½ inches in length. In a well-balanced head there should be little apparent difference in length between skull and foreface. If, however, the foreface is noticeably shorter, it amounts to a fault, the head looking weak and "unfinished." On the other hand, when the eyes are set too high up in the skull and too near the ears, it also amounts to a fault, the head being said to have a "foreign appearance." Although the foreface should gradually taper from eye to muzzle and should dip slightly at its juncture with the forehead, it should not "dish" or fall away quickly below the eyes, where it should be full and well made up, but relieved from "wedginess" by a little delicate chiseling. While well-developed jaw-bones, armed with a set of strong, white teeth, impart that appearance of strength to the foreface which is so desirable, an excessive bony or muscular development of the jaws is both unnecessary and unsightly, as it is partly responsible for the full and rounded contour of the cheeks to which the term "cheeky" is applied. *Nose* should be black. **Eyes**—Should be dark in color, moderately small, rather deep-set not prominent , and full of fire, life, and intelligence; as nearly as possible circular in shape, and not too far apart. Anything approaching a yellow eye is most objectionable. *Ears*—Should be small and V-shaped and of moderate thickness, the flaps neatly folded over and drooping forward close to the cheeks. The top line of the folded ear should be well above the level of the skull. A pendulous ear, hanging dead by the side of the head like a Hound's, is uncharacteristic of the Terrier, while an ear which is semi-erect is still more undesirable. *Mouth*—Both upper and lower jaws should be strong and muscular, the teeth as nearly as possible level and capable of closing together like a vise—the lower canines locking in front of the upper and the points of the upper incisors slightly overlapping the lower.

Neck—Should be clean, muscular, of fair length, free from throatiness and presenting a graceful curve when viewed from the side.

Forequarters—Shoulders when viewed from the front should slope steeply downwards from their juncture, with the neck towards the points, which should be fine. When viewed from the side they should be long, well laid back, and should slope obliquely backwards from points to withers, which should always be clean cut. A shoulder well laid back gives the long fore-hand which, in combination with a short back, is so desirable in Terrier or Hunter. Chest deep and not broad, a too narrow chest being almost as undesirable as a very broad one. Excessive depth of chest and brisket is an impediment to a Terrier when going to ground. Viewed from any direction the legs should be straight, the bone of the forelegs strong right down to the feet. The elbows should hang perpendicular to the body, working free of the sides, carried straight through in traveling.

Body—The back should be short and level with no appearance of slackness—the loins muscular and very slightly arched. The brisket should be deep, the front ribs moderately arched, and the back ribs deep, and well sprung. The term "slackness" is applied both to the portion of the back immediately behind the withers when it shows any tendency to dip, and also the flanks when there is too much space between the back-ribs and hip-bone. When there is little space between the ribs and hips, the dog is said to be "short in couplings," "short-coupled," or "well-ribbed up." A Terrier can scarely be too short in back, provided he has sufficient length of neck and liberty of movement. The bitch may be slightly longer in couplings than the dog.

Hindquarters—Should be strong and muscular, quite free from droop or crouch; the thighs long and powerful; the stifles well curved and turned neither in nor out; the hock-joints well bent and near the ground; the hocks perfectly upright and parallel with each other when viewed from behind. The worst possible form of hindquarters consists of a short second-thigh and a straight stifle, a combination which causes the hind legs to act as props rather than instruments of propulsion. The hind legs should be carried straight through in traveling.

Feet—Should be round, compact, and not large—the pads tough and well cushioned, and the toes moderately arched and turned neither in nor out. A Terrier with good-shaped forelegs and feet will wear his nails down short by contact with the road surface, the weight of the body being evenly distributed between the toe-pads and the heels.

Tail—Should be set on rather high and carried gaily but not curled. It should be of good strength and substance and of fair length—a three-quarters dock is about right—since it affords the only safe grip when handling working Terriers. A very short tail is suitable neither for work nor show.

Coat—The best coats appear to be broken, the hairs having a tendency to twist, and are of dense, wiry texture—like coconut matting—the hairs growing so closely and strongly together that when parted with the fingers the skin cannot be seen. At the base of these stiff hairs is a shorter growth of finer and softer hair—termed the undercoat. The coat on the sides is never quite so hard as that on the back and quarters. Some of the hardest coats are "crinkly" or slightly waved, but a curly coat is very objectionable. The hair on the upper and lower jaws should be crisp and only sufficiently long to impart an appearance of strength to the fore-face. The hair on the forelegs should also be dense and crisp. The coat should average in length from ¾ to 1 inch on shoulders and neck, lengthening to 1½ inches on withers, backs, ribs, and quarters. These measurements are given rather as a guide to exhibitors than as an infallible rule, since the length of coat depends on the climate, seasons, and individual animal. The judge must form his own opinion as to what constitutes a "sufficient" coat on the day.

Color—White should predominate; brindle, red, liver or slaty blue are objectionable. Otherwise, color is of little or no importance.

Weight and Size—Bone and strength in a small compass are essential, but this must not be taken to mean that a Terrier should be "cloddy," or in any way coarse—speed and endurance being requisite as well as power. The Terrier must on no account be leggy, nor must he be too short on the leg. He should stand like a cleverly-made, short-backed hunter, covering a lot of ground. According to present-day requirements, a full-sized, well-balanced dog should not exceed 15½ inches at the withers—the bitch being proportiontely lower—nor should the length of back from withers to root of tail exceed 12 inches, while to maintain the relative proportions, the head—as before mentioned—should not exceed 7¼ inches or be less than 7 inches. A dog with these measurements should scale 18 lbs. in show condition—a bitch weighing some 2 lbs. less—with a margin of 1 lb. either way.

Disqualifications

Nose—White, cherry, or spotted to a considerable extent with either of these colors. **Ears**—Prick, tulip, or rose. **Mouth**—Much undershot or much overshot.

N.B.—Old scars or injuries, the result of work or accident, should not be allowed to prejudice a Terrier's chance in the show ring, unless they interfere with its movement or with its utility for work or stud.

Scale of Points

Head and Ears	10	Stern	5
Neck	5	Legs and Feet	10
Shoulders and Chest	10	Coat	10
Back and Loins	10	Symmetry, Size and	
Hind Quarters	10	Character	15
		Movement	15
			100

Approved December 11, 1984
Effective June 1, 1985

SOME NOTES ON THE BRITISH STANDARDS FOR FOX TERRIERS

The requirements for both Smooth and Wire Fox Terriers in Great Britain are closely similar to one another except where size is concerned, and of course the type and quality of coat. The description in each case is similar to that for these breeds in the U.S., where the Standards are based closely on the British.

Regarding size, British Smooths are to be weighed rather than measured, ideally tipping the scales between 16-18 pounds for dogs and 15-17 pounds for bitches. In Wires, both height and weight have their stipulations, the words being "Height at withers not exceeding 39 cms (15½ ins) in dogs, bitches slightly less." Ideal weight in show condition 8.25 kg (18 lbs) for dogs, bitches slightly less.

Further more, the British Standards for both breeds, give neither a Standard of Points nor breed disqualifications as in the U. S.

Fortune's Hickory Daquiri Doc, C.D., watches her owner, Lynne Bockelman, dig a hole in the sand. Daq found this role reversal to be fascinating.

Chapter 7

On Living with a Fox Terrier

To us, a Fox Terrier, either Smooth or Wire, makes a truly outstanding dog for family membership; especially if that family is a young one, with energetic children growing up who want a dog to play with, to romp with, and to enjoy.

Fox Terriers are hardy, full of fun, and keep things lively wherever they may be. They are generally gentle and loving with people; but not always that way with other dogs, as they are inclined, especially if provoked, to enjoy a fight upon occasion. And many a cat has found itself up a tree when beating a hasty retreat from the path of an agitated Fox Terrier (or any other sort of terrier, for that matter).

The terrier personality is feisty, alert, and always ready for whatever may occur. Their alertness makes them good watch dogs; they are hardy in constitution, and require little, if any, special coddling.

For all their activity and hardiness, terriers make devoted companions, enjoying just as much as any breed the comforts of home, and the pleasure of human companionship. They develop a rapport with their owners, by whom they are usually adored.

We think that they enjoy, more than do many other breeds, being the lone dog in a household, thus not having to tolerate other canines and so the subject of your undivided affection and attention. Their loyalty knows no bounds.

Introduction at a terrier trial! This Jack Russell and Wire Fox Terrier have just been introduced, and the Wire responds to the new friend with a kiss. Courtesy of Lisa Sachs, Huntington, New York.

Ch. Sunnybrook Spot On on his daily walk with then owner Dan Kiedrowski, editor-publisher of *Terrier Type*. Dan and Spot On were devoted pals and Spot On lived out a canine "dream-come-true" retirement.

These two Smooths, Ch. Quissex Proclamation, C.D. and C.G., and Ch. Quissex Vestral Virgin, C.D., are lure-coursing with the Working Collie Association of Long Island. Another activity for which the Smooths seem to be especially keen. Lisa Sachs, owner, Fortune's Kennels, Huntington, New York.

Terriers are great little dogs to have around a farm, or stable, or country home as they are members of the canine family developed to "go to ground," i.e. rout rodents or other critters from underground tunnels. Thus they can keep the rodent population nicely under control. Most owners of pack hounds have a few of the small terrier breeds around to accompany them on hunts, where they are useful for routing foxes or rabbits from underground or underbrush.

Fox Terriers are a nice size for city living, and one sees many of them being walked, smartly and happily, on leads around the streets of New York. Depending on how you have raised yours, you may or may not find the dog agreeable to being left alone in the apartment all day if you are a business person. Some of them, especially older dogs, rise to the occasion and keep out of mischief until your return. But a young terrier may not be so placid about this, and you may come home to complaints from the neighbors regarding barking and to various damage to your possessions from chewing. As I have said, this depends on the individual dog and on how it has been raised; but it is possible that they may be too busy in temperament to be reliable under these circumstances.

Fox Terriers are not difficult dogs to raise or keep in good condition. We have discussed upbringing, care, feeding, and grooming in other chapters. Usually they are good "doers," and in the case of Fox Terriers, of a size to keep healthy in the city if taken for a real walk at least once daily—not just to the curb and back. They are long-lived under usual circumstances.

225

Am. and Can. Ch. Rosecliffe Top Choice, sire of Ch. Wendywyre Independence, the homebred class dog who went Best in Show. Both owned by Richard and Laura Forkel, Wendywyre, Orange, California.

226

Chapter 6

The Purchase of Your Fox Terrier

Careful consideration should be given to what breed of dog you wish to own prior to your purchase of one. If several breeds are attractive to you, and you are undecided as to which you prefer, learn all you can about the characteristics of each before making your decision. As you do so, you are thus preparing yourself to make an intelligent choice; and this is very important when buying a dog who will be, with reasonable luck, a member of your household for at least a dozen years or more. Obviously, since you are reading this book, you have decided on the breed—so now all that remains is to make a good choice.

It is never wise to just rush out and buy the first cute puppy who catches your eye. Whether you wish a dog to show, one with whom to compete in obedience, or one as a family dog purely for his (or her) companionship, the more time and thought you invest as you plan the purchase, the more likely you are to meet with complete satisfaction. The background and early care behind your pet will reflect in the dog's future health and temperament. Even if you are planning the purchase purely as a pet, with no thoughts of showing or breeding in the dog's or puppy's future, it is essential that, if the dog is to enjoy a trouble-free future, you assure yourself of a healthy, properly raised puppy or adult from sturdy, well-bred stock.

Throughout the pages of this book you will find the names and locations of many well-known and well-established kennels in various areas. Another source of information is the American Kennel

227

Ch. Boreham Burlesque, by Ch. Newmaidley Whistling Jeremy ex Ch. Boreham Ballerina, owned by Mrs. J. T. Winstanley, Fordingbridge, Hants, England. Born in 1968, a representative of the type and quality Smooth raised at Boreham Kennels.

Ch. Teesford Trier, winner of nine C.C.s, five reserve C.C.s, including the C.C. at Crufts in 1978; C.C. and Best of Breed, Smooth Fox Terrier Association in 1978; and C.C. and Best of Breed, Crufts 1979. This famed English winner, by Teesford Tartar ex Teesford Twink, was bred by Mr. and Mrs. F. Brown, Teesford Kennels, England, and born in 1975. Sold to Dr. Dagradi in Italy. Photo courtesy of Mrs. Brown.

Club (51 Madison Avenue, New York, New York 10010), from whom you can obtain a list of recognized breeders in the vicinity of your home. If you plan to have your dog campaigned by a professional handler, by all means let the handler help you locate and select a good dog. Through their numerous clients, handlers have access to a variety of interesting show prospects; and the usual arrangement is that the handler re-sells the dog to you for what his cost has been, with the agreement that the dog be campaigned for you by him throughout the dog's career. It is most strongly recommended that prospective purchasers follow these suggestions, as you thus will be better able to locate and select a satisfactory puppy or dog.

Your first step in searching for your puppy is to make appointments at kennels specializing in your breed, where you can visit and inspect the dogs, both those available for sale and the kennel's basic breeding stock. You are looking for an active, sturdy puppy with bright eyes and intelligent expression and who is friendly and alert; avoid puppies who are hyperactive, dull, or listless. The coat should be clean and thick, with no sign of parasites. The premises on which he was raised should look (and smell) clean and be tidy, making it obvious that the puppies and their surroundings are in capable hands. Should the kennels featuring the breed you intend to own be sparse in your area or not have what you consider attractive, do not hesitate to contact others at a distance and purchase from them if they seem better able to supply a puppy or dog who will please you—*so long as it is a recognized breeding kennel of that breed.* Shipping dogs is a regular practice nowadays, with comparatively few problems when one considers the number of dogs shipped each year. A reputable, well-known breeder wants the customer to be satisfied; thus, he will represent the puppy fairly. Should you not be pleased with the puppy upon arrival, a breeder, such as described, will almost certainly permit its return. A conscientious breeder takes real interest and concern in the welfare of the dogs he or she causes to be brought into the world. Such a breeder also is proud of a reputation for integrity. Thus on two counts, for the sake of the dog's future and the breeder's reputation, to such a person a *satisfied* customer takes precedence over a sale at any cost.

If your puppy is to be a pet or "family dog," the earlier the age at which it joins your household the better. Puppies are weaned and ready to start out on their own, under the care of a sensible new owner, at about six weeks old; and if you take a young one, it is often easier to train it to the routine of your household and to your requirements of it than is the case with an older dog which, even though still technically a puppy, may have already started habits you will find difficult to change. The younger puppy is usually less costly, too, as it stands to reason the breeder will not have as much expense invested in it. Obviously, a puppy that has been raised to five or six months old represents more in care and cash expenditure on the breeder's part than one sold earlier; therefore he should be, and generally is, priced accordingly.

There is an enormous amount of truth in the statement that "bargain" puppies seldom turn out to be that. A "cheap" puppy, raised purely for sale and profit, can and often does lead to great heartbreak, including problems and veterinarian's bills which can add up to many times the initial cost of a properly reared dog. On the other hand, just because a puppy is expensive does not assure one that is healthy and well reared. There have been numerous cases where unscrupulous dealers have sold, for several hundred dollars, puppies that were sickly, in poor condition, and such poor specimens that the breed of which they were supposedly members was barely recognizable. So one cannot always judge a puppy by price alone. Common sense must guide a prospective purchaser, plus the selection of a *reliable*, well-recommended dealer whom you know to have well-satisfied customers or, best of all, a specialized breeder. You will probably find the fairest pricing at the kennel of a breeder. Such a person, experienced with the breed in general and with his or her own stock in particular, through extensive association with these dogs, has watched enough of them mature to have obviously learned to assess quite accurately each puppy's potential—something impossible where such background is non-existent.

One more word on the subject of pets. Bitches make a fine choice for this purpose as they are usually quieter and more gentle than the males, easier to house train, more affectionate, and less inclined to roam. If you do select a bitch and have no intention of breeding or showing her, by all means have her spayed, for your sake and for hers. The advantages to the owner of a spayed bitch include avoiding the nuisance of "in season" periods which normally occur twice yearly—with the accompanying eager canine

Ch. Clowngirl of Notts is representative of the magnificent Fox Terriers from the kennels of The Duchess of Newcastle. The Duchess has played an important role in the history of this breed both for the quality of the "Notts" dogs and her thorough knowledge of the breed.

Ch. Kraehollow Katy O'Della, by Ch. Toofox Blazin' Saddler ex Ch. Kandihill Digger O'Della, owned by Jane Swanson, Erie, Illinois. Dam of the noted winner Ch. Foxtrot Fast Lane.

swains haunting your premises in an effort to get close to your female—plus the unavoidable messiness and spotting of furniture and rugs at this time, which can be annoying if she is a household companion in the habit of sharing your sofa or bed. As for the spayed bitch, she benefits as she grows older because this simple operation almost entirely eliminates the possibility of breast cancer ever occurring. It is recommended that all bitches eventually be spayed—even those used for show or breeding when their careers have ended—in order that they may enjoy a happier, healthier old age. Please take note, however, that a bitch who has been spayed (or an altered dog) *cannot be shown at American Kennel Club dog shows once this operation has been performed*. Be certain that you are *not* interested in showing her before taking this step.

Also, in selecting a pet, never underestimate the advantages of an older dog, perhaps a retired show dog or a bitch no longer needed for breeding, who may be available and quite reasonably priced by a breeder anxious to place such a dog in a loving home. These dogs are settled and can be a delight to own, as they make wonderful companions, especially in a household of adults where raising a puppy can sometimes be a trial.

Ch. Viscum Vellum, one of the foundations there, is to be found behind many of the currently winning Quissex dogs. An important dog in the history of the breed pictured here taking Best of Opposite Sex.

Ch. Foxglen's Spellbinder, by Can. Ch. Foxglen Man in Command ex Ch. Foxglen Envoy's Tamora. Bred and owned by Irene Rhodes, Foxglen Kennels, Sharpsville, Pennsylvania.

Everything that has been said about careful selection of your pet puppy and its place of purchase applies, but with many further considerations, when you plan to buy a show dog or foundation stock for a future breeding program. Now is the time for an indepth study of the breed, starting with every word and every illustration in this book and all others you can find written on the subject. The Standard of the breed has now become your guide, and you must learn not only the words but also how to interpret them and how to apply them to actual dogs before you are ready to make an intelligent selection of a show dog.

If you are thinking in terms of a dog to show, obviously you must have learned about dog shows and must be in the habit of attending them. This is fine, but now your activity in this direction should be increased, with your attending every single dog show within a reasonable distance from your home. Much can be learned about a breed at ringside at these events. Talk with the breeders who are exhibiting. Study the dogs they are showing. Watch the judging with concentration, noting each decision made, and attempt to follow the reasoning by which the judge has reached it. Note carefully the attributes of the dogs who win and, for your later use, the manner in which each is presented. Close your ears to the ringside know-it-alls, usually novice owners of a dog or two and very new to the Fancy, who have only derogatory remarks to make about all that is taking place unless they happen to win. This is the type of exhibitor who "comes and goes" through the Fancy and whose interest is usually of very short duration, owing to lack of knowledge and dissatisfaction caused by the failure to recognize the need to learn. You, as a fancier whom we hope will last and enjoy our sport over many future years, should develop independent thinking at this stage; you should learn to draw your own conclusions about the merits, or lack of them, seen before you in the ring and, thus, sharpen your own judgement in preparation for choosing wisely and well.

Note carefully which breeders campaign winning dogs—not just an occasional isolated good one, but consistent, homebred winners. It is from one of these people that you should select your own future "star."

If you are located in an area where dog shows take place only occasionally or where there are long travel distances involved, you will need to find another testing ground for your ability to select a worthy show dog. Possibly, there are some representative kennels raising this breed within a reasonable distance. If so, by all means ask permission of the owners to visit the kennels and do so when permission is granted. You may not necessarily buy then and there, as they may not have available what you are seeking that very day, but you will be able to see the type of dog being raised there and to discuss the dogs with the breeder. Every time you do this, you add to your knowledge. Should one of these kennels have dogs which especially appeal to you, perhaps you could reserve a show-prospect puppy from a coming litter. This is frequently done, and it is often worth waiting for a puppy, unless you have seen a dog with which you truly are greatly impressed and which is immediately available.

The purchase of a puppy has already been discussed. Obviously this same approach applies in a far greater degree when the purchase involved is a future show dog. The only place from which to purchase a show prospect is a breeder who raises show-type stock; otherwise, you are almost certainly doomed to disappointment as

234

Penda Pied Piper and Worsbro Wink, straight from quarantine in 1971. Important members of the Canbury Wire Kennels. Barbara A. Withers, Ebenezer, Australia.

the puppy matures. Show and breeding kennels obviously cannot keep all of their fine young stock. An active breeder-exhibitor is, therefore, happy to place promising youngsters in the hands of people also interested in showing and winning with them, doing so at a fair price according to the quality and prospects of the dog involved. Here again, if no kennel in your immediate area has what you are seeking, do not hesitate to contact top breeders in other areas and to buy at long distance. Ask for pictures, pedigrees, and a complete description. Heed the breeder's advice and recommendations, after truthfully telling exactly what your expectations are for the dog you purchase. Do you want something with which to win just a few ribbons now and then? Do you want a dog who can complete his championship? Are you thinking of the real "big time" (*i.e.*, seriously campaigning with Best of Breed, Group wins, and possibly even Best in Show as your eventual goal)? Consider it all carefully in advance; then honestly discuss your plans with the breeder. You will be better satisfied with the results if you do this, as the breeder is then in the best position to help you choose the dog who is most likely to come through for you. A breeder selling a show dog is just as anxious as the buyer for the dog to succeed, and the breeder will represent the dog to you with truth and honesty. Also, this type of breeder does not lose interest the moment the sale has been made but, when necessary, will be right there to assist you with beneficial advice and suggestions based on years of experience.

This is the famous breeder, Mrs. E.A. Kraft, Wynwyre Kennels in Michigan, watching with approval as handler George Ward sets up Ch. Wynwyre's Saddle for her inspection. Wynwyre produced many outstanding Wires who made names for themselves in the show ring. This photo is from the 1950s.

As you make inquiries of at least several kennels, keep in mind that show-prospect puppies are less expensive than mature show dogs, the latter often costing close to four figures, and sometimes more. The reason for this is that, with a puppy, there is always an element of chance, the possibility of it's developing unexpected faults as it matures or failing to develop the excellence and quality that earlier had seemed probable. There definitely is a risk factor in buying a show-prospect puppy. Sometimes all goes well, but occasionally the swan becomes an ugly duckling. Reflect on this as you consider available puppies and young adults. It just might be a good idea to go with a more mature, though more costly, dog if one you like is available.

When you buy a mature show dog, "what you see is what you get," and it is not likely to change beyond coat and condition, which are dependent on your care. Also advantageous for a novice owner is the fact that a mature dog of show quality almost certainly will have received show-ring training and probably match-show experience, which will make your earliest handling ventures much easier.

Frequently it is possible to purchase a beautiful dog who has completed championship but who, owing to similarity in bloodlines, is not needed for the breeder's future program. Here you have the opportunity of owning a champion, usually in the two-to-five-year-old range, which you can enjoy campaigning as a special (for Best of Breed competition) and which will be a settled, handsome dog for you and your family to enjoy with pride.

If you are planning foundation for a future kennel, concentrate on acquiring one or two really superior bitches. These need not be top show-quality, but they should represent your breed's finest producing bloodlines from a strain noted for producing quality, generation after generation. A proven matron who is already the dam of show-type puppies is, of course, the ideal selection; but these are usually difficult to obtain, no one being anxious to part with so valuable an asset. You just might strike it lucky, though, in which case you are off to a flying start. If you cannot find such a matron available, select a young bitch of finest background from top-producing lines who is herself of decent type, free of obvious faults, and of good quality.

Great attention should be paid to the pedigree of the bitch from whom you intend to breed. If not already known to you, try to see the sire and dam. It is generally agreed that someone starting with a breed should concentrate on a fine collection of topflight bitches and raise a few litters from these before considering keeping one's own stud dog. The practice of buying a stud and then breeding everything you own or acquire to that dog does not always work out well. It is better to take advantage of the many noted sires who are available to be used at stud, who represent all of the leading strains, and, in each case, to carefully select the one who in type and pedigree seems most compatible to each of your bitches, at least for your first several litters.

To summarize, if you want a "family dog" as a companion, it is best to buy it young and raise it according to the habits of your household. If you are buying a show dog, the more mature it is, the more certain you can be of its future beauty. If you are buying foundation stock for a kennel, then bitches are better, but they must be from the finest *producing* bloodlines.

When you buy a pure-bred dog that you are told is eligible for registration with the American Kennel Club, you are entitled to receive from the seller an application form which will enable you to register your dog. If the seller cannot give you the application form, you should demand and receive an identification of your dog, consisting of the name of the breed, the registered names and numbers of the sire and dam, the name of the breeder, and your dog's date of birth. If the litter of which your dog is a part is already recorded with the American Kennel Club, then the litter number is sufficient identification.

An amusing story accompanies this photo of Ted and George Ward taken years back at a Michigan Specialty. Ted Ward (proudly holding the trophy) had brought the Wire, Ch. Deko Druid, down from Canada to this show which Mrs. Thomas Carruthers III was judging. After she had made him Winners Dog, and without her knowledge, Mr. Carruthers bought the dog for their Hetherington Kennels. Mrs. Carruthers, still unaware that this had taken place, made Druid the Best of Variety. Upon leaving the ring, she was greeted with the news that the dog she had put up now was one of theirs.

A famous dog and famous people! Mrs. Joseph Urmston, judge, making the top award at the Western Fox Terrier Club of the Central States Specialty to Ch. Wynwyre's Satrap owned by Mr. and Mrs. John F. Kane of Miami, Florida, for whom George Ward is handling.

Do not be misled by promises of papers at some later date. Demand a registration application form or proper identification as described above. If neither is supplied, do not buy the dog. So warns the American Kennel Club, and this is especially important in the purchase of show or breeding stock.

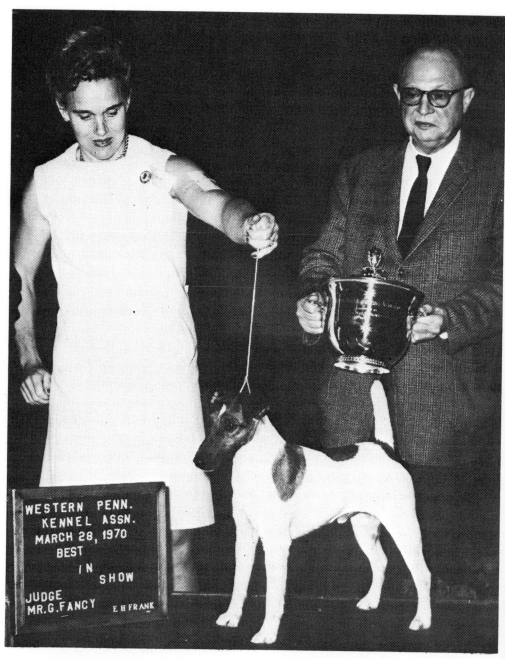

WESTERN PENN.
KENNEL ASSN.
MARCH 28, 1970
BEST
IN
SHOW
JUDGE
MR. G. FANCY   E.H.FRANK

Ch. Ellastone Fireflash taking Best in Show at Western Pennsylvania Kennel Association, March 1970. Jane Forsyth handling for Mr. and Mrs. James A. Farrell, Jr., Foxden Kennels, Darien, Connecticut.

Chapter 12

The Care of Your Fox Terrier Puppy

The moment you decide to be the new owner of a puppy is not one second too soon to start planning for the puppy's arrival in your home. Both the new family member and you will find the transition period easier if your home is geared in advance of the arrival.

The first things to be prepared are a bed for the puppy and a place where you can pen him up for rest periods. Every dog should have a crate of its own from the very beginning, so that he will come to know and love it as his special place where he is safe and happy. It is an ideal arrangement, for when you want him to be free, the crate stays open. At other times you can securely latch it and know that the pup is safely out of mischief. If you travel with him, his crate comes along in the car; and, of course, in traveling by plane there is no alternative but to have a carrier for the dog. If you show your dog, you will want him upon occasion to be in a crate a good deal of the day. So from every consideration, a crate is a very sensible and sound investment in your puppy's future safety and happiness and for your own peace of mind.

The crates most desirable are the wooden ones with removable side panels, which are ideal for cold weather (with the panels in place to keep out drafts) and in hot weather (with the panels removed to allow better air circulation). Wire crates are all right in the summer, but they give no protection from cold or drafts. Alu-

241

minum crates, due to the manner in which the metal reflects surrounding temperatures, are not recommended. If it is cold, so is the metal of the crate; if it is hot, the crate becomes burning hot.

When you choose the puppy's crate, be certain that it is roomy enough not to become outgrown. The crate should have sufficient height so the dog can stand up in it as a mature dog and sufficient area so that he can stretch out full length when relaxed. When the puppy is young, first give him shredded newspaper as a bed; the papers can be replaced with a mat or turkish towels when the dog is older. Carpet remnants are great for the bottom of the crate, as they are inexpensive and in case of accidents can be quite easily replaced. As the dog matures and is past the chewing age, a pillow or blanket in the crate is an appreciated comfort.

Sharing importance with the crate is a safe area in which the puppy can exercise and play. If you are an apartment dweller, a baby's playpen works out well for a young dog; for an older puppy use a portable exercise pen which you can use later when travelling with your dog or for dog shows. If you have a yard, an area where he can be outside in safety should be fenced in prior to the dog's arrival at your home. This area does not need to be huge, but it does need to be made safe and secure. If you are in a suburban area where there are close neighbors, stockade fencing works out best, as then the neighbors are less aware of the dog and the dog cannot see and bark at everything passing by. If you are out in the country where no problems with neighbors are likely to occur, then regular chain-link fencing is fine. For added precaution in both cases, use a row of concrete blocks or railroad ties inside against the entire bottom of the fence; this precludes or at least considerably lessens the chances of your dog digging his way out.

Be advised that if yours is a single dog, it is very unlikely that it will get sufficient exercise just sitting in the fenced area, which is what most of them do when they are there alone. Two or more dogs will play and move themselves around, but one by itself does little more than make a leisurely tour once around the area to check things over and then lie down. You must include a daily walk or two in your plans if your puppy is to be rugged and well. Exercise is extremely important to a puppy's muscular development and to keep a mature dog fit and trim. So make sure that those exercise periods, or walks, a game of ball, and other such activities, are part of your daily program as a dog owner.

If your fenced area has an outside gate, provide a padlock and key and a strong fastening for it, and use them, so that the gate cannot be opened by others and the dog taken or turned free. The ultimate convenience in this regard is, of course, a door (unused for other purposes) from the house around which the fenced area can be enclosed, so that all you have to do is open the door and out into his area he goes. This arrangement is safest of all, as then you need not be using a gate, and it is easier in bad weather since then you can send the dog out without taking him and becoming soaked yourself at the same time. This is not always possible to manage, but if your house is arranged so that you could do it this way, you would never regret it due to the convenience and added safety thus provided. Fencing in the entire yard, with gates to be opened and closed whenever a caller, deliveryman, postman, or some other person comes on your property, really is not safe at all because people not used to gates are frequently careless about closing and latching them *securely*. Many heartbreaking incidents have been brought about by someone carelessly half closing a gate (which the owner had thought to be firmly latched) and the dog wandering out. For greatest security a fenced *area* definitely takes precedence over a fenced *yard*.

The puppy will need a collar (one that fits now, not one to be grown into) and a lead from the moment you bring him home. Both should be an appropriate weight and type for his size. Also needed are a feeding dish and a water dish, both made preferably of unbreakable material. Your pet supply shop should have an interesting assortment of these and other accessories from which you can choose. Then you will need grooming tools of the type the breeder recommends and some toys. Equally satisfactory is Nylabone®, a nylon bone that does not chip or splinter and that "frizzles" as the puppy chews, providing healthful gum massage. Avoid plastics and any sort of rubber toys, *particularly those with squeakers* which the puppy may remove and swallow. If you want a ball for the puppy to use when playing with him, select one of very hard construction made for this purpose and do not leave it alone with him because he may chew off and swallow bits of the rubber. Take the ball with you when the game is over. This also applies to some of those "tug of war" type rubber toys which are fun when used with the two of you for that purpose but again should *not* be left behind for the dog to work on with his teeth.

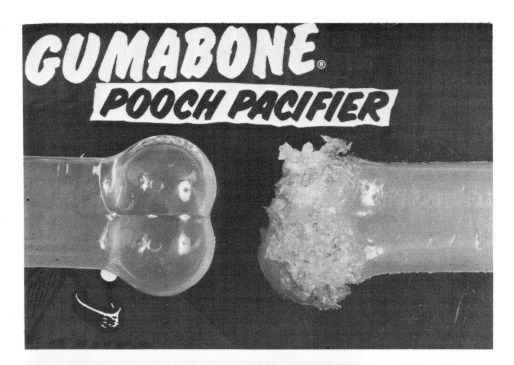

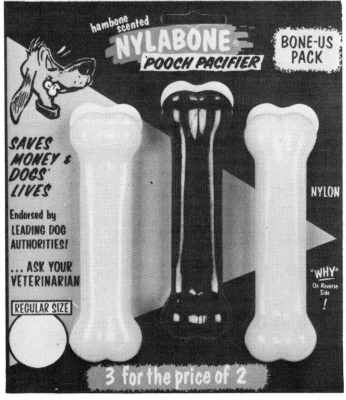

Gumabones® and Nylabones® are therapeutic devices, not toys, manufactured in a range of sizes (petite to giant). Made of non-toxic synthetic materials, they will not harm a dog's gums and teeth. Any tiny sliver swallowed is eliminated harmlessly.

Bits of swallowed rubber, squeakers, and other such foreign articles can wreak great havoc in the intestinal tract—do all you can to guard against them.

Too many changes all at once can be difficult for a puppy. For at least the first few days he is with you, keep him on the food and feeding schedule to which he is accustomed. Find out ahead of time from the breeder what he feeds his puppies, how frequently, and at what times of the day. Also find out what, if any, food supplements the breeder has been using and recommends. Then be prepared by getting in a supply of the same food so that you will have it there when you bring the puppy home. Once the puppy is accustomed to his new surroundings, then you can switch the type of food and schedule to fit your convenience, but for the first several days do it as the puppy expects.

Your selection of a veterinarian should also be attended to before the puppy comes home, because you should stop at the vet's office for the puppy to be checked over as soon as you leave the breeder's premises. If the breeder is from your area, ask him for recommendations. Ask you dog-owning friends for their opinions of the local veterinarians, and see what their experiences with those available have been. Choose someone whom several of your friends recommend highly, then contact him about your puppy, perhaps making an appointment to stop in at his office. If the premises are clean, modern, and well equipped, and if you like the veterinarian, make an appointment to bring the puppy in on the day of purchase. Be sure to obtain the puppy's health record from the breeder, including information on such things as shots and worming that the puppy has had.

JOINING THE FAMILY

Remember that, exciting and happy an occasion as it is for you, the puppy's move from his place of birth to your home can be, for him, a traumatic experience. His mother and littermates will be missed. He quite likely will be awed or frightened by the change of surroundings. The person on whom he depended will be gone. Everything should be planned to make his arrival at your home pleasant—to give him confidence and to help him realize that yours is a pretty nice place to be after all.

Never bring a puppy home on a holiday. There is just too much going on with people and gifts and excitement. If he is in honor of an "occasion," work it out so that his arrival will be a few days earlier, or perhaps even better, a few days later than the "occasion." Then your home will be back to its normal routine and the puppy can enjoy your undivided attention. Try not to bring the puppy home in the evening. Early morning is the ideal time, as then he has the opportunity of getting acquainted and the initial strangeness should wear off before bedtime. You will find it a more peaceful night that way. Allow the puppy to investigate as he likes, under your watchful eye. If you already have a pet in the household, keep a careful watch that the relationship between the two gets off to a friendly start or you may quickly find yourself with a lasting problem. Much of the future attitude of each toward the other will depend on what takes place that first day, so keep your mind on what they are doing and let your other activities slide for the moment. Be careful not to let your older pet become jealous by paying more attention to the puppy than to him, as that will start a bad situation immediately.

If you have a child, here again it is important that the relationship start out well. Before the puppy is brought home, you should have a talk with the youngster. He must clearly understand that puppies are fragile and can easily be injured; therefore, they should not be teased, hurt, mauled, or overly rough-housed. A puppy is not an inanimate toy; it is a living thing with a right to be loved and handled respectfully, treatment which will reflect in the dog's attitude toward your child as both mature together. Never permit your children's playmates to mishandle the puppy, tormenting the puppy until it turns on the children in self-defense. Children often do not realize how rough is too rough. You, as a responsible adult, are obligated to assure that your puppy's relationship with children is a pleasant one.

Do not start out by spoiling your puppy. A puppy is usually pretty smart and can be quite demanding. What you had considered to be "just for tonight" may be accepted by the puppy as "for keeps." Be firm with him, strike a routine, and stick to it. The puppy will learn more quickly this way, and everyone will be happier as a result. A radio playing softly or a dim night light are often comforting to a puppy as it gets accustomed to new surroundings and should be provided in preference to bringing the puppy to bed with you—unless, of course, you intend him to share the bed as a permanent arrangement.

SOCIALIZING AND TRAINING

Socialization and training of your puppy should start the very day of his arrival in your home. Never address him without calling him by name. A short, simple name is the easiest to teach as it catches the dog's attention quickly; avoid elaborate call names. Always address the dog by the same name, not a whole series of pet names; the latter will only confuse the puppy.

Use his name clearly, and call the puppy over to you when you see him awake and wandering about. When he comes, make a big fuss over him for being such a good dog. He thus will quickly associate the sound of his name with coming to you and a pleasant happening.

Several hours after the puppy's arrival is not too soon to start accustoming him to the feel of a light collar. He may hardly notice it; or he may struggle, roll over, and try to rub it off his neck with his paws. Divert his attention when this occurs by offering a tasty snack or a toy (starting a game with him) or by petting him. Before long he will have accepted the strange feeling around his neck and no longer appear aware of it. Next comes the lead. Attach it and then immediately take the puppy outside or otherwise try to divert his attention with things to see and sniff. He may struggle against the lead at first, biting at it and trying to free himself. Do not pull him with it at this point; just hold the end loosely and try to follow him if he starts off in any direction. Normally his attention will soon turn to investigating his surroundings if he is outside or you have taken him into an unfamiliar room in your house; curiosity will take over and he will become interested in sniffing around the surroundings. Follow him with the lead slackly held until he seems to have completely forgotten about it; then try with gentle urging to get him to follow you. Don't be rough or jerk at him; just tug gently on the lead in short quick motions (steady pulling can become a battle of wills), repeating his name or trying to get him to follow your hand which is holding a bite of food or an interesting toy. If you have an older lead-trained dog, then it should be a cinch to get the puppy to follow along after *him*. In any event the average puppy learns quite quickly and will soon be trotting along nicely on the lead. Once that point has been reached, the next step is to teach him to follow on your left side, or heel. This will not likely be accomplished all in one day; it should be done with short training periods over the course of sev-

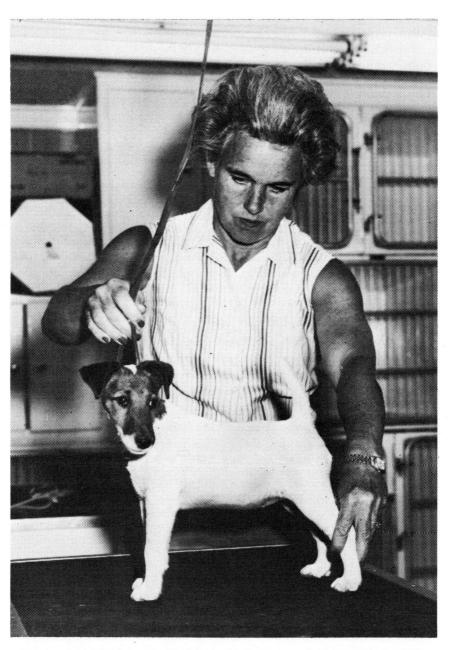

Show prospect puppies should be taught from an early age to stand and be "stacked" on a table. Note the sophistication of the future Foxden Smooth champion as Jane Forsyth teaches the fundamentals of good table manners.

eral days until you are satisfied with the result.

During the course of house training your puppy, you will need to take him out frequently and at regular intervals: first thing in the morning directly from the crate, immediately after meals, after the puppy has been napping, or when you notice that the puppy is looking for a spot. Choose more or less the same place to take the puppy each time so that a pattern will be established. If he does not go immediately, do not return him to the house as he will probably relieve himself the moment he is inside. Stay out with him until he has finished; then be lavish with your praise for his good behavior. If you catch the puppy having an accident indoors, grab him firmly and rush him outside, sharply saying "No!" as you pick him up. If you do not see the accident occur, there is little point in doing anything except cleaning it up, as once it has happened and been forgotten, the puppy will most likely not even realize why you are scolding him.

If you live in a big city or are away many hours at a time, having a dog that is trained to go on paper has some very definite advantages. To do this, one proceeds pretty much the same way as taking the puppy outdoors, except now you place the puppy on the newspaper at the proper time. The paper should always be kept in the same spot. An easy way to paper train a puppy if you have a playpen for it or an exercise pen is to line the area with newspapers; then gradually, every day or so, remove a section of newspaper until you are down to just one or two. The puppy acquires the habit of using the paper; and as the prepared area grows smaller, in the majority of cases the dog will continue to use whatever paper is still available. It is pleasant, if the dog is alone for an excessive length of time, to be able to feel that if he needs it the paper is there and will be used.

The puppy should form the habit of spending a certain amount of time in his crate, even when you are home. Sometimes the puppy will do this voluntarily, but if not, he should be taught to do so, which is accomplished by leading the puppy over by his collar, gently pushing him inside, and saying firmly, "Down" or "Stay." Whatever expression you use to give a command, stick to the very same one each time for each act. Repetition is the big thing in training—and so is association with what the dog is expected to do. When you mean "Sit," always say exactly that. "Stay" should mean *only* that the dog should remain where he receives the command. "Down" means something else again. Do not confuse the dog by shuffling the commands, as this will create training problems for you.

As soon as he had had his immunization shots, take your puppy with you whenever and wherever possible. There is nothing that will build a self-confident, stable dog like socialization, and it is extremely important that you plan and give the time and energy necessary for this, whether your dog is to be a show dog or a pleasant, well-adjusted family member. Take your puppy in the car so that he will learn to enjoy riding and not become carsick, as dogs may do if they are infrequent travelers. Take him any-where you are going where you are certain he will be welcome: visiting friends and relatives (if they do not have housepets who may resent the visit), busy shopping centers (keeping him always on lead), or just walking around the streets of your town. If some-one admires him (as always seems to happen when one is out with puppies), encourage the stranger to pet and talk with him. Social-ization of this type brings out the best in your puppy and helps him to grow up with a friendly outlook, liking the world and its inhabitants. The worst thing that can be done to a puppy's per-sonality is to shelter him. By always keeping him at home away from things and people unfamiliar to him, you may be creating a personality problem for the mature dog that will be a cross for you to bear later on.

FEEDING YOUR DOG

Time was when providing nourishing food for dogs involved a far more complicated procedure than people now feel is necessary. The old school of thought was that the daily ration must consist of fresh beef, vegetables, cereal, egg yolks, and cottage cheese as basics with such additions as brewer's yeast and vitamin tablets on a daily basis.

During recent years, however, many minds have changed re-garding this procedure. Eggs, cottage cheese, and supplements to the diet are still given, but the basic method of feeding dogs has changed; and the change has been, in the opinion of many author-ities, definitely for the better. The school of thought now is that you are doing your dogs a favor when you feed them some of the fine commercially prepared dog foods in preference to your own home-cooked concoctions.

250

Fortune's Blackjack was a Christmas gift from Winnie Stout to Lisa Sachs. At his first show he went Winners Dog for a 5-point major, owner-handled, age ten months. Lisa hopes that he will complement the Quissex bitches in her kennel, and that eventually he will take over as "top dog" at her kennel.

The reason behind this new outlook is easily understandable. The dog food industry has grown to be a major one, participated in by some of the best known and most respected names in America. These trusted firms, it is agreed, turn out excellent products, so people are feeding their dog food preparations with confidence and the dogs are thriving, living longer, happier, and healthier lives than ever before. What more could one want?

There are at least half a dozen absolutely top-grade dry foods to be mixed with broth or water and served to your dog according to directions. There are all sorts of canned meats, and there are several kinds of "convenience foods," those in a packet which you open and dump out into the dog's dish. It is just that simple. The convenience foods are neat and easy to use when you are away from home, but generally speaking a dry food mixed with hot water (or soup) and meat is preferred. It is the opinion of many that the canned meat, with its added fortifiers, is more beneficial to the dogs than the fresh meat. However, the two can be alternated or, if you prefer and your dog does well on it, by all means use fresh ground beef. A dog enjoys changes in the meat part of his diet, which is easy with the canned food since all sorts of beef are available (chunk, ground, stewed, and so on), plus lamb, chicken, and even such concoctions as liver and egg, plain liver flavor, and a blend of five meats.

There is also prepared food geared to every age bracket of your dog's life, from puppyhood on through old age, with special additions or modifications to make it particularly nourishing and beneficial. Previous generations never had it so good where the canine dinner is concerned, because these commercially prepared foods are tasty and geared to meeting the dog's gastronomic approval.

Additionally, contents and nutrients are clearly listed on the labels, as are careful instructions for feeding just the right amount for the size, weight, and age of each dog.

With these foods the addition of extra vitamins is not necessary, but if you prefer there are several kinds of those, too, that serve as taste treats as well as being beneficial. Your pet supplier has a full array of them.

Of course there is no reason not to cook up something for your dog if you would feel happier doing so. But it seems unnecessary when such truly satisfactory rations are available with so much less trouble and expense.

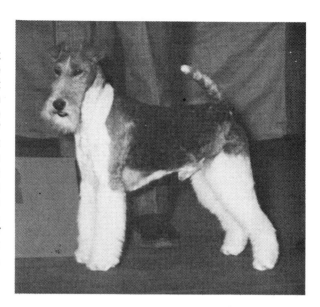

Ch. Sunnybrook Spot On winning the Terrier Group at Westminster in 1974. One of the outstanding "greats" among Wire Fox Terriers, Spot On soon after this win retired to live as "family dog" with Dan Kiedrowski, publisher of *Terrier Type* magazine, in California.

How often you feed your dog is a matter of how it works out best for you. Many owners prefer to do it once a day. It is generally agreed that two meals, each of smaller quantity, are better for the digestion and more satisfying to the dog, particularly if yours is a household member who stands around and watches preparations for the family meals. Do not overfeed. This is the shortest route to all sorts of problems. Follow directions and note carefully how your dog is looking. If your dog is overweight, cut back the quantity of food a bit. If the dog looks thin, then increase the amount. Each dog is an individual and the food intake should be adjusted to his requirements to keep him feeling and looking trim and in top condition.

From the time puppies are fully weaned until they are about twelve weeks old, they should be fed four times daily. From three months to six months of age, three meals should suffice. At six months of age the puppies can be fed two meals, and the twice daily feedings can be continued until the puppies are close to one year old, at which time feeding can be changed to once daily if desired. If you do feed just once a day, do so by early afternoon at the latest and give the dog a snack, a biscuit or two, at bedtime.

Remember that plenty of fresh water should always be available to your puppy or dog for drinking. This is of utmost importance to his health.

Westminster 1983. This photo snapped during the judging of the Terrier Group shows Wood Wornall (*right*) with the Wire Ch. Dynamic Super Sensation; and Ch. Kraehollow Morning Mist, by Ch. Kraehollow Kavalier ex Kraehollow The Boxer, owned by Martha Riekenberg and Lynn Sparks, handled by "Fitzie" who was an assistant to Ric Chashoudian. These two Fox Terriers had been adjudged Best Wire and Best Smooth at this event.

254

Chapter 13

The Making of a Show Dog

If you have decided to become a show dog exhibitor, you have accepted a very real and very exciting challenge. The groundwork has been accomplished with the selection of your future show prospect. If you have purchased a puppy, it is assumed that you have gone through all the proper preliminaries concerning good care, which should be the same if the puppy is a pet or future show dog, with a few added precautions for the latter.

GENERAL CONSIDERATIONS

Remember the importance of keeping your future winner in trim, top condition. Since you want him neither too fat nor too thin, his appetite for his proper diet should be guarded, and children and guests should not be permitted to constantly feed him "goodies." The best treat of all is a small wad of raw ground beef or a packaged dog treat. To be avoided are ice cream, cake, cookies, potato chips, and other fattening items which will cause the dog to put on weight and may additionally spoil his appetite for the proper, nourishing, well-balanced diet so essential to good health and condition.

The importance of temperament and showmanship cannot possibly be overestimated. They have put many a mediocre dog across, while lack of them can ruin the career of an otherwise outstanding specimen. From the day your dog joins your family, socialize him. Keep him accustomed to being with people and to being handled by people. Encourage your friends and relatives to "go over" him as the judges will in the ring so this will not seem a strange and upsetting experience. Practice showing his "bite" (the manner in which his teeth meet) quickly and deftly. It is quite simple to slip the lips apart with your fingers, and the puppy should be willing to accept this from you or the judge without struggle.

Some judges prefer that the exhibitors display the dog's bite and other mouth features themselves. These are the considerate ones, who do not wish to chance the spreading of possible infection from dog to dog with their hands on each one's mouth—a courtesy particularly appreciated in these days of virus epidemics. But the old-fashioned judges still persist in doing it themselves, so the dog should be ready for either possibility.

Ch. Trucote Surprise was one of the early Wires owned by Mrs. Leonard J.A. Smit prior to her marriage to Joseph Urmston. This 1946 photo depicts Surprise winning under judge Tom Keator (*right*), as George Hartman (*center*) presents trophy to George Ward who is handling.

Take your future show dog with you in the car, thus accustoming him to riding so that he will not become carsick on the day of a dog show. He should associate pleasure and attention with going in the car, van, or motor home. Take him where it is crowded: downtown, to the shops, everywhere you go that dogs are permitted. Make the expeditions fun for him by frequent petting and words of praise; do not just ignore him as you go about your errands.

Do not overly shelter your future show dog. Instinctively you may want to keep him at home where he is safe from germs or danger. This can be foolish on two counts. The first reason is that a puppy kept away from other dogs builds up no natural immunity against all the things with which he will come in contact at dog shows, so it is wiser to keep him up-to-date on all protective shots and then let him become accustomed to being among dogs and dog owners. Also, a dog who is never among strange people, in strange places, or among strange dogs may grow up with a shyness or timidity of spirit that will cause you real problems as his show career draws near.

Keep your show prospect's coat in immaculate condition with frequent grooming and daily brushing. When bathing is necessary, use a mild dog shampoo or whatever the breeder of your puppy may suggest. Several of the brand-name products do an excellent job. Be sure to rinse thoroughly so as not to risk skin irritation by traces of soap left behind, and protect against soap entering the eyes by a drop of castor oil in each before you lather up. Use warm water (be sure it is not uncomfortably hot or chillingly cold) and a good spray. Make certain you allow your dog to dry thoroughly in a warm, draft-free area (or outdoors, if it is warm and sunny) so that he doesn't catch cold. Then proceed to groom him to perfection.

A show dog's teeth must be kept clean and free of tartar. Hard dog biscuits can help toward this, but if tartar accumulates, see that it is removed promptly by your veterinarian. Bones for chewing are not suitable for show dogs as they tend to damage and wear down the tooth enamel.

Assuming that you will be handling the dog yourself, or even if he will be professionally handled, a few moments each day of dog show routine is important. Practice setting him up as you have seen the exhibitors do at the shows you've attended, and teach him to hold this position once you have him stacked to your satis-

Ch. Mutiny Mainstay of Glenarden, owned by Denny Ross and handled by Ric Chashoudian, was a Best in Show dog, and also a Santa Barbara Terrier Group winner during a short career in the show ring.

faction. Make the learning period pleasant by being firm but lavish in your praise when he responds correctly. Teach him to gait at your side at a moderate rate on a loose lead. When you have mastered the basic essentials at home, then hunt out and join a training class for future work. Training classes are sponsored by show-giving clubs in many areas, and their popularity is steadily increasing. If you have no other way of locating one, perhaps your veterinarian would know of one through some of his other clients; but if you are sufficiently aware of the dog show world to want a show dog, you will probably be personally acquainted with other people who will share information of this type with you.

Accustom your show dog to being in a crate (which you should be doing with a pet dog as well). He should relax in his crate at the shows "between times" for his own well being and safety.

MATCH SHOWS

Your show dog's initial experience in the ring should be in match show competition. This type of event is intended as a learning experience for both the dog and the exhibitor. You will not feel embarrassed or out of place no matter how poorly your puppy may behave or how inept your attempts at handling may be, as you will find others there with the same type of problems. The important thing is that you get the puppy out and into a show ring where the two of you can practice together and learn the ropes.

Only on rare occasions is it necessary to make match show entries in advance, and even those with a pre-entry policy will usually accept entries at the door as well. Thus you need not plan several weeks ahead, as is the case with point shows, but can go when the mood strikes you. Also there is a vast difference in the cost, as match show entries only cost a few dollars while entry fees for the point shows may be over ten dollars, an amount none of us needs to waste until we have some idea of how the puppy will behave or how much more pre-show training is needed.

Match shows are frequently judged by professional handlers who, in addition to making the awards, are happy to help new exhibitors with comments and advice on their puppies and their presentation of them. Avail yourself of all these opportunities before heading out to the sophisticated world of the point shows.

POINT SHOWS

As previously mentioned, entries for American Kennel Club point shows must be made in advance. This must be done on an official entry blank of the show-giving club. The entry must then be filed either personally or by mail with the show superintendent or the show secretary (if the event is being run by the club members alone and a superintendent has not been hired, this information will appear on the premium list) in time to reach its destination prior to the published closing date or filling of the quota. These entries must be made carefully, must be signed by the owner of the dog or the owner's agent (your professional handler), and must be accompanied by the entry fee; otherwise they will not be accepted. Remember that it is not when the entry leaves your hands that counts, but the date of arrival at its destination. If you are relying on the mails, which are not always dependable, get the entry off well before the deadline to avoid disappointment.

A dog must be entered at a dog show in the name of the actual owner at the time of the entry closing date of that specific show. If a registered dog has been acquired by a new owner, it must be entered in the name of the new owner in any show for which entries close after the date of acquirement, regardless of whether the new owner has or has not actually received the registration certificate indicating that the dog is recorded in his name. State on the entry form whether or not transfer application has been mailed to the American Kennel Club, and it goes without saying that the latter should be attended to promptly when you purchase a registered dog.

In filling out your entry blank, type, print, or write clearly, paying particular attention to the spelling of names, correct registration numbers, and so on. Also, if there is more than one variety in your breed, be sure to indicate into which category your dog is being entered.

The **Puppy Class** is for dogs or bitches who are six months of age and under twelve months and who are not champions. The age of a dog shall be calculated up to and inclusive of the first day of a show. For example, the first day a dog whelped on January 1st is eligible to compete in a Puppy Class at a show is July 1st of the same year; and he may continue to compete in Puppy Classes up to and including a show on December 31 of the same year, but

Ms. Marcia A. Foy (*left*), co-author, with Am. and Can. Ch. Bullseye Seasprite. By Ch. Foxmoor Macho Macho Man ex Ch. Battle Cry Bionic. This Smooth is one of the current champions from Quissex Smooth Fox Terriers, Mrs. Winifred Stout, Foster, Rhode Island.

BEST OF
OPPOSITE
TROY
KENNEL CLUB
1985   DAVE ASHBEY

Here, at Morris and Essex in 1946, Ch. Wynwyre's Pamela won under the famed authority Stanley J. Halle (Halleston Kennels) for Mr. and Mrs. E.A. Kraft. Handled by George Ward.

he is *not* eligible to compete in a Puppy Class at a show held on or after January 1 of the following year.

The Puppy Class is the first one in which you should enter your puppy. In it a certain allowance will be made for the fact that they *are* puppies, thus an immature dog or one displaying less than perfect showmanship will be less severely penalized than, for instance, would be the case in Open. It is also quite likely that others in the class will be suffering from these problems, too. When you enter a puppy, be sure to check the classification with care, as some shows divide their Puppy Class into a 6-9 months old section and a 9-12 months old section.

The **Novice Class** is for dogs six months of age and over, whelped in the United States or Canada, who *prior to the official closing date for entries* have *not* won three first prizes in the Novice Class, any first prize at all in the Bred-by-Exhibitor, American-bred, or Open Classes, or one or more points toward championship. The provisions for this class are confusing to many people, which is probably the reason exhibitors do not enter in it more frequently. A dog may win any number of first prizes in the Puppy Class and still retain his eligibility for Novice. He may place second, third, or fourth not only in Novice on an unlimited number of occasions, but also in Bred-by-Exhibitor, American-bred and Open and still remain eligible for Novice. But he may no longer be shown in Novice when he has won three blue ribbons in that class, when he has won even one blue ribbon in either Bred-by-Exhibitor, American-bred, or Open, or when he has won a single championship point.

In determining whether or not a dog is eligible for the Novice Class, keep in mind the fact that previous wins are calculated ac-

Ch. Holmwire Tudor Reliant, by Holmwire Tudor Renown ex Secichad Girl, was imported by Ric Chashoudian from Charlie Higginson in England, then sold to Steve and Bella Farber in Englewood, Colorado. He was a Westminster Group winner and had 24 all-breed Bests in Show under Mr. Chashoudian's handling.

Ch. Brimtina Quissex Bella, by Am. and Can. Ch. Battle Cry Brimstone ex Foxden Gleam, was bred by Phyllis Gratton (Canada) and is owned by George O'Donnell. Taking Winners at Westchester in 1985.

cording to the official published date for closing of entries, not by the date on which you may actually have made the entry. So if in the interim, between the time you made the entry and the official closing date, your dog makes a win causing him to become ineligible for Novice, change your class *immediately* to another for which he will be eligible, preferably either Bred-by-Exhibitor or American-bred. To do this, you must contact the show's superintendent or secretary, at first by telephone to save time and then in writing to confirm it. The Novice Class always seems to have the fewest entries of any class, and therefore it is a splendid "practice ground" for you and your young dog while you are getting the "feel" of being in the ring.

Bred-by-Exhibitor Class is for dogs whelped in the United States or, if individually registered in the American Kennel Club Stud Book, for dogs whelped in Canada who are six months of age or older, are not champions, and are owned wholly or in part by the person or by the spouse of the person who was the breeder or one of the breeders of record. Dogs entered in this class must be handled in the class by an owner or by a member of the immediate family of the owner. Members of an immediate family for this purpose are husband, wife, father, mother, son, daughter, brother, or sister. This is the class which is really the "breeders' showcase," and the one which breeders should enter with particular pride to show off their achievements.

The **American-bred Class** is for all dogs excepting champions, six months of age or older, who were whelped in the United States by reason of a mating which took place in the United States.

The **Open Class** is for any dog six months of age or older (this is the only restriction for this class). Dogs with championship points compete in it, dogs who are already champions are eligible to do so, dogs who are imported can be entered, and, of course, American-bred dogs compete in it. This class is, for some strange reason, the favorite of exhibitors who are "out to win." They rush to enter their pointed dogs in it, under the false impression that by doing so they assure themselves of greater attention from the judges. This really is not so, and some people feel that to enter in one of the less competitive classes, with a better chance of winning it and thus earning a second opportunity of gaining the judge's approval by returning to the ring in the Winners Class, can often be a more effective strategy.

One does not enter the **Winners Class.** One earns the right to compete in it by winning first prize in Puppy, Novice, Bred-by-Exhibitor, American-bred, or Open. No dog who has been defeated on the same day in one of these classes is eligible to compete for Winners, and every dog who has been a blue-ribbon winner in one of them and not defeated in another, should he have been entered in more than one class (as occasionally happens), *must* do so. Following the selection of the Winners Dog or the Winners Bitch, the dog or bitch receiving that award leaves the ring. Then the dog or bitch who placed second in that class, unless previously beaten by another dog or bitch in another class at the same show, re-enters the ring to compete against the remaining first-prize winners for Reserve. The latter award indicates that the dog or bitch selected for it is standing "in reserve" should the one who received Winners be disqualified or declared ineligible through any technicality when the awards are checked at the American Kennel Club. In that case, the one who placed Reserve is moved up to Winners, at the same time receiving the appropriate championship points.

Winners Dog and Winners Bitch are the awards which carry points toward championship with them. The points are based on the number of dogs or bitches actually in competition, and the points are scaled one through five, the latter being the greatest number available to any one dog or bitch at any one show. Three-, four-, or five-point wins are considered majors. In order to become a champion, a dog or bitch must have won two majors under two different judges, plus at least one point from a third judge, and the additional points necessary to bring the total to fifteen. When your dog has gained fifteen points as described above, a championship certificate will be issued to you, and your dog's name will be published in the champions of record list in the *Pure-Bred Dogs/American Kennel Gazette*, the official publication of the American Kennel Club.

The scale of championship points for each breed is worked out by the American Kennel Club and reviewed annually, at which time the number required in competition may be either changed (raised or lowered) or remain the same. The scale of championship points for all breeds is published annually in the May issue of the *Gazette*, and the current ratings for each breed within that area are published in every show catalog.

Ch. Foxbank Entertainer was handled by George Ward in the early 1950s for Harold and Sue Florsheim. Winner of 30 Group 1sts and who went on to Best in Show 20 times. A truly superb Wire with a most prestigious record.

Ch. Dundrum Super Star winning the Terrier Group at Wheaton K.C. in 1966. A Best In Show and Multiple Group winner, George Ward handled this noted Wire for Jean Holmes and Betty Scott.

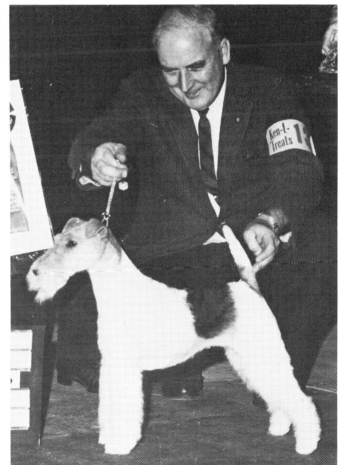

When a dog or bitch is adjudged Best of Winners, its champion-ship points are, for that show, compiled on the basis of which sex had the greater number of points. If there are two points in dogs and four in bitches and the dog goes Best of Winners, then *both* the dog and the bitch are awarded an equal number of points, in this case four. Should the Winners Dog or the Winners Bitch go on to win Best of Breed or Best of Variety, additional points are accorded for the additional dogs and bitches defeated by so doing, provided, of course, that there were entries specifically for Best of Breed competition or Specials, as these specific entries are called.

If your dog or bitch takes Best of Opposite Sex after going Win-ners, points are credited according to the number of the same sex defeated in both the regular classes and Specials competition. If Best of Winners is also won, then whatever additional points for each of these awards are available will be credited. Many a one- or two-point win has grown into a major in this manner.

Moving further along, should your dog win its **Variety Group** from the classes (in other words, if it has taken either Winners Dog or Winners Bitch), you then receive points based on the greatest number of points awarded to any member of any breed included within that Group during that show's competition. Should the day's winning also include Best in Show, the same rule of thumb applies, and your dog or bitch receives the highest num-ber of points awarded to any other dog of any breed at that event.

Best of Breed competition consists of the Winners Dog and the Winners Bitch, who automatically compete on the strength of those awards, in addition to whatever dogs and bitches have been entered specifically for this class for which champions of record are eligible. Since July 1980, dogs who, according to their owner's records, have completed the requirements for a championship af-ter the closing of entries for the show (but whose championships are unconfirmed) may be transferred from one of the regular classes to the Best of Breed competition, provided this transfer is made by the show superir tendent or show secretary *prior to the start of any judging at the show.*

This has proved an extremely popular new rule, as under it a dog can finish on Saturday and then be transferred and compete as a Special on Sunday. It must be emphasized that *the change must be made prior to the start of any part of the day's judging, not for just your individual breed.*

In the United States, Best of Breed winners are entitled to compete in the Variety Group which includes them. This is not mandatory; it is a privilege which exhibitors value. (In Canada, Best of Breed winners *must* compete in the Variety Group or they lose any points already won.) The dogs winning *first* in each of the seven Variety Groups *must* compete for Best in Show. Missing the opportunity of taking your dog in for competition in its Group is foolish, as it is there where the general public is most likely to notice your breed and become interested in learning about it.

Non-regular classes are sometimes included at the all-breed shows, and they are almost invariably included at Specialty shows. These include Stud Dog Class and Brood Bitch Class, which are judged on the basis of the quality of the two offspring accompanying the sire or dam. The quality of the latter two is beside the point and should not be considered by the judge; it is the youngsters who count, and the quality of *both* are to be averaged to decide which sire or dam is the best and most consistent producer. Then there is the Brace Class (which, at all-breed shows, moves up to Best Brace in each Variety Group and then Best Brace in Show) which is judged on the similarity and evenness of appearance of the two brace members. In other words, the two dogs should look like identical twins in size, color, and conformation and should move together almost as a single dog, one person handling with precision and ease. The same applies to the Team Class competition, except that four dogs are involved and, if necessary, two handlers.

The Veterans Class is for the older dog, the minimum age of whom is seven years. This class is judged on the quality of the dogs, as the winner competes in Best of Breed competition and has, on a respectable number of occasions, been known to take that top award. So the point is *not* to pick out the oldest dog, as some judges seem to believe, but the best specimen of the breed, exactly as in the regular classes.

Then there are Sweepstakes and Futurity Stakes sponsored by many Specialty clubs, sometimes as part of their regular Specialty shows and sometimes as separate events on an entirely different occasion. The difference between the two stakes is that Sweepstakes entries usually include dogs from six to eighteen months of age with entries made at the same time as the others for the show, while for a Futurity the entries are bitches nominated when bred and the individual puppies entered at or shortly following their birth.

JUNIOR SHOWMANSHIP COMPETITION

If there is a youngster in your family between the ages of ten and sixteen, there is no better or more rewarding hobby than becoming an active participant in Junior Showmanship. This is a marvelous activity for young people. It teaches responsibility, good sportsmanship, the fun of competition where one's own skills are the deciding factor of success, proper care of a pet, and how to socialize with other young folks. Any youngster may experience the thrill of emerging from the ring a winner and the satisfaction of a good job well done.

Entry in Junior Showmanship Classes is open to any boy or girl who is at least ten years old and under seventeen years old on the day of the show. The Novice Junior Showmanship Class is open to youngsters who have not already won, at the time the entries close, three firsts in this class. Youngsters who have won three firsts in Novice may compete in the Open Junior Showmanship Class. Any junior handler who wins his third first-place award in Novice may participate in the Open Class at the same show, provided that the Open Class has at least one other junior handler entered and competing in it that day. The Novice and Open Classes may be divided into Junior and Senior Classes. Youngsters between the ages of ten and twelve, inclusively, are eligible for the Junior division; and youngsters between thirteen and seventeen, inclusively, are eligible for the Senior division.

Any of the foregoing classes may be separated into individual classes for boys and for girls. If such a division is made, it must be so indicated on the premium list. The premium list also indicates the prize for Best Junior Handler, if such a prize is being offered at the show. Any youngster who wins a first in any of the regular classes may enter the competition for this prize, provided the youngster has been undefeated in any other Junior Showmanship Class at that show.

Junior Showmanship Classes, unlike regular conformation classes in which the quality of the dog is judged, are judged solely on the skill and ability of the junior handling the dog. Which dog is best is not the point—it is which youngster does the best job with the dog that is under consideration. Eligibility requirements for the dog being shown in Junior Showmanship, and other detailed information, can be found in *Regulations for Junior Showmanship*, available from the American Kennel Club.

A junior who has a dog that he or she can enter in both Junior Showmanship and conformation classes has twice the opportunity for success and twice the opportunity to get into the ring and work with the dog, a combination which can lead to not only awards for expert handling, but also, if the dog is of sufficient quality, for making a conformation champion.

PRE-SHOW PREPARATIONS

Preparation of the items you will need as a dog show exhibitor should not be left until the last moment. They should be planned and arranged several days in advance of the show in order for you to remain calm and relaxed as the countdown starts.

The importance of the crate has already been mentioned and should already be part of your equipment. Of equal importance is the grooming table, which very likely you have also already acquired for use at home. You should take it along with you to the shows, as your dog will need last minute touches before entering the ring. Should you have not yet made this purchase, folding tables with rubber tops are made specifically for this purpose and can be purchased at most dog shows, where concession booths with marvelous assortments of "doggy" necessities are to be found, or at your pet supplier. You will also need a sturdy tack box (also available at the dog show concessions) in which to carry your grooming tools and equipment. The latter should include: brushes; combs; scissors; nail clippers; whatever you use for last minute clean-up jobs; cotton swabs; first-aid equipment; and anything you are in the habit of using on the dog, including a leash or two of the type you prefer, some well-cooked and dried-out liver or any of the small packaged "dog treats" for use as bait in the ring, an atomizer in case you wish to dampen your dog's coat when you are preparing him for the ring, and so on. A large turkish towel to spread under the dog on the grooming table is also useful.

Take a large thermos or cooler of ice, the biggest one you can accommodate in your vehicle, for use by "man and beast." Take a jug of water (there are lightweight, inexpensive ones available at all sporting goods shops) and a water dish. If you plan to feed the

269

dog at the show, or if you and the dog will be away from home more than one day, bring food for him from home so that he will have the type to which he is accustomed.

You may or may not have an exercise pen. While the shows do provide areas for exercise of the dogs, these are among the most likely places to have your dog come in contact with any illnesses which may be going around, and having a pen of your own for your dog's use is excellent protection. Such a pen comes in handy while you're travelling; since it is roomier than a crate, it becomes a comfortable place for your dog to relax and move around in, especially when you're at motels or rest stops. These pens are available at the show concession stands and come in a variety of heights and sizes. A set of "pooper scoopers" should also be part of your equipment, along with a package of plastic bags for cleaning up after your dog.

Bring along folding chairs for the members of your party, unless all of you are fond of standing, as these are almost never provided by the clubs. Have your name stamped on the chairs so that there will be no doubt as to whom the chairs belong. Bring whatever you and your family enjoy for drinks or snacks in a picnic basket

Ch. Gosmore Kirkmoor Storm, born in October 1963, by Zeloy Emperor ex Model Taste, bred by Mr. T. Walker. Still another "great" owned by William Myers Jones, Encino, California. This winner of 20 Bests in Show and many Terrier Groups was handled by Ric Chashoudian.

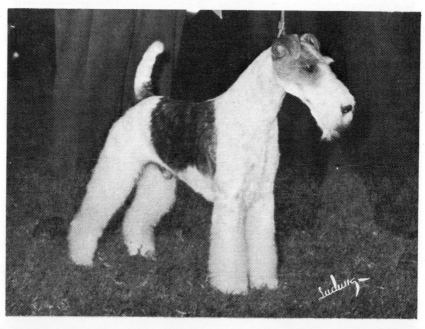

Ch. Sunnybrook's Special Choice in 1957, an importation whom Ric Chashoudian considers to be the finest Wire he ever handled, was schooled by Billy Mitchell in England where he was also a winner. In the U.S. his wins included three Bests in Show, a Fox Terrier Specialty and the Terrier Group at Harbor Cities. The morning after the latter victory, he was unfortunately stolen from his owners' backyard.

or cooler, as show food, in general, is expensive and usually not great. You should always have a pair of boots, a raincoat, and a rain hat with you (they should remain permanently in your vehicle if you plan to attend shows regularly), as well as a sweater, a warm coat, and a change of shoes. A smock or big cover-up apron will assure that you remain tidy as you prepare the dog for the ring. Your overnight case should include a small sewing kit for emergency repairs, bandaids, headache and indigestion remedies, and any personal products or medications you normally use.

In your car, you should always carry maps of the area where you are headed and an assortment of motel directories. Generally speaking, Holiday Inns have been found to be the nicest about taking dogs. Ramadas and Howard Johnsons generally do so cheerfully (with a few exceptions). Best Western generally frowns on pets (not always, but often enough to make it necessary to find out which do). Some of the smaller chains welcome pets; the majority of privately-owned motels do not.

Have everything prepared the night before the show to expedite your departure. Be sure that the dog's identification and your judging program and other show information are in your purse or

Amer. and Braz. Ch. Waybroke Smooth Operator. A Top Ten Smooth who won the Homer Gage Memorial Trophy offered by the American Fox Terrier Club for the Top American-bred Smooth. After a very successful career in the U.S., this dog went to Brazil where he became also a multi-Group and Best in Show winner. Owners, Hubert M. Thomas, Madison M. Weeks, and Sergio Nerigo. Judge, the esteemed Terrier authority, the late Robert Braithwaite.

The imported Ch. Jokyl Lady Advocate, owned by Pool Forge Kennels, was handled in 1965 to Best of Breed at the Fox Terrier Club of Chicago Specialty by Peter Green.

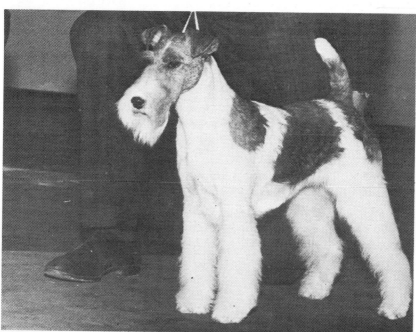

briefcase. If you are taking sandwiches, have them ready. Anything that goes into the car the night before the show will be one thing less to remember in the morning. Decide upon what you will wear and have it out and ready. If there is any question in your mind about what to wear, try on the possibilities before the day of the show; don't risk feeling you may want to change when you see yourself dressed a few moments prior to departure time!

In planning your outfit, make it something simple that will not detract from your dog. Remember that a dark dog silhouettes attractively against a light background and vice-versa. Sport clothes always seem to look best at dog shows, preferably conservative in type and not overly "loud" as you do not want to detract from your dog, who should be the focus of interest at this point. What you wear on your feet is important. Many types of flooring can be hazardously slippery, as can wet grass. Make it a habit to wear rubber soles and low or flat heels in the ring for your own safety, especially if you are showing a dog that likes to move out smartly.

Your final step in pre-show preparation is to leave yourself plenty of time to reach the show that morning. Traffic can get amazingly heavy as one nears the immediate area of the show, finding a parking place can be difficult, and other delays may occur. You'll be in better humor to enjoy the day if your trip to the show is not fraught with panic over fear of not arriving in time!

ENJOYING THE DOG SHOW

From the moment of your arrival at the show until after your dog has been judged, keep foremost in your mind the fact that he is your reason for being there and that he should therefore be the center of your attention. Arrive early enough to have time for those last-minute touches that can make a great difference when he enters the ring. Be sure that he has ample time to exercise and that he attends to personal matters. A dog arriving in the ring and immediately using it as an exercise pen hardly makes a favorable impression on the judge.

When you reach ringside, ask the steward for your arm-card and anchor it firmly into place on your arm. Make sure that you are where you should be when your class is called. The fact that you have picked up your arm-card does not guarantee, as some seem to think, that the judge will wait for you. The judge has a full schedule which he wishes to complete on time. Even though you may be nervous, assume an air of calm self-confidence. Remember that this is a hobby to be enjoyed, so approach it in that state of mind. The dog will do better, too, as he will be quick to reflect your attitude.

Always show your dog with an air of pride. If you make mistakes in presenting him, don't worry about it. Next time you will do better. Do not permit the presence of more experienced exhibitors to intimidate you. After all, they, too, were once newcomers.

The judging routine usually starts when the judge asks that the dogs be gaited in a circle around the ring. During this period the judge is watching each dog as it moves, noting style, topline, reach and drive, head and tail carriage, and general balance. Keep your mind and your eye on your dog, moving him at his most becoming gait and keeping your place in line without coming too close to the exhibitor ahead of you. Always keep your dog on the inside of the circle, between yourself and the judge, so that the judge's view of the dog is unobstructed.

Calmly pose the dog when requested to set up for examination. If you are at the head of the line and many dogs are in the class, go all the way to the end of the ring before starting to stack the dog, leaving sufficient space for those behind you to line theirs up as well, as requested by the judge. If you are not at the head of the line but between other exhibitors, leave sufficient space ahead of your dog for the judge to examine him. The dogs should be spaced so that the judge is able to move among them to see them from all angles. In practicing to "set up" or "stack" your dog for the judge's examination, bear in mind the importance of doing so quickly and with dexterity. The judge has a schedule to meet and only a few moments in which to evaluate each dog. You will immeasurably help yours to make a favorable impression if you are able to "get it all together" in a minimum amount of time. Practice at home before a mirror can be a great help toward bringing this about, facing the dog so that you see him from the same side that the judge will and working to make him look right in the shortest length of time.

Listen carefully as the judge describes the manner in which the dog is to be gaited, whether it is straight down and straight back; down the ring, across, and back; or in a triangle. The latter has become the most popular pattern with the majority of judges. "In a triangle" means the dog should move down the outer side of the

274

ring to the first corner, across that end of the ring to the second corner, and then back to the judge from the second corner, using the center of the ring in a diagonal line. Please learn to do this pattern without breaking at each corner to twirl the dog around you, a senseless maneuver that has been noticed on occasion. Judges like to see the dog in an uninterrupted triangle, as they are thus able to get a better idea of the dog's gait.

It is impossible to overemphasize that the gait at which you move your dog is tremendously important and considerable study and thought should be given to the matter. At home, have someone move the dog for you at different speeds so that you can tell which shows him off to best advantage. The most becoming action almost invariably is seen at a moderate gait, head up and topline holding. Do not gallop your dog around the ring or hurry him into a speed atypical of his breed. Nothing being rushed appears at its best; give your dog a chance to move along at his (and the breed's) natural gait. For a dog's action to be judged accurately, that dog should move with strength and power, but not excessive speed, holding a straight line as he goes to and from the judge.

As you bring the dog back to the judge, stop him a few feet away and be sure that he is standing in a becoming position. Bait him to show the judge an alert expression, using whatever tasty morsel he has been trained to expect for this purpose or, if that works better for you, use a small squeak-toy in your hand. A reminder, please, to those using liver or treats: take them with you when you leave the ring. Do not just drop them on the ground where they will be found by another dog.

When the awards have been made, accept yours graciously, no matter how you actually may feel about it. What's done is done, and arguing with a judge or stomping out of the ring is useless and a reflection on your sportsmanship. Be courteous, congratulate the winner if your dog was defeated, and try not to show your disappointment. By the same token, please be a gracious winner; this, surprisingly, sometimes seems to be still more difficult.

SPEAKING OF FOX TERRIER COATS

The amount of work involved in coat and grooming of either a Wire or a Smooth Fox Terrier depends on your plans for the dog. If grooming worries you, then a Smooth would be your better choice. But many people truly enjoy the challenge of turning out

Famous historic dog, Am. and Can. Ch. Tavabob, by Eng. Ch. Seedfield Meritor Superflash ex Tavaclaire, was bred by Robert and Arthur Davison in England. Owned by Mr. and Mrs. Raymond M. Splawn, Wyrequest Kennels, Spokane, Washington. Pictured winning under the late judge Alva Rosenberg.

a properly presented Wire, and to someone with that point of view, the effort seems well worthwhile. Certainly there is no sadder sight than a neglected, bedraggled-looking terrier; nor one more handsome than a Wire "groomed to the teeth." If you are able to create the latter, there is pride and satisfaction in doing so.

If you would however, dread the work and be inclined to cut corners, then the more simply maintained Smooth is the one you will enjoy, as his "handsome best" is certainly far easier to attain.

If you do not have dog shows on your mind, then it really matters little which of the breeds you choose, as the work of keeping either a Smooth or a Wire family dog in presentable shape is not all that complicated, provided that the dog is strictly a pet. For example, the pet Wire can be clipped to a neat and tidy appearance; although using clippers on this type of coat (where *hardness of texture* is so tremendously important in a show dog) would be utter disaster to the future possibilities of a show prospect Wire, as the process completely removes the harsh outer coat, which the Wire exhibitor holds his breath to encourage. Read the words of the breed standard and you will understand the reason.

Clipping off the top coat, which you are doing when using clippers on a dog, leaves that dog with only the soft undercoat, where once the coat texture may well have been correct. This is a condition which does *not* correct itself, as hair once removed in this manner never returns; nor does the hard texture replace itself. The coat that grows in will be *soft* coat, and that is what you will have if you start clipping any of the hard-coated terriers, of which the Wire is one. So please consider well before you start clipping, for while the soft coat makes a Wire no less desirable as a *pet,* it certainly can be the ruination of a show dog or show prospect. So "think before you clip," and if you feel there is any possibility that you may ever wish to show that particular dog, keep the clippers off it. Later on, if the dog does not prove to be show quality or if you know for certain that no matter what you will not show him, there is plenty of time to then change over to the more informal pet-type coat care. But do not risk it even once until your decision is definite. Again, due to its effect on coat texture, Fox Terriers (especially Wires) should *not* be bathed too frequently. As dogs with large amounts of white, they do require more bathing or cleaning than some breeds. However, rinseless shampoos made especially for dogs can be used on legs and on the face furnishings

George Ward in the 1950s with Ch. Edswyre Supermaid owned by Mrs. Mable Farr, Florham Park, New Jersey.

of Wires. This is rubbed into the coat and then wiped dry with a turkish towel. Using such shampoos will leave the dog looking and smelling clean and beautiful, and they are very useful products that can be purchased from your pet supply shop.

Whether Smooth or Wire, accustom your Fox Terrier, from puppyhood on, to being groomed. Start at about six weeks by taking the Wire puppy on your lap and lightly brush with a soft bristle brush. For the Smooth puppy, use a "hound glove," which is like a very short bristle brush but in the form of a mitt you place over your hand to work on the dog. This will teach the puppy that grooming is pleasant and not to be feared. As soon as the puppy becomes accustomed to this, however, teach him to stand on a grooming table (rubber-topped and made exactly for this purpose), which has been equipped with a post and noose to steady him, all of which are available from pet supply shops or the concession booths at dog shows. The rubber top keeps the puppy from slipping, thus giving him a feeling of security; the noose steadies him, enabling you to have your hands free for your work. The puppy should also learn to have his nails trimmed on the table.

A *pet* Wire puppy should be accustomed to the sound of the electric clippers (if you are *sure* you will not be showing the dog), as their sound can terrorize the puppy if they are used on him too suddenly. Let the clippers run in the puppy's presence; "introduce" him to them by encouraging him to look and sniff at them in your hand; then when he seems to no longer be startled at the

One of the author's favorite photos! Ch. Waybrook Smooth Trick, Bayberry's Miss Pumpkin Patch, Bayberry's Miss Goblin Girl, and Waybroke's Buster of Bayberry in September 1985 at Summerland Key, Florida. Owned by Gilbert Aleman and Jack Lindsay, Miami, Florida.

sound, start working with them. The clippers will be used to take down the coat on the back, neck, tail and head. The coat on the legs and the muzzle can be scissored. Just be *sure*, before you touch the clippers to the dog, that you realize you can never repair a clipped coat, and make sure that you know whether or not you have a show-quality dog before taking the clippers to him. Perhaps we seem repetitious on that subject, but it is an *important* fact to be realized.

A pet Smooth puppy, or grown dog, does not require much more than a daily rub down with your "hound glove," plus trimming the nails every two or three weeks according to their rate of growth.

The coat care for showing both the Smooth and the Wire Fox Terrier is a complicated and specialized process which cannot be learned by reading about it in a book. The best way to learn is to go to a professional handler who specializes in terriers, or to a long-time breeder who is adept at putting down coats; and arrange with them to teach you how to do it. Hand-plucking, which is what it takes for a Wire coat to be kept in show form, sounds simple and is, once you have learned to do it. *But* it must be done *correctly* or you will make a mess of the dog's appearance. If you

Standing perfectly on the table for the scrutiny of the judge, Ch. Jonwyre's Galaxy of Foxden is handled here by Jane Forsyth for Mrs. James A. Farrell, Jr. Note neck and topline, front and rear of this excellent, well-known winner. Photo courtesy of Frank Jones, Jonwyre Kennels, England.

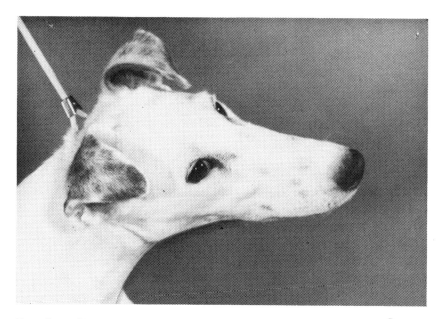

Crag Crest Signal Dancer, "Mischa," is the dam of Crag Crest All Clear. By Ch. Watteau Snufsed of Crag Crest ex Foxformee Joan. She represents the Crag Crest homebreds; nearly all of them follow her type and style. Note the truly classic head of this lovely bitch. Crag Crest Kennels, Mr. and Mrs. Fred Kuska, Colfax, California.

are placing the dog in the hands of a professional to be shown, watch like a hawk as that person works on the dog, and ask questions as the job progresses. Actually, this is a good investment; for you will have the opportunity to see your dog done up by an expert, *and* the opportunity of noting the manner in which the dog is presented in the ring as well as how he is groomed. All of this will help you enormously if your plans are to eventually personally groom and show. Many owner-handlers are successful with Fox Terriers; but *not* until they have learned to become professional in their grooming and handling technique.

Again a word of caution. Do *not* take a Wire you plan to show to just any dog groomer, but only to a successful and respected *terrier* person. The average pet groomer often does not do the dog as well as you could yourself, and certainly no one who is inexperienced with show terriers carrying this type of coat will turn one out to compare favorably with the work of a specialist.

The Smooth also requires considerable technique in his show grooming which, although simpler than that of the Wire, must be done *correctly* for the dog to hold his own in competition.

281

Praise while heeling helps to keep the dog in position and happy. Illustrated by Fortune's Daquiri Doc, C.D., and owner-trainer Lynne Bockelman.

Chapter 10

Your Fox Terrier and Obedience

For its own protection and safety, every dog should be taught, at the very least, to recognize and obey the commands "Come," "Heel," "Down," "Sit," and "Stay." Doing so at some time might save the dog's life and in less extreme circumstances will certainly make him a better behaved, more pleasant member of society. If you are patient and enjoy working with your dog, study some of the excellent books available on the subject of obedience and then teach your canine friend these basic manners. If you need the stimulus of working with a group, find out where obedience training classes are held (usually your veterinarian, your dog's breeder, or a dog-owning friend can tell you) and you and your dog can join. Alternatively, you could let someone else do the training by sending the dog to class, but this is not very rewarding because you lose the opportunity of working with your dog and the pleasure of the rapport thus established.

If you are going to do it yourself, there are some basic rules which you should follow. You must remain calm and confident in attitude. Never lose your temper and frighten or punish your dog unjustly. Be quick and lavish with praise each time a command is correctly followed. Make it fun for the dog and he will be eager to please you by responding correctly. Repetition is the keynote, but it should not be continued without recess to the point of tedium. Limit the training sessions to ten- or fifteen-minute periods at a time.

Formal obedience training can be followed, and very frequently is, by entering the dog in obedience competition to work toward an obedience degree, or several of them, depending on the dog's aptitude and your own enjoyment. Obedience trials are held in conjunction with the majority of all-breed conformation dog shows, with Specialty shows, and frequently as separate Specialty events. If you are working alone with your dog, a list of trial dates might be obtained from your dog's veterinarian, your dog breeder, or a dog-owning friend; the AKC *Gazette* lists shows and trials to be scheduled in the coming months; and if you are a member of a training class, you will find the information readily available.

The goals for which one works in the formal AKC Member or Licensed Trials are the following titles: Companion Dog (C.D.), Companion Dog Excellent (C.D.X.), and Utility Dog (U.D.). These degrees are earned by receiving three "legs," or qualifying scores, at each level of competition. The degrees must be earned in order, with one completed prior to starting work on the next. For example, a dog must have earned C.D. prior to starting work on C.D.X.; then C.D.X. must be completed before U.D. work begins. The ultimate title attainable in obedience work is Obedience Trial Champion (O.T.Ch.)

When you see the letters C.D. following a dog's name, you will know that this dog has satisfactorily completed the following exercises: heel on leash and figure eight, heel free, stand for examination, recall, long sit, and long down. C.D.X. means that tests have been passed on all of those just mentioned plus heel free and figure eight, drop on recall, retrieve on flat, retrieve over high jump, broad jump, long sit, and long down. U.D. indicates that the dog has additionally passed tests in scent discrimination (leather article), scent discrimination (metal article), signal exercise, directed retrieve, directed jumping, and group stand for examination. The letters O.T.Ch. are the abbreviation for the only obedience title which precedes rather than follows a dog's name. To gain an obedience trial championship, a dog who already holds a Utility Dog degree must win a total of one hundred points and must win three firsts, under three different judges, in Utility and Open B Classes.

There is also a Tracking Dog title (T.D.) which can be earned at tracking trials. In order to pass the tracking tests the dog must follow the trail of a stranger along a path on which the trail was

Fortune's Hickory Daquiri Doc, C.D., illustrated proper heel position and good eye contact as she worked with trainer-owner Lynne Bockelman.

laid between thirty minutes and two hours previously. Along this track there must be more than two right-angle turns, at least two of which are well out in the open where no fences or other boundaries exist for the guidance of the dog or the handler. The dog wears a harness and is connected to the handler by a lead twenty to forty feet in length. Inconspicuously dropped at the end of the track is an article to be retrieved, usually a glove or wallet, which the dog is expected to locate and the handler to pick up. The letters T.D.X. are the abbreviation for Tracking Dog Excellent, a more difficult version of the Tracking Dog test with a longer track and more turns to be worked through.

FOXTERRIERS IN OBEDIENCE

Lisa Sachs, whose Fortune Smooth Fox Terriers are at Huntington, New York, is a show dog enthusiast who has won well with Fox Terriers. However, she is even more into obedience work, having trained dogs for it over a more than twenty-year period prior to becoming active with her Smooths in the show ring. And so, of course, when she started with Smooths, it was inevitable that they would find their way into the obedience rings as well. Their success in many fields is impressive, as I am sure that you will agree after reading of some of their accomplishments.

The foundation bitch at Fortune Kennels, Champion Quissex Vestal Virgin, was quick to prove special talent in this regard. Bianca, as she was called, brought satisfaction and pleasure to her owner when she became, to quote Lisa's own words, "one of the most reliable obedience dogs I have trained." Finishing her C.D. in her first three shows, she was Highest Scoring Champion of Record at her third trial. She also qualified at her two back-up shows, and at the last one was Highest Scoring Dog of the Terrier Group.

Another of Lisa's Smooths, Champion Quissex Proclamation, C.D., C.G., also has a talent for obedience and was going happily along the route to a Tracking Dog Degree when his owner had to give that up due to lack of time.

The very special "pride and joy" at Fortune is a most notable dog, Fortune's Kid Smoothie, C.D., known as "Jack," who, since about 1973, has been in continuous demand for all aspects of modeling. Of him, his owner says, "I owe him a great deal. Not only has he taught me an enormous amount about dog psychology,

Fun time! Matthew Black with two of his Smooth pals, Kevin and Robbie (Springbox Smooths, New South Wales, Australia) enjoy games in the water with their young master. Mr. and Mrs. R. Black, owners.

Ch. Wyrelee Double Trouble, C.D., learning the "sit-stay" command. Nancy Lee Wolf, owner, Scotts Valley, California.

he has also introduced me to several phases of dogs that I never dreamed within my reach.

Jack is known to millions of Americans as the "Breakstone Dog," for he is the Fox Terrier who has appeared on about fourteen of that company's commercials. Additionally, he has acted in a Broadway show; taken part in three movies; has done four kennel spots; a Singer Sewing Machine commercial; one for Whatchamacallit Candy Bars; a commercial for Sleepys Bedding Centers; and numerous others, not to mention print work and personal appearances. His "spare" time is spent as his owner's much loved personal pet.

Lisa Sachs is also the breeder of Fortune's Hickory Daquiri Dog, C.D., who finished that title in three straight shows with two additional qualifying scores at her other novice sorties. "Daq" was Highest Scoring Dog in Trial at the American Foxterrier Club Centenary, June 1985. Daq is owned, trained and shown in obedience by Lynne Bockelman.

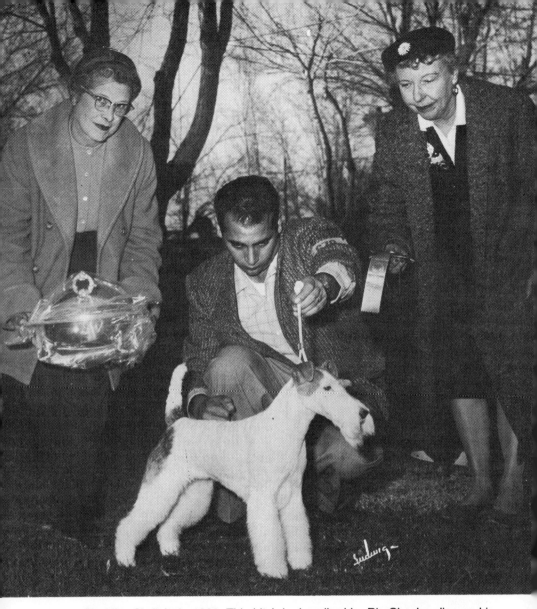

Ch. Miss Skylight in 1961. This bitch is described by Ric Chashoudian as his "personal all-time favorite of Fox Terriers," whom he handled for Wyldwest Kennels. She was imported by Anton Rost, purchased from a hog farmer in Ireland, and was in the U.S. originally turned over to professional handler Ben Brown, for whom Ric Chashoudian was trimming then. Ben labeled her "a great one," which she proved to be on her first Texas circuit where she promptly won two Bests in Show. She was turned over to Ric by Ben. Her show record included winning the Top Dog All Breeds. She had 29 Bests in Show plus well over 100 Group 1sts, and she won the breed twice at Westminster, once taking 2nd in the Group there. She was Ric's first important winner and her record is most noteworthy.

288

Chapter 18

Breeding Your Fox Terrier

The first responsibility of any person breeding dogs is to do so with care, forethought, and deliberation. It is inexcusable to breed more litters than you need to carry on your show program or to perpetuate your bloodlines. A responsible breeder should not cause a litter to be born without definite plans for the safe and happy disposition of the puppies.

A responsible dog breeder makes absolutely certain, so far as is humanly possible, that the home to which one of his puppies will go is a good home, one that offers proper care and an enthusiastic owner. To be admired are those breeders who insist on visiting (although doing so is not always feasible) the prospective owners of their puppies to see if they have suitable facilities for keeping a dog, to find out if they understand the responsibility involved, and to make certain if all members of the household are in accord regarding the desirability of owning one. All breeders should carefully check out the credentials of prospective purchasers to be sure that the puppy is being placed in responsible hands.

No breeder ever wants a puppy or grown dog he has raised to wind up in an animal shelter, in an experimental laboratory, or as a victim of a speeding car. While complete control of such a situation may be impossible, it is important to make every effort to turn over dogs to responsible people. When selling a puppy, it is a good idea to do so with the understanding that should it become necessary to place the dog in other hands, the purchaser will first contact you, the breeder. You may want to help in some way, possibly by buying or taking back the dog or placing it elsewhere. It is not fair to sell puppies and then never again give a thought to their welfare. Family problems arise, people may be forced to move where dogs are prohibited, or people just grow bored with a dog and its care. Thus the dog becomes a victim. You, as the dog's breeder, should concern yourself with the welfare of each of your dogs and see to it that the dog remains in good hands.

The final obligation every dog owner shares, be there just one dog or an entire kennel involved, is that of making detailed, explicit plans for the future of these dearly loved animals in the event of the owner's death. Far too many people are apt to procrastinate and leave this very important matter unattended to, feeling that everything will work out or that "someone will see to them." Neither is too likely, at least not to the benefit of the dogs, unless you have done some advance planning which will assure their future well-being.

Life is filled with the unexpected, and even the youngest, healthiest, most robust of us may be the victim of a fatal accident or sudden illness. The fate of your dogs, so entirely in your hands, should never be left to chance. If you have not already done so, please get together with your lawyer and set up a clause in your will specifying what you want done with each of your dogs, to whom they will be entrusted (after first making absolutely certain that the person selected is willing and able to assume the responsibility), and telling the locations of all registration papers, pedigrees, and kennel records. Just think of the possibilities which might happen otherwise! If there is another family member who shares your love of the dogs, that is good and you have less to worry about. But if your heirs are not dog-oriented, they will hardly know how to proceed or how to cope with the dogs themselves, and they may wind up disposing of or caring for your dogs in a manner that would break your heart were you around to know about it.

It is advisable to have in your will specific instructions concerning each of your dogs. A friend, also a dog person who regards his or her own dogs with the same concern and esteem as you do, may agree to take over their care until they can be placed accordingly and will make certain that all will work out as you have planned. This person's name and phone number can be prominently displayed in your van or car and in your wallet. Your lawyer can be made aware of this fact. This can be spelled out in your will. The friend can have a signed check of yours to be used in case of an emergency or accident when you are traveling with the dogs; this check can be used to cover his or her expense to come and take over the care of your dogs should anything happen to make it impossible for you to do so. This is the least any dog owner should do in preparation for the time their dogs suddenly find themselves alone. There have been so many sad cases of dogs unprovided for by their loving owners, left to heirs who couldn't care less and who disposed of them in any way at all to get rid of them, or left to heirs who kept and neglected them under the misguided idea that they were providing them "a fine home with lots of freedom." These misfortunes must be prevented from befalling your own dogs who have meant so much you!

Conscientious breeders feel quite strongly that the only possible reason for producing puppies is the ambition to improve and uphold quality and temperament within the breed—definitely *not* because one hopes to make a quick cash profit on a mediocre litter, which never seems to work out that way in the long run and which accomplishes little beyond perhaps adding to the nation's heartbreaking number of unwanted canines. The only reason ever for breeding a litter is, with conscientious people, a desire to improve the quality of dogs in their own kennel or, as pet owners, to add to the number of dogs they themselves own with a puppy or two from their present favorites. In either case, breeding should not take place unless one definitely has prospective owners for as many puppies as the litter may contain, lest you find yourself with several fast-growing young dogs and no homes in which to place them.

THE BROOD BITCH

Bitches should not be mated earlier than their second season, by which time they should be from fifteen to eighteen months old. Many breeders prefer to wait and finish the championships of their show bitches before breeding them, as pregnancy can be a disaster to a show coat and getting the bitch back in shape again takes time. When you have decided what will be the proper time, start watching at least several months ahead for what you feel would be the perfect mate to best complement your bitch's quality and bloodlines. Subscribe to the magazines which feature your breed exclusively and to some which cover all breeds in order to familiarize yourself with outstanding stud dogs in areas other than your own, for there is no necessity nowadays to limit your choice to a local dog unless you truly like him and feel that he is the most suitable. It is quite usual to ship a bitch to a stud dog a distance away, and this generally works out with no ill effects. The important thing is that you need a stud dog strong in those features where your bitch is weak, a dog whose bloodlines are compatible with hers. Compare the background of both your bitch and the stud dog under consideration, paying particular attention to the

Littermates from 1972, these were two out of four who finished. Ch. Raylu Lynwal Lyrist (*left*) and Ch. Raylu Lynwal Lightning, the latter finishing with three 5-point majors, Atlanta Fox Terrier Club Specialty and Old Dominion K.C. in 1973. Bred, owned, and shown by Gene S. Bigelow, Raylu Kennels, Yorktown, Virginia.

Ch. Zeloy's Envoy's kids at Foxglen Kennels. Irene Rhodes, owner. Sharpsville, Pennsylvania.

quality of the puppies from bitches with backgrounds similar to your bitch's. If the puppies have been of the type and quality you admire, then this dog would seem a sensible choice for yours, too.

Stud fees may be a few hundred dollars, sometimes even more under special situations for a particularly successful sire. It is money well spent, however. *Do not* ever breed to a dog because he is less expensive than the others unless you honestly believe that he can sire the kind of puppies who will be a credit to your kennel and your breed.

Contacting the owners of the stud dogs you find interesting will bring you pedigrees and pictures which you can then study in relation to your bitch's pedigree and conformation. Discuss your plans with other breeders who are knowledgeable (including the one who bred your own bitch). You may not always receive an entirely unbiased opinion (particularly if the person giving it also has an available stud dog), but one learns by discussion so listen to what they say, consider their opinions, and then you may be better qualified to form your own opinion.

As soon as you have made a choice, phone the owner of the stud dog you wish to use to find out if this will be agreeable. You will be asked about the bitch's health, soundness, temperament, and freedom from serious faults. A copy of her pedigree may be requested, as might a picture of her. A discussion of her background over the telephone may be sufficient to assure the stud's owner that she is suitable for the stud dog and that she is of type, breeding, and quality herself, capable of producing the kind of puppies for which the stud is noted. The owner of a top-quality stud is

Ch. Quissex Calliope taking Winners Bitch at Ox Ridge in 1971. By Ch. Watteau Musical Box ex an Ebony Box daughter. Owned by Mrs. Winifred Stout, Quissex Smooths.

often extremely selective in the bitches permitted to be bred to his dog, in an effort to keep the standard of his puppies high. The owner of a stud dog may require that the bitch be tested for brucellosis, which should be attended to not more than a month previous to the breeding.

Check out which airport will be most convenient for the person meeting and returning the bitch, if she is to be shipped, and also what airlines use that airport. You will find that the airlines are also apt to have special requirements concerning acceptance of animals for shipping. These include weather limitations and types of crates which are acceptable. The weather limits have to do with extreme heat and extreme cold at the point of destination, as some airlines will not fly dogs into temperatures above or below certain levels, fearing for their safety. The crate problem is a simple one, since, if your own crate is not suitable, most of the airlines have specially designed crates available for purchase at a fair and moderate price. It is a good plan to purchase one of these if you intend to be shipping dogs with any sort of frequency. They are made of fiberglass and are the safest type to use for shipping.

Normally you must notify the airline several days in advance to make a reservation, as they are able to accommodate only a certain number of dogs on each flight. Plan on shipping the bitch on about her eighth or ninth day of season, but be careful to avoid shipping her on a weekend when schedules often vary and freight offices are apt to be closed. Whenever you can, ship your bitch on a direct flight. Changing planes always carries a certain amount of risk of a dog being overlooked or wrongly routed at the middle stop, so avoid this danger if at all possible. The bitch must be accompanied by a health certificate which you must obtain from your veterinarian before taking her to the airport. Usually it will be necessary to have the bitch at the airport about two hours prior to flight time. Before finalizing arrangements, find out from the stud's owner at what time of day it will be most convenient to have the bitch picked up promptly upon arrival.

It is simpler if you can bring the bitch to the stud dog yourself. Some people feel that the trauma of the flight may cause the bitch to not conceive; and, of course, undeniably there is a slight risk in shipping which can be avoided if you are able to drive the bitch to her destination. Be sure to leave yourself sufficient time to assure your arrival at the right time for her for breeding (normally

Aust. Ch. Canbury The Countess, by Conock Count (U.K. imported) ex Canbury Miss Chief, photographed prior to whelping her litter by the U.K. importation, Penda Pepo, in February 1986. Owned by Canbury Kennels, Ebenezer, Australia.

the tenth to fourteenth day following the first signs of color); and remember that if you want the bitch bred twice, you should allow a day to elapse between the two matings. Do not expect the stud's owner to house you while you are there. Locate a nearby motel that takes dogs and make that your headquarters.

Just prior to the time your bitch is due in season, you should take her to visit your veterinarian. She should be checked for worms and should receive all the booster shots for which she is due plus one for parvovirus, unless she has had the latter shot fairly recently. The brucellosis test can also be done then, and the health certificate can be obtained for shipping if she is to travel by air. Should the bitch be at all overweight, now is the time to get the surplus off. She should be in good condition, neither underweight nor overweight, at the time of breeding.

The moment you notice the swelling of the vulva, for which you should be checking daily as the time for her season approaches, and the appearance of color, immediately contact the stud's owner and settle on the day for shipping or make the appointment for your arrival with the bitch for breeding. If you are shipping the bitch, the stud fee check should be mailed immediately, leaving ample time for it to have been received when the bitch arrives and the mating takes place. Be sure to call the airline, making her reservation at that time, too.

Do not feed the bitch within a few hours before shipping her. Be certain that she has had a drink of water and been well exercised before closing her in the crate. Several layers of newspapers, topped with some shredded newspaper, make a good bed and can be discarded when she arrives at her destination; these can be replaced with fresh newspapers for her return home. Remember that the bitch should be brought to the airport about two hours before flight time, as sometimes the airlines refuse to accept late arrivals.

If you are taking your bitch by car, be certain that you will arrive at a reasonable time of day. Do not appear late in the evening. If your arrival in town is not until late, get a good night's sleep at your motel and contact the stud's owner first thing in the morning. If possible, leave children and relatives at home, as they will only be in the way and perhaps unwelcome by the stud's owner. Most stud dog owners prefer not to have any unnecessary people on hand during the actual mating.

After the breeding has taken place, if you wish to sit and visit for awhile and the stud's owner has the time, return the bitch to her crate in your car (first ascertaining, of course, that the temperature is comfortable for her and that there is proper ventilation). She should not be permitted to urinate for at least one hour following the breeding. This is the time when you attend to the business part of the transaction. Pay the stud fee, upon which you should receive your breeding certificate and, if you do not already have it, a copy of the stud dog's pedigree. The owner of the stud dog does not sign or furnish a litter registration application until the puppies have been born.

Upon your return home, you can settle down and plan in happy anticipation a wonderful litter of puppies. A word of caution! Remember that although she has been bred, your bitch is still an interesting target for all male dogs, so guard her carefully for the next week or until you are absolutely certain that her season has entirely ended. This would be no time to have any unfortunate incident with another dog.

THE STUD DOG

Choosing the best stud dog to complement your bitch is often ,very difficult. The two principal factors to be considered should be the stud's conformation and his pedigree. Conformation is fairly obvious; you want a dog that is typical of the breed in the words of the Standard of perfection. Understanding pedigrees is a bit more subtle since the pedigree lists the ancestry of the dog and involves individuals and bloodlines with which you may not be entirely familiar.

To a novice in the breed, the correct interpretation of a pedigree may at first be difficult to grasp. Study the pictures and text of this book and you will find many names of important bloodlines and members of the breed. Also make an effort to discuss the various dogs behind the proposed stud with some of the more experienced breeders, starting with the breeder of your own bitch. Frequently these folks will be familiar with many of the dogs in question, will be able to offer opinions of them, and may have access to additional pictures which you would benefit by seeing. It is very important that the stud's pedigree be harmonious with that of the bitch you plan on breeding to him. Do not rush out and breed to the latest winner with no thought of whether or not he

Ch. Falstaff Lady Fayre in 1963. One of the winning Wires owned by William Myers Jones, Lady Fayre was bred by Mrs. E. Pinket, sired by Mitre Advocate ex Falstaff Fragrance. Imported by Anton Rost, then sold to Wyldwest Kennels in the U.S. after winning six tickets in Great Britain by 1½ years old. On one circuit alone, she won seven out of a possible ten Bests in Show, and she had many additional top awards. She twice won Best of Breed at Westminster when over seven years of age.

can produce true quality. By no means are all great show dogs great producers. It is the producing record of the dog in question, and the dogs and bitches from which he has come, that should be the basis on which you make your choice.

Breeding dogs is never a money-making operation. By the time you pay a stud fee, care for the bitch during pregnancy, whelp the litter, and rear the puppies through their early shots, worming, and so on, you will be fortunate to break even financially once the puppies have been sold. Your chances of doing this are greater if you are breeding for a show-quality litter which will bring you higher prices, as the pups are sold as show prospects. Therefore, your wisest investment is to use the best dog available for your bitch regardless of the cost; then you should wind up with more valuable puppies. Remember that it is equally costly to raise mediocre puppies as it is top ones, and your chances of financial return are better on the latter. Breeding to the most excellent, most suitable stud dog you can find is the only sensible thing to do, and it is poor economy to quibble over the amount you are paying in a stud fee.

298

It will be your decision as to which course you follow when you breed your bitch, as there are three options: linebreeding, inbreeding, and outcrossing. Each of these methods has its supporters and its detractors! Linebreeding is breeding a bitch to a dog belonging originally to the same canine family, being descended from the same ancestors, such as half brother to half sister, grandsire to granddaughter, niece to uncle (and vice-versa) or cousin to cousin. Inbreeding is breeding father to daughter, mother to son, or full brother to sister. Outcross breeding is breeding a dog and a bitch with no or only a few mutual ancestors.

Linebreeding is probably the safest course, and the one most likely to bring results, for the novice breeder. The more sophisticated inbreeding should be left to the experienced, longtime breeders who throroughly know and understand the risks and the possibilities involved with a particular line. It is usually done in an effort to intensify some ideal feature in that strain. Outcrossing is the reverse of inbreeding, an effort to introduce improvement in a specific feature needing correction, such as a shorter back, better movement, more correct head or coat, and so on.

It is the serious breeder's ambition to develop a strain or bloodline of their own, one strong in qualities for which their dogs will become distinguished. However, it must be realized that this will involve time, patience, and at least several generations before the

Ch. Ayree Dominator, Top Winning Fox Terrier of all time, retired following a show career which included 76 All Breed Bests in Show; and 157 Terrier Group 1sts. Sire of 32 champions Including No. 1 American Bred Ch. Terrikane's Tulliver and No. 2 American Bred Wire Ch. Bev Wyre Sovereign Escort. Owned by Michael and Florence Weissman, Yonkers, New York.

achievement can be claimed. The safest way to embark on this plan, as previously mentioned, is by the selection and breeding of one or two bitches, the best you can buy and from top-producing kennels. In the beginning you do *not* really have to own a stud dog. In the long run it is less expensive and sounder judgement to pay a stud fee when you are ready to breed a bitch than to purchase a stud dog and feed him all year; a stud dog does not win any popularity contests with owners of bitches to be bred until he becomes a champion, has been successfully Specialed for a while, and has been at least moderately advertised, all of which adds up to quite a healthy expenditure.

The wisest course for the inexperienced breeder just starting out in dogs is to keep the best bitch puppy from the first several litters. After that you may wish to consider keeping your own stud dog, if there has been a particularly handsome male in one of your litters that you feel has great potential or if you know where there is one available that you are interested in, with the feeling that he would work in nicely with the breeding program on which you have embarked. By this time, with several litters already born, your eye should have developed to a point enabling you to make a wise choice, either from one of your own litters or from among dogs you have seen that appear suitable.

The greatest care should be taken in the selection of your own stud dog. He must be of true type and highest quality as he may be responsible for siring many puppies each year, and he should come from a line of excellent dogs on both sides of his pedigree which themselves are, and which are descended from, successful producers. This dog should have no glaring faults in conformation; he should be of such quality that he can hold his own in keenest competition within his breed. He should be in good health, be virile and be a keen stud dog, a proven sire able to transmit his correct qualities to his puppies. Need one say that such a dog will be enormously expensive unless you have the good fortune to produce him in one of your own litters? To buy and use a lesser stud dog, however, is downgrading your breeding program unnecessarily since there are so many dogs fitting the description of a fine stud whose services can be used on payment of a stud fee.

You should *never* breed to an unsound dog or one with any serious disqualifying faults according to the breed's standard. Not all

300

champions by any means pass along their best features; and by the same token, occasionally you will find a great one who can pass along his best features but never gained his championship title due to some unusual circumstances. The information you need about a stud dog is what type of puppies he has produced, and with what bloodlines, and whether or not he possesses the bloodlines and attributes considered characteristic of the best in your breed.

If you go out to buy a stud dog, obviously he will not be a puppy, but rather a fully mature and proven male with as many of the best attributes as possible. True, he will be an expensive investment, but if you choose and make his selection with care and forethought, he may well prove to be one of the best investments you have ever made.

Of course, the most exciting of all is when a young male you have decided to keep from one of your litters, due to his tremendous show potential, turns out to be a stud dog such as we have described. In this case he should be managed with care, for he is a valuable property that can contribute inestimably to this breed as a whole and to your own kennel specifically.

Do not permit your stud dog to be used until he is about a year old, and even then he should be bred to a mature, proven matron accustomed to breeding who will make his first experience pleasant and easy. A young dog can be put off forever by a maiden bitch who fights and resists his advances. Never allow this to happen. Always start a stud dog out with a bitch who is mature, has been bred previously, and is of even temperament. The first breeding should be performed in quiet surroundings with only you and one other person to hold the bitch. Do not make it a circus, as the experience will determine the dog's outlook about future stud work. If he does not enjoy the first experience or associates it with any unpleasantness, you may well have a problem in the future.

Your young stud must permit help with the breeding, as later there will be bitches who will not be cooperative. If right from the beginning you are there helping him and praising him, whether or not your assistance is actually needed, he will expect and accept this as a matter of course when a difficult bitch comes along.

Things to have handy before introducing your dog and the bitch are K-Y jelly (the only lubricant which should be used) and a length of gauze with which to muzzle the bitch should it be neces-

301

sary to keep her from biting you or the dog. Some bitches put up a fight; others are calm. It is best to be prepared.

At the time of the breeding, the stud fee comes due, and it is expected that it will be paid promptly. Normally a return service is offered in case the bitch misses or fails to produce one live puppy. Conditions of the service are what the stud dog's owner makes them, and there are no standard rules covering this. The stud fee is paid for the act, not the result. If the bitch fails to conceive, it is customary for the owner to offer a free return service; but this is a courtesy and not to be considered a right, particularly in the case of a proven stud who is siring consistently and whose fault the failure obviously is *not*. Stud dog owners are always anxious to see their clients get good value and to have, in the ring, winning young stock by their dog; therefore, very few refuse to mate the second time. It is wise, however, for both parties to have the terms of the transaction clearly understood at the time of the breeding.

If the return service has been provided and the bitch has missed a second time, that is considered to be the end of the matter and the owner would be expected to pay a further fee if it is felt that the bitch should be given a third chance with the stud dog. The management of a stud dog and his visiting bitches is quite a task, and a stud fee has usually been well earned when one service has been achieved, let alone by repeated visits from the same bitch.

The accepted litter is one live puppy. It is wise to have printed a breeding certificate which the owner of the stud dog and the owner of the bitch both sign. This should list in detail the conditions of the breeding as well as the dates of the mating.

Upon occasion, arrangements other than a stud fee in cash are made for a breeding, such as the owner of the stud taking a pick-of-the-litter puppy in lieu of money. This should be clearly specified on the breeding certificate along with the terms of the age at which the stud's owner will select the puppy, whether it is to be a specific sex, or whether it is to be the pick of the entire litter.

The price of a stud fee varies according to circumstances. Usually, to prove a young stud dog, his owner will allow the first breeding to be quite inexpensive. Then, once a bitch has become pregnant by him, he becomes a "proven stud" and the fee rises accordingly for bitches that follow. The sire of championship quality puppies will bring a stud fee of at least the purchase price of one show puppy as the accepted "rule-of-thumb." Until at least one champion by your stud dog has finished, the fee will remain equal to the price of one pet puppy. When his list of champions starts to grow, so does the amount of the stud fee. For a top-producing sire of champions, the stud fee will rise accordingly.

Almost invariably it is the bitch who comes to the stud dog for the breeding. Immediately upon having selected the stud dog you wish to use, discuss the possibility with the owner of that dog. It is the stud dog owner's prerogative to refuse to breed any bitch deemed unsuitable for this dog. Stud fee and method of payment should be stated at this time and a decision reached on whether it is to be a full cash transaction at the time of the mating or a pick-of-the-litter puppy, usually at eight weeks of age.

If the owner of the stud dog must travel to an airport to meet the bitch and ship her for the flight home, an additional charge will be made for time, tolls, and gasoline based on the stud owner's proximity to the airport. The stud fee includes board for the day on the bitch's arrival through two days for breeding, with a day in between. If it is necessary that the bitch remain longer, it is very likely that additional board will be charged at the normal per-day rate for the breed.

Be sure to advise the stud's owner as soon as you know that your bitch is in season so that the stud dog will be available. This is especially important because if he is a dog being shown, he and his owner may be unavailable, owing to the dog's absence from home.

As the owner of a stud dog being offered to the public, it is essential that you have proper facilities for the care of visiting bitches. Nothing can be worse than a bitch being insecurely housed and slipping out to become lost or bred by the wrong dog. If you are taking people's valued bitches into your kennel or home, it is imperative that you provide them with comfortable, secure housing and good care while they are your responsibility.

There is no dog more valuable than the proven sire of champions, Group winners, and Best in Show dogs. Once you have such an animal, guard his reputation well and do *not* permit him to be bred to just any bitch that comes along. It takes two to make the puppies; even the most dominant stud cannot do it all himself, so never permit him to breed a bitch you consider unworthy. Remember that when the puppies arrive, it will be your stud dog who will be blamed for any lack of quality, while the bitch's short-comings will be quickly and conveniently overlooked.

Going into the actual management of the mating is a bit super-fluous here. If you have had previous experience in breeding a dog and bitch, you will know how the mating is done. If you do not have such experience, you should not attempt to follow directions given in a book but should have a veterinarian, breeder friend, or handler there to help you with the first few times. You do not turn the dog and bitch loose together and await developments, as too many things can go wrong and you may altogether miss getting the bitch bred. Someone should hold the dog and the bitch (one person each) until the "tie" is made and these two people should stay with them during the entire act.

If you get a complete tie, probably only the one mating is abso-lutely necessary. However, especially with a maiden bitch or one that has come a long distance for this breeding, a follow-up with a second breeding is preferred, leaving one day in between the two matings. In this way there will be little or no chance of the bitch missing.

Once the tie has been completed and the dogs release, be cer-tain that the male's penis goes completely back within its sheath. He should be allowed a drink of water and a short walk, and then he should be put into his crate or somewhere alone where he can settle down. Do not allow him to be with other dogs for a while as they will notice the odor of the bitch on him, and, particularly with other males present, he may become involved in a fight.

PREGNANCY, WHELPING, AND THE LITTER

Once the bitch has been bred and is back at home, remember to keep an ever watchful eye that no other males get to her until at least the twenty-second day of her season has passed. Until then, it will still be possible for an unwanted breeding to take place, which at this point would be catastrophic. Remember that she actually can have two separate litters by two different dogs, so take care.

In other ways, she should be treated normally. Controlled exer-cise is good and necessary for the bitch throughout her pregnancy, tapering it off to just several short walks daily, preferably on lead, as she reaches her seventh week. As her time grows close, be care-ful about her jumping or playing too roughly.

Ch. Meritor Bang On, owned by Mr. and Mrs. William Myers Jones, was bred by N. Seddon and sired by Zeloy Emperor. Pictured winning the Terrier Group at South Oregon K.C. in 1967 handled by Ric Chashoudian. The dog was purchased from Ric at age nine months by Henry Sayres, then later going to Mr. and Mrs. Jones. Bang On was a multi Best in Show winner and a dominant stud force from whom numerous winners have descended.

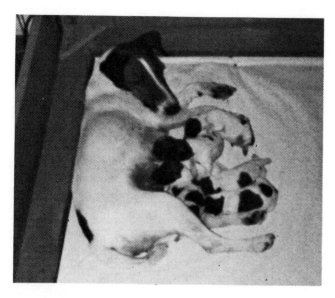

Sugarland Saucy Buttons with her several day-old puppies. Note construction of the whelping box. Charbonne Kennels, owner, Highland, California.

The theory that a bitch should be overstuffed with food when pregnant is a poor one. A fat bitch is never an easy whelper, so the overfeeding you consider good for her may well turn out to be a hindrance later on. During the first few weeks of pregnancy, your bitch should be fed her normal diet. At four to five weeks along, calcium should be added to her food. At seven weeks her food may be increased if she seems to crave more than she is getting, and a meal of canned milk (mixed with an equal amount of water) should be introduced. If she is fed just once a day, add another meal rather than overload her with too much at one time. If twice a day is her schedule, then a bit more food can be added to each feeding.

A week before the pups are due, your bitch should be introduced to her whelping box so that she will be accustomed to it and feel at home there when the puppies arrive. She should be encouraged to sleep there but permitted to come and go as she wishes. The box should be roomy enough for her to lie down and stretch out in but not too large, lest the pups have more room than is needed in which to roam and possibly get chilled by going too far away from their mother. Be sure that the box has a "pig rail"; this will prevent the puppies from being crushed against the sides. The room in which the box is placed, either in your home or in the kennel, should be kept at about 70 degrees Fahrenheit. In winter

306

it may be necessary to have an infrared lamp over the whelping box, in which case be careful not to place it too low or close to the puppies.

Newspapers will become a very important commodity, so start collecting them well in advance to have a big pile handy for the whelping box. With a litter of puppies, one never seems to have papers enough, so the higher pile to start with, the better off you will be. Other necessities for whelping time are clean, soft turkish towels, scissors, and a bottle of alcohol.

You will know that her time is very near when your bitch becomes restless, wandering in and out of her box and out of the room. She may refuse food, and at that point her temperature will start to drop. She will dig at and tear up the newspapers in her

Ch. Watteau Snuff Box, famous English winner with 23 Challenge Certificates to his credit, the Fox Terrier Club's Gold Cup winner for two successive years, and the sire of some highly influential stud dogs. Watteau Kennels, Mrs. A. Blake, West Scrafton, Yorks, England.

box, shiver, and generally look uncomfortable. Only you should be with your bitch at this time. She does not need spectators; and several people hanging over her, even though they may be family members whom she knows, may upset her to the point where she may harm the puppies. You should remain nearby, quietly watching, not fussing or hovering; speak calmly and frequently to her to instill confidence. Eventually she will settle down in her box and begin panting; contractions will follow. Soon thereafter a puppy will start to emerge, sliding out with the contractions. The mother immediately should open the sac, sever the cord with her teeth, and then clean up the puppy. She will also eat the placenta, which you should permit. Once the puppy is cleaned, it should be placed next to the bitch unless she is showing signs of having the next one immediately. Almost at once the puppy will start looking for a nipple on which to nurse, and you should ascertain that it is able to latch on successfully.

If the puppy is a breech (*i.e.*, born feet first), you must watch carefully for it to be completely delivered as quickly as possible and for the sac to be removed quickly so that the puppy does not drown. Sometimes even a normally positioned birth will seem extremely slow in coming. Should this occur, you might take a clean towel, and as the bitch contracts, pull the puppy out, doing so gently and with utmost care. If, once the puppy is delivered, it shows little signs of life, take a rough turkish towel and massage the puppy's chest by rubbing quite briskly back and forth. Continue this for about fifteen minutes, and be sure that the mouth is free of liquid. It may be necessary to try mouth-to-mouth breathing, which is begun by pressing the puppy's jaws open and, using a finger, depressing the tongue which may be stuck to the roof of the mouth. Then place your mouth against the puppy's and blow hard down the puppy's throat. Rub the puppy's chest with the towel again and try artificial respiration, pressing the sides of the chest together slowly and rhythmically—in and out, in and out. Keep trying one method or the other for at least twenty minutes before giving up. You may be rewarded with a live puppy who otherwise would not have made it.

If you are successful in bringing the puppy around, do not immediately put it back with the mother as it should be kept extra warm. Put it in a cardboard box on an electric heating pad or, if it is the time of year when your heat is running, near a radiator

308

or near the fireplace or stove. As soon as the rest of the litter has been born, it then can join the others.

An hour or more may elapse between puppies, which is fine so long as the bitch seems comfortable and is neither straining nor contracting. She should not be permitted to remain unassisted for more than an hour if she does continue to contract. This is when you should get her to your veterinarian, whom you should already have alerted to the possibility of a problem existing. He should examine her and perhaps give her a shot of Pituitrin. In some cases the veterinarian may find that a Caesarean section is necessary due to a puppy being lodged in a manner making normal delivery impossible. Sometimes this is caused by an abnormally large puppy, or it may just be that the puppy is simply turned in the wrong position. If the bitch does require a Caesarean section, the puppies already born must be kept warm in their cardboard box with a heating pad under the box.

Once the section is done, get the bitch and the puppies home. Do not attempt to put the puppies in with the bitch until she has regained consciousness, as she may unknowingly hurt them. But do get them back to her as soon as possible for them to start nursing.

Should the mother lack milk at this time, the puppies must be fed by hand, kept very warm, and held onto the mother's teats several times a day in order to stimulate and encourage the secretion of milk, which should start shortly.

Assuming that there has been no problem and that the bitch has whelped naturally, you should insist that she go out to exercise, staying just long enough to make herself comfortable. She can be offered a bowl of milk and a biscuit, but then she should settle down with her family. Freshen the whelping box for her with newspapers while she is taking this respite so that she and the puppies will have a clean bed.

Unless some problem arises, there is little you must do for the puppies until they become three to four weeks old. Keep the box clean and supplied with fresh newspapers the first few days, but then turkish towels should be tacked down to the bottom of the box so that the puppies will have traction as they move about.

If the bitch has difficulties with her milk supply, or if you should be so unfortunate as to lose her, then you must be prepared to either hand-feed or tube-feed the puppies if they are to survive. Tube-feeding is so much faster and easier. If the bitch is available, it is best that she continues to clean and care for the puppies in the normal manner, excepting for the food supplements you will provide. If it is impossible for her to do this, then after every feeding you must gently rub each puppy's abdomen with wet cotton to make it urinate, and the rectum should be gently rubbed to open the bowels.

Newborn puppies must be fed every three to four hours around the clock. The puppies must be kept warm during this time. Have your veterinarian teach you how to tube-feed. You will find that it is really quite simple.

After a normal whelping, the bitch will require additional food to enable her to produce sufficient milk. In addition to being fed twice daily, she should be given some canned milk several times each day.

When the puppies are two weeks old, their nails should be clipped, as they are needle sharp at this age and can hurt or damage the mother's teats and stomach as the pups hold on to nurse.

Between three and four weeks of age, the puppies should begin to be weaned. Scraped beef (prepared by scraping it off slices of beef with a spoon so that none of the gristle is included) may be offered in very small quantities a couple of times daily for the first few days. Then by the third day you can mix puppy chow with warm water as directed on the package, offering it four times daily. By now the mother should be kept away from the puppies and out of the box for several hours at a time so that when they have reached five weeks of age she is left in with them only overnight. By the time the puppies are six weeks old, they should be entirely weaned and receiving only occasional visits from their mother.

Most veterinarians recommend a temporary DHL (distemper, hepatitis, leptospirosis) shot when the puppies are six weeks of age. This remains effective for about two weeks. Then at eight weeks of age, the puppies should receive the series of permanent shots for DHL protection. It is also a good idea to discuss with your vet the advisability of having your puppies inoculated against the dreaded parvovirus at the same time. Each time the pups go to the vet for shots, you should bring stool samples so that they can be examined for worms. Worms go through various stages of development and may be present in a stool sample even though

Ch. Harwire Hetman of Whitlatter was the Ken-L-Ration Top Terrier of the Year for winning most Terrier Groups of any dog in America during 1977. Owned by the late Constance C. Jones, handled by Clifford Hallmark, Hetman won 81 Bests in Group during that year.

the sample does not test positive in every checkup. So do not neglect to keep careful watch on this.

The puppies should be fed four times daily until they are three months old. Then you can cut back to three feedings daily. By the time the puppies are six months of age, two meals daily are sufficient. Some people feed their dogs twice daily throughout their lifetime; others go to one meal daily when the puppy becomes one year of age.

The ideal age for puppies to go to their new homes is between eight and twelve weeks, although some puppies successfully adjust to a new home when they are six weeks old. Be sure that they go to their new owners accompanied by a description of the diet you've been feeding them and a schedule of the shots they have already received and those they still need. These should be included with the registration application and a copy of the pedigree.

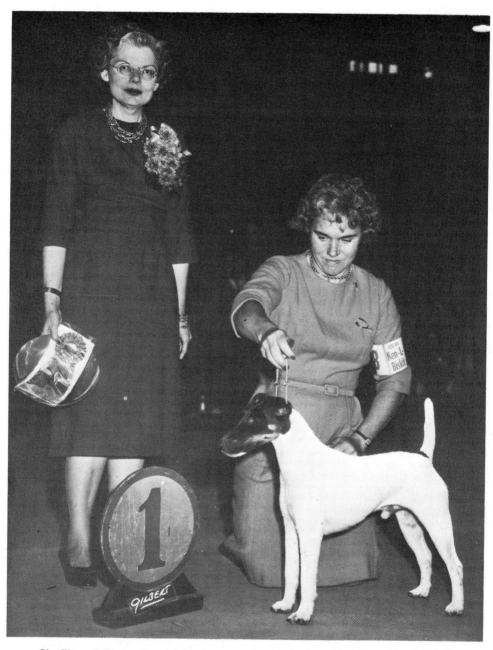

Ch. Flornell Ebony Box of Foxden was the Montgomery County Kennel Club Best in Show winner for 1960. Owned by Mr. and Mrs. James A. Farrell, Jr., Foxden Kennels, Darien, Connecticut, Ebony Box was handled by Jane Kamp Forsyth. Pictured winning the Terrier Group with the author (A.K.N.) as the judge at Springfield K.C. en route to Best in Show.

Chapter 19

Traveling with Your Fox Terrier

When you travel with your dog, to shows or on vacation or wherever, remember that everyone does not share your enthusiasm or love for dogs and that those who do not, strange creatures though they seem to us, have their rights too. These rights, on which you should not encroach, include not being disturbed, annoyed, or made uncomfortable by the presence and behavior of other people's pets. Your dog should be kept on lead in public places and should recognize and promptly obey the commands: "Down," "Come," "Sit," and "Stay."

Take along his crate if you are going any distance with your dog, and keep him in it when riding in the car. A crated dog has a far better chance of escaping injury than one riding loose in the car, should an accident occur or an emergency arise. If you do permit your dog to ride loose, never allow him to hang out a window, ears blowing in the breeze. An injury to his eyes could occur in this manner. He could also become overly excited by something he sees and jump out, or he could lose his balance and fall out.

Never, ever, under any circumstances, should a dog be permitted to ride loose in the back of a pick-up truck. Some people do transport dogs in this manner, which is cruel and shocking. How easily such a dog can be thrown out of the truck by sudden jolts or an impact! Doubtless many dogs have jumped out at the sight of something exciting along the way. Some unthinking individuals tie the dog, probably not realizing that were he to jump under those circumstances, his neck would be broken, he could be dragged alongside the vehicle, or he could be hit by another vehicle. If for any reason you are taking your dog in an open-back truck, please have sufficient regard for that dog to at least provide a crate for him; and then remember that, in or out of a crate, a dog riding under the direct rays of the sun in hot weather can suffer and have his life endangered by the heat.

If you are staying at a hotel or motel with your dog, exercise him somewhere other than in the flower beds and parking lot of the property. People walking to and from their cars really are not thrilled at "stepping in something" left by your dog. Should an accident occur, pick it up with a tissue or paper towel and deposit it in a proper receptacle; do not just walk off, leaving it to remain there. Usually there are grassy areas on the sides of and behind motels where dogs can be exercised. Use them rather than the more conspicuous, usually carefully tended, front areas or those close to the rooms. If you are becoming a dog show enthusiast, you will eventually need an exercise pen to take with you to the show. Exercise pens are ideal to use when staying at motels, too, as they permit you to limit the dog's roaming space and to pick up after him more easily.

Never leave your dog unattended in the room of a motel unless you are absolutely certain that he will stay there quietly and not damage or destroy anything. You do not want a long list of complaints from irate guests, caused by the annoying barking or whining of a lonesome dog in strange surroundings, or an overzealous watch dog barking furiously each time a footstep passes the door or he hears a sound from an adjoining room. And you certainly do not want to return to torn curtains or bedspreads, soiled rugs, or other embarrassing evidence of the fact that your dog is not really house-reliable after all.

If yours is a dog accustomed to traveling with you and you are positive that his behavior will be acceptable when left alone, that is fine. But if the slightest uncertainty exists, the wise course is to leave him in the car while you go to dinner or elsewhere; then bring him into the room when you are ready to retire for the night.

Ch. Dounburn Alexander wins Best in Show in 1961 for owner Barbara Keenan with Ted Ward handling. Mrs. Keenan is more frequently thought of in connection with Westies and Beagles, but as you see here, top winning Wires also have been among her noted dogs.

Ch. Bevwyre Conbrio Tim, a Best in Show winner owned by Mr. Max Gilberg, New York. Handled by Peter Green to win Best Puppy in Show in Bermuda.

When you travel with a dog, it is often simpler to take along from home the food and water he will need rather than to buy food and look for water while you travel. In this way he will have the rations to which he is accustomed and which you know agree with him, and there will be no fear of problems due to different drinking water. Feeding on the road is quite easy now, at least for short trips, with all the splendid dry foods and high-quality canned meats available. A variety of lightweight, refillable water containers can be bought at many types of stores.

Always be careful to leave sufficient openings to ventilate your car when the dog will be alone in it. Remember that during the summer, the rays of the sun can make an inferno of a closed car within only a few minutes, so leave enough window space open to provide air circulation. Again, if your dog is in a crate, this can be done quite safely. The fact that you have left the car in a shady spot is not always a guarantee that you will find conditions the same when you return. Don't forget that the position of the sun changes in a matter of minutes, and the car you left nicely shaded half an hour ago can be getting full sunlight far more quickly than you may realize. So, if you leave a dog in the car, make sure there is sufficient ventilation and check back frequently to ascertain that all is well.

If you are going to another country, you will need a health certificate from your veterinarian for each dog you are taking with you, certifying that each has had rabies shots within the required time preceding your visit.

316

Index

319